Guyasuta
and the
FALL
of
INDIAN
AMERICA

GEORGE WASHINGTON
PRESIDENT.
1792.

Guyasuta

and the

FALL

of

INDIAN

AMERICA

BRADY J. CRYTZER

WESTHOLME
Yardley

Frontispiece: An etching of the silver medal presented to the Seneca sachem Red Jacket by President George Washington to commemorate the Treaty of Canandaigua, signed on November 11, 1794, establishing friendship between the Iroquois Nations and the new American republic. It was essentially a surrender of control of the Ohio Country and some of the Nations' own lands to the Americans. Three months earlier, the Legion of the United States led by General "Mad" Anthony Wayne destroyed a confederacy of Indian Nations in the Ohio Country at the Battle of Fallen Timbers, the final Indian resistance to American expansion in the Old Northwest. That same year, the Mingo sachem Guyasuta, died. He had inspired the Ohio Indians and had struggled to maintain an American Indian polity for nearly fifty years. (*Library of Congress*)

©2013 Brady J. Crytzer
Maps by Tracy Dungan
Maps ©2013 Westholme Publishing

Westholme Publishing, LLC
904 Edgewood Road
Yardley, Pennsylvania 19067
Visit our Web site at www.westholmepublishing.com

First Printing May 2013
10 9 8 7 6 5 4 3 2 1
ISBN: 978-1-59416-174-2
Also available as an eBook.

Printed in the United States of America.

In Memory of David Dixon
1954–2008

Nous Sommes Tous Sauvages
"We are all Savages."

CONTENTS

List of Maps

PROLOGUE

The role of America's native peoples in the formation of the United States has emerged from the shadows of history over the past fifty years and continues to develop. Colonial North America was a highly complex, deeply divided world, contested by two distant empires, the British and the French, a multitude of indigenous peoples with varying alliances—including what was for all intents and purposes another empire, the Iroquois Confederacy—and a growing settler population along the eastern seaboard. Colonial American history emphasizes events in the East, and while the American identity may have been penned in Philadelphia, it was born on the frontier.

Through the life of one of Native America's most important early leaders, Guyasuta, this book will trace the evolution of Indian America alongside the expansion of the colonies at a time when its impact on the emergence of the United States was its most profound. It will also reveal how by the end of Guyasuta's long life, the world of the American Indian was changed forever, with the possibility of any future independent Indian nation gone with the presence of the new United States of America.

To begin to understand Guyasuta's world, one must understand his times and his home, the frontier. By his birth in 1724, political geography was far from clearly defined in North America. On one side of the continent, settlements both large and small huddled against the Atlantic Coast and were fully aware that the order and power of Europe were only an ocean away. To their west though, beyond the Appalachian Mountain chain, most colonists described a dark and mysterious land called simply "the backcountry." They thought of the land in terms of only what was known and unknown. It is startling to consider that many colonists felt safer sailing the vast and featureless ocean than stepping beyond the limits of their own property.

Yet if the overwhelming majority of Europeans in North America never considered exploring the great distant regions of the continent, others did. Beyond the mountains the frontier settler found a world of fertile lowlands, imposing mountains, rushing streams, and seemingly endless forest. It was a veritable paradise of raw materials, and home to many unique native peoples. This was the world that Guyasuta was born into; in the colonies it became known as the Ohio Country.

In the most specific sense the Ohio Country was the vast stretch of untouched wilderness that today is comprised of western Pennsylvania, the states of Ohio and West Virginia, and parts of Indiana, yet from the restricted vantage point of the colonists it might as well have stretched to infinity. The Ohio Country embodied the frontier; it was densely forested with trees over seventy feet in circumference and home to a staggering wealth of flora and fauna that dazzled the Eurocentric communities of Philadelphia, Boston, and New York. Its rugged valleys and mountains were seen as untouched canvas, and memories of the terribly crowded and filthy streets of London and Paris vanished at the prospects of settling it. If the New World was the land of opportunity, there was no doubt that the Ohio Country was its prize. The great powers of Europe were tempted by the fortunes that could be made by exploiting the land, so much so that they were considered well worth the cost of war if necessary.

The defining feature of the Ohio Country that captivated policy makers in London and Paris alike was a parcel of land where not two, but three rivers joined. Known as the Forks of the Ohio, it was a point where the southward-flowing Allegheny and northbound Monongahela combined to form the great westward driven Ohio River. To control those waters was to control North America's great gateway to the West and the timbers and furs that Europeans craved. Both Britain and France knew that whoever could control North America and its resources could shift the tightly defined balance of power that had characterized their rivalry for centuries.

In London and Paris, the administrators of two empires began to devise competing, expensive strategies to acquire North America's most precious assets. In spite of their differences in style and imperial ambition, the French and British approaches to North American domination both hinged on one common, critical truth: the key to the continent was found in the hearts and minds of the Indian peoples who called it home.

North America was under the yoke of imperialism long before the any European planted his flag there. Since the thirteenth century oral tradition tells of long and bloody conquests by a variety of peoples that laid claim to its many locales, and first among them was the mighty Iroquois Confederacy. Made up initially of five separate Indian nations all bound together in pursuit of a common goal, notably protecting their shared way of life, the Iroquois reigned supreme in North America as its most politically successful imperial power. As early as 1200 the collection of peoples that called themselves *Haudenosaunee*, or "People of the Longhouse," had purged much of today's New York of its traditional inhabitants and laid claim to it themselves.

Made up of the Seneca, Cayuga, Onandaga, Oneida, and Mohawk nations, the Iroquois Confederacy ruled the American northeast with impunity; they soon found that subjugating the peoples that they defeated rather than exterminating them only served to bolster their growing empire. One area of particular importance to the Five Nations was that of the Ohio Country. Like the Europeans years later, the Haudenosaunee coveted its rich hunting grounds. As Europeans first began to reach the shores of America's East Coast the Iroquois had just completed their first attempts at ravaging the small clans of people that called the Ohio River valley home.

By the time that the first Europeans had entered the political affairs of the New World the Iroquois were already feeling the effects of their powerful new empire. In 1608, French explorer Samuel de Champlain was sent to claim as much territory for His Most Christian Majesty as possible. While he navigated the dense wilderness of the Great Lakes region, Champlain stumbled across the long and bloody war between the Huron and the Iroquois. In an effort to best suit his own needs, Champlain sided with the Huron, and though the Iroquois would be victorious, they would hold a lasting animosity toward the French.

As the European presence, and therefore intervention, increased in North America, the Iroquois and their neighbors greatly benefitted from the steady supply of firearms that followed. While hunting became much easier, sustaining the natural environment became almost impossible. The natives had been proficient hunters with the bow and arrow for centuries already, but it was a weapon of great skill and limited success. The new powder musket, however, eliminated much of the skill and concentration required to handle a bow, and the results were much higher kill counts. In addition, due to European demand, by the mid-seventeenth century, beaver, the most prized game of the continent, had grown scarce, and a war began for rights to its fertile trapping grounds. In the Beaver Wars, the Iroquois decimated their Algonquin-speaking counterparts. Because much of the fighting took place away from European view, historians can only estimate the casualties of the war. All told, considering the total victory wrought by the Haudenosaunee, the Beaver Wars were one of the bloodiest periods of combat in North American history.

With the close of hostilities the Northeast belonged to the Iroquois, and they were as powerful as ever. The Ohio Country's Algonquin population had been all but exterminated, and the land was the Iroquois' to colonize. In the midst of the chaotic period of fighting, the English saw opportunity. Knowing that they shared a common enemy in the empire of France, the English and Iroquois joined in a relationship of goodwill referred to as the Covenant Chain. While the agreement seemed to benefit the Iroquois as well as the English, what King Charles

II had perpetrated was actually a devious tactic employed in empires throughout history.

It has been said that imperialism is not the art of conquest, but the science of collaboration; the Covenant Chain was a perfect example. By the seventeenth century it had become clear to the empires of Europe that it was much easier to conquer a foreign land by forming a bond with the existing ruling power structure rather than by marching an army into it. In forming an alliance with the Iroquois, the English were able to use the Indian power's previously set channels of influence to simply apply their own. It was a brilliant strategy, but it was fully designed to allow the glory of England to supersede any other on the continent.

With the Ohio Country firmly in their hands, the Haudenosaunee were forced to devise a policy that shifted their influence from conquest to control, and the method they chose was decidedly European. With most of their newly won territory drained of its native communities, the Iroquois turned to a policy of strategic relocation to solidify their claims to the Ohio Country. Indian families poured into the region, and as most of them were members of the western Iroquois Seneca and Cayuga nations, this migration can be viewed in its simplest terms as colonization.

The dynamics of empire in North America were strikingly similar whether it concerned Europeans or indigenous groups. Just as would be the case in the American Revolution, the original British colonists of North America had suddenly developed their own "American" identity. Subsequently rebellion and ultimately revolution was the natural order of establishing themselves as a free people; in Iroquoia, a similar shift occurred on a much smaller scale. As generations passed, the descendants of those original Iroquois migrants to the Ohio Country likewise developed their own identity, and rather than adhering to their imperial roots they suddenly began distinguishing themselves by a new name: Mingo.

Just as the American colonists threw off their Britishness and latched onto this new Americanism, the Ohio Country Iroquois did the same with their identity. Although they technically remained as Iroquois as any of their northern counterparts, the

Mingo's search for self-governance had led to the foundation of an entirely new political minority. At the same time that the Mingo were finding their voice, the Delaware refugees from the east, pushed away by the British Pennsylvanians, were settling in the region as well. Although Pennsylvania's proprietor William Penn envisioned it to be his Peaceable Kingdom where people of all faiths and races could live in harmony, his successors had a much less noble perspective. In 1737 the colony of Pennsylvania underhandedly defrauded over 1.2 million acres of land from the native Delaware peoples and forced them out of their ancestral homelands into the great wilds of the Ohio Country. Joining the Mingo and Delaware were the migrating peoples called the Shawnees, and while the circumstances were not ideal they too found a home in the Ohio Country. Separately the nations were their own people, yet they shared the reality that they were all the imperial subjects of the Iroquois Confederacy. Suddenly an area that had been rendered empty by Iroquoian ethnic cleansing a century earlier was now inhabited by three distinctly different nations, and it was their common ground that allowed them to form a political alliance unique to the region. Out of this turbulent political world the figure of the New Ohioan emerges.

It was under these circumstances that Guyasuta was raised. Although he was born to Seneca parents in New York's Genesee River valley, he spent his most formative years among the Delaware and Shawnee. Unlike his father, who had spent his whole life as a Seneca, Guyasuta's upbringing in the distant Ohio Country drew him into the culture of the New Ohioan in a way that his parents could never understand. He was the son of a Seneca colonist, and he would be among the first generation to consider itself Mingo.

Guyasuta's father had to have come from some form of powerful family lineage, as Guyasuta was held in high regard by the Ohioans. He was not a chief, or sachem, at birth, but he was well on his way by the time that he was twenty. In the Indian world a leader had to earn the respect of his followers, and since Guyasuta was technically a Seneca in the way the Americans were technically British, the Ohioans looked on him as a potential leader in the future. Despite his bloodline and heritage, however, Guyasuta would not simply assume a position of power as was the case in European empires; he had to earn it on the field of battle. It is his martial experience that also makes Guyasuta's life notable: he served as a guide for George Washington's first diplomatic mission to confront the French in 1753; he was at the destruction of Braddock's expedition; he fought during Pontiac's Rebellion, a movement he helped inspire, and at Oriskany during the American Revolution when the Iroquois nations first took up arms against one another.

But in the Iroquois hubris lay the great weakness of empire, and just as the Crown would be blindsided by the American Patriot rebellion, the imperial Iroquois would fall victim as well. The figure of Guyasuta and the New Ohioan was largely unseen by the Iroquois. Although they were aware of this new name, Mingo, they had little understanding of what potential the Mingo had for upsetting the Iroquois way of life. From the perspective of the great council fire that was the center of all Indian life in the territory of the Onondaga, the Mingo were simply western Seneca. The Iroquois believed that the Western Seneca, despite identifying themselves as Mingo, could not have possibly considered themselves as equals to the rest of the Ohioans, and likewise could not share their distaste for Iroquois rule.

For all the signs that the Iroquois and their British allies missed, however, one very interested party was able to recognize its potential: New France. Operating from its base of Quebec, France was desperate to gain an upper hand. The French had already succeeded in wooing the native peoples of the Great Lakes to their side in the absence of British action in the region, and while the Iroquois would clearly never join them in partnership, there was no reason the French could not try to win over the Iroquois subjects. It was in the figure of the New Ohioan that King Louis found his greatest ally in the great war that was emerging in North America. The French promised the Ohioans the freedom and independence Great Britain could never give them, and the choice was clear; if Great Britain fell, so did the Iroquois.

Britain and France appeared destined for a bloody conflagration to secure control of the Ohio Country, and while the Covenant Chain rested over the British-allied Iroquois

Confederacy, the majority of Iroquois had no idea that the very ground they stood on was crumbling beneath their feet.

Witness to these world-changing events was Guyasuta, whom history first records as a young man on the precipice of a revolution, forced to straddle two worlds. It was a stance that would persist over his long life, through war, rebellion, and revolution, and in the end, the realization that the world he had once known was gone forever.

ONE

The Hunter

BRITISH POSTURING IN THE OHIO COUNTRY, 1753

Situated along the right bank of the icy Ohio River, the nearly thirty-year old village of Logstown was abuzz with excitement. Peoples from all walks of Indian life had frequented the site, and at any given point members of over a dozen local groups could be found indulging in the sweet and profitable commercial activities of the small, yet bustling community. The sun was beginning to set, and the plateau above the river on which the town sat was increasingly glowing as new fires were being lit, and as old ones rekindled.

For the people of Logstown, a population that was always changing, foreign visitors were a welcomed sight. As the largest village in the river valley, it was the hub of economic, commercial, and diplomatic activities in the whole of the Ohio Country. On a regular basis, well-equipped European and native investors could barter and trade at hefty profits nearly seven days a week. Native trappers could trade their fur elsewhere in the region, and often times they would, at a considerable loss. It was therefore the unique position and heavy traffic that brought dozens of people to Logstown on this night, much as it had for the last six years.

For all of those reasons and many more, the twenty-eight-year-old Guyasuta found himself at this busy spot. In Logstown he could stay informed of the region's recent developments and truly sense the pulse of the native peoples of the Ohio River valley. It would have been a trying time for the young sachem, and the shifting patterns of identity and new visions of independence galvanized by recent French interventions had pressed him into a personal quagmire. As the son of the Seneca father, he had familial obligations to the Iroquoian worldview, and he had benefited from it.[1]

Yet, as he sat in Logstown and saw the familiar faces around him, those he culturally related to most, he would have been unsettled by the undeniable fact that they were not Iroquois. He heard the whispers of the Shawnees, the legendary yarns spun by the Delawares, and learned the farming practices of the Wyandots. His birthright had been Iroquois; his experiences had been something else. He would have been confronted with the unavoidable conclusion that his allegiance to the old Haudenosaunee, the People of the Longhouse, was becoming less tangible, and more in name alone.[2]

Guyasuta was by no means responsible for this shifting perspective; as one of thousands staying afloat in a churning tide of political and social upheaval, he was not alone. Where he did stand unique was in the role that he would begin to play. As a man of Seneca (and therefore Iroquoian) lineage, the peoples traditionally subjugated by the Six Nations were naturally inclined to respect him. But, as the French continued to woo the subjects of the Haudenosaunee toward an alliance, the Iroquois-style of empire was quickly transforming from a valuable commodity to a disturbing liability. He had walked this thin line for most of the last five years, but as events unfolded and French aggressiveness increased, he could not hide behind the veil of indifference for long.

Logstown presented a unique opportunity for Guyasuta, and in many ways over the next several days his decision may have been made for him. In the village with him at the time were two particularly conservative and aging elder sachems, and as an Iroquois he would need to defer to their decisions. The first and most immediate above him was a fellow Seneca Kaghswaghtaniunt, or Belt of Wampum. A traditionalist in the highest regard, Kaghswaghtaniunt had lived his entire life in a world dominated by Iroquoian principles. While there is a distinct lack of source material on the long-time policy maker, he would play a very obvious role in the formation of Guyasuta's worldview; he offered a clear image of what the young Seneca *was not*. Kaghswaghtaniunt had enjoyed the fruits of the native empire since his youth, and his mind was so fixed on the once-great strength of the Iroquois Confederacy that it clouded his view of its current state: a leaning tower on a crumbling foundation. The foundation, for centuries, had been that the Haudenosaunee had a stable supply of subjected people to dominate and exploit. No empire can remain without copious, if not loyal, subjects; the Iroquois Empire was no different.

For Guyasuta, the Ohio Indians' emerging values of freedom and quest for autonomy were a legitimate movement led by deserving and reputable peoples. For the Iroquois Empire to continue, it would need to alter its present course to accommodate them, for without them it would fall. Guyasuta would have been formulating scenarios in which this could be accomplished, a balance of his traditional worldview with his new progressive perspectives. He would soon see however that such a balance could never be struck, and his experiences with Kaghswaghtaniunt made it clear that the elders of the Six Nations would never recognize any increased independence for the Ohio Indians. At worst many Iroquois traditionalists, Kaghswaghtaniunt among them, failed to even recognize the New Ohioans as an actual figure, virtually guaranteeing their failure when confronting the new minority in future engagements.[3]

As the sun had met the horizon in the skies above Logstown, a commotion in the village instantly drew Guyasuta's attention. A delegation of eight men had just been escorted into the town, and they were calling for a general meeting with all sachems present. The men were wet, tired, and worn. They claimed to be from Virginia and wished to speak on behalf of King George; they were British.[4]

The dramatic shift that had troubled Guyasuta so deeply was evolving before his eyes.

The years leading to 1753 saw the relatively stable balance of daily Indian life transform drastically when the old rivalries and contentions of Europe descended quickly into the well-connected economy of the Ohio Country. In villages around the region new, unfamiliar faces appeared seeking economic and diplomatic fortunes among the more susceptible nations of the New World. While the French and British versions of empire were both motivated by similar goals, the nature of those goals often left the two massive nations competing for limited resources. The result was often an economic state of continuous gamesmanship for the affections of any available tribal affiliations. Goods ranging from firearms to alcohol flooded the villages and footpaths of the Ohio Country. For the native peoples of the region, it was clear by 1750 that the deep and intense history between the European empires was able to provide an economic stimulus that their relatively closed economy desperately needed.[5]

For the administration of New France in Quebec, a reliable and stable relationship among the major nations of the Great Lakes, or *pays d'en haut,* primarily supported their North American imperial ambitions. This nearly fifty-year affiliation was encouraged, and maintained, by the establishment of Fort Detroit in 1701. With a large and busy fortification strategically placed in the midst of the Great Lakes, France remained relatively uncontested by their Anglo-enemies on America's eastern seaboard.[6]

Beginning in 1744, however, existing tensions from the Old World disrupted New France's economic exceptionalities in the New World. Known in North America as King George's War (in Europe, the War of the Austrian Succession), the four-year stretch of open North American combat proved costly to the French. After temporarily losing their St. Lawrence River stronghold of Louisbourg to a force of British-Americans, Fort Detroit began to feel the strain of an effective blockade that made goods normally traded to the Great Lakes peoples almost unaffordable. Though the war-ending Treaty of Aix-la-Chapelle in 1748 effectively retained the *status quo antebellum* of North America, including the return of the fortress of Louisbourg to the

French, the damage due to the high price of trade goods appeared to have been done; many formerly allied Indians began to look elsewhere for their flow of valuable European commodities.

With political upheaval comes seemingly endless opportunity, and with many of the Great Lakes nations open for new business, the British could not resist for long. In the midst of King George's War, one of the first great entrepreneurs of the English-speaking world would make an early, yet profound, impact on the economy of New France. George Croghan, an opportunist by birth and an Irishman by the grace of God, expanded one of his many operations in the Ohio Country northward toward Lake Erie, and soon within fifty-five miles of Fort Detroit itself at Sandusky Bay.

As the French recovered from four years of tenuous combat in 1749, Quebec watched furiously as the St. Lawrence River reopened, yet trade at Fort Detroit never fully recovered. It soon stagnated, followed by the realization that a large percentage of their regular customers had trickled over to the British side. Among the defecting nations were the powerful Miamis, who had relocated to the village of Pickawillany, strategically located between the Mississippi River and Fort Detroit. Croghan and his associates had brilliantly redirected regular commercial routes by maintaining a well-positioned trading post at the village.[7]

While French policy was primarily focused on the *pays d'en haut* region, the scope of British ambition prompted Comte de la Galissonière, the governor of New France, to dispatch Captain Pierre-Joseph Céleron de Blainville on a simple mission: establish French control over the Ohio Country. In the fall of 1749 Céleron's expedition, along with 265 regular Canadian infantrymen, traversed the Allegheny and Ohio river valleys, proclaiming the domain of King Louis XV of France. Along the way, the French placed a series of lead plates at strategic waterways to solidify their claims. Of the six placed, only two have been recovered intact; when translated they read:

> In the year 1749, of the reign of Louis the 15th, King of France, we Céloron, commander of a detachment sent by Monsieur the Marquis de la Galissonière, Governor General of New France, to reestablish tranquility in some Indian vil-

lages of these cantons, have buried this Plate of Lead at the
confluence of the Ohio and the Chatauqua, this 29th day of
July, near the river Ohio, otherwise Belle Rivière, as a monu-
ment of the renewal of the possession we have taken of the
said river Ohio and of all those which empty into it, and of
all the lands on both sides as far as the sources of the said
rivers, as enjoyed or ought to have been enjoyed by the kings
of France preceding and as they have there maintained themselves by arms and by treaties, especially those of Ryswick,
Utrecht and Aix la Chapelle.

Historically, many view the limited scope of Céleron's expedition as a success. While he did "assert" French intentions in a
generally hollow way, he also was able to record and report
Indian activities throughout the region, particularly that of the
troublesome Miamis. They were, in fact, trading with the
British, most specifically the Pennsylvanians. What neither
Céleron nor the marquis de La Jonquière, the newly appointed
governor of New France, failed to recognize was that British
trading interests in the region were unique, and diverse. While
George Croghan and the Pennsylvanians were the most obvious
culprits, their ambitions stopped at open trade; they had done
most of the damage to the French cause that they would ever do.

The true cause for concern in Quebec should have been the
involvement of a group that they never recognized, largely due
to the fact that the French saw all British settlers as one and the
same. While Croghan's mission of open trade was accomplished,
he had very little interest in actually buying land. In 1752 however the game changed dramatically when the colony of Virginia
entered the fray looking to do exactly that. The governor of New
France made the mistake of thinking there was little difference
between a Pennsylvanian and a Virginian, a lesson that he would
learn the hard way.[8]

In 1752 a cabal of power and wealth based in the Old
Dominion formed an investment association known as the
Ohio Company of Virginia. Made up of affluent members of
the colony's upper crust, most notably Lieutenant Governor
Robert Dinwiddie and two brothers, Lawrence and Augustine
Washington, the Ohio Company devised a concerted strategy to

speculate on and sell the rich lands of the Ohio Country. A fortune was to be had, and King George's empire was to benefit. While Croghan and his men were modest traders, the Ohio Company represented a physical manifestation of the sheer profitability of the New World, and the capital invested would be viewed as a threat to the French way of life. Money and power in politics was as much a part of policy-making in the eighteenth century as it is in the twenty-first.[9]

With a clear agenda in mind, Dinwiddie dispatched a trusted advisor and experienced frontiersman named Christopher Gist into the Ohio Country to meet with and arrange possible land sales with the existing power bases in the region. In 1752, Gist sat at council in Logstown with the Iroquois sachem Tanacharison. Tanacharison, a Seneca appointed by the Council Fire at Ononodoga, was central to the success of the Ohio Company as his blessings could potentially open the strategic Forks of the Ohio for speculation. Known pejoratively as "Half-King" by the Ohio Indians, Tanacharison was given the unenviable task of serving as regent and representative of the Iroquois Confederacy among the subjected peoples of the Ohio River valley. His task was to give these people a sense of connection to the imperial metropole in New York, and more important to ensure that they did not stir into rebellion against their Iroquois oppressors. Because he was only a representative, Tanacharison's role was limited to that of a middle manager; he was the official that would hear all orders of business in the region, but he had almost no power to approve any meaningful legislation. All matters were to be forwarded north to the Council Fire for final approval. While he attempted to maintain a dignified presence, the Ohio Indians saw how weak he truly was.[10]

For the old Seneca, European intervention into the region was nothing unusual. In his lifetime, the French and British had always been dual pillars of power in the New World. Yet Tanacharison was becoming increasingly alarmed at the recent exploits by the French into his jurisdiction; as the French became more ambitious, so the Ohio Indians became bolder. While many of the elder policymakers at the Council Fire failed to recognize the New Ohioan, Tanacharison saw the entire situation unfolding. When Gist met with him at Logstown and asked permission to build a fort at the Forks of the Ohio, that sacred place where two rivers become three, the "Half-King" had little choice but to accept. Although the Iroquois would have preferred to retain their autonomy over the area, British intrusion would at least keep the balance of power in his favor: French success could very well mean open rebellion in Iroquoia.

Upon the death of La Jonquière, the next governor of New France, Charles Le Moyne de Longueil, decided to smash the new Anglo power play for Indian trade that had developed at the village of Pickawillany. Mostly fueled by British Pennsylvanians, Pickawillany had emerged as a new bustling center of trade that proved itself to be quite viable by leaving Fort Detroit desolate to the north. Therefore, only days after the Logstown conference between Gist and Tanacharison, two hundred French-allied Ojibwa and Ottawa warriors raided and destroyed the small village. As long-time power brokers in the Great Lakes region and therefore traditional French allies, the Ottawa and Ojibwa would have been pleased to restore the trading prowess at Fort Detroit. Five of the six traders at Pickawillany were captured; the sixth and a prominent Miami sachem were killed. Their hearts were publicly boiled and eaten by the warriors, sending a clear message to the Miamis: return to Fort Detroit or suffer the consequences. This was only reinforced when the Pennsylvanians fled back across the Alleghenies with no apparent intention of returning.

With the absence of viable trade now evident, the Ohio Company moved forward with their plans for regional hegemony despite the aggressive efforts of New France. Although the Forks of the Ohio had been the original goal, the Virginians pushed ahead by building a fortification at the confluence of the Monongahela River and Red Stone Creek. Called Red Stone Fort, this new post served as the Ohio Company's launching point into a profitable and prosperous future. It sat just thirty-seven miles from the Forks of the Ohio.[11]

The British interest in the Ohio Country proved to be the first true test of the new governor of New France, Marquis Duquesne. Reflecting the fluidity of colonial governorships in the eighteenth century, which were royal appointments with no tenure of office, Duquesne was the third governor of the massive territory of New France in as many years. An aggressive naval officer who had battled the British his entire career, Duquesne proposed a controversial new aggressive strategy to enforce the French way of life upon of the Ohio Country: full-scale military occupation. His plan would entail using maps drawn by Céleron three years earlier to fortify positions he believed to be most strategic. The enormous venture would run almost four million livres.

Aside from the financial cost, the cost of filling these new forts with active garrisons would take an even greater toll on the colony. Historian Fred Anderson estimates that the two-year building project would have required over two thousand French and Canadian soldiers to be successful. That figure, when compared to the only eleven thousand men between the ages of sixteen and sixty available in all of New France, is an enormous investment.[12] By the spring of 1753, Duquesne's plans had unfolded in the completion of two forts, Presque Isle on Lake Erie and Le Boeuf fifteen miles to its south, with two more on the docket for the following year. Fort Machault would be built at the prominent Indian village of Venango, and the modestly named Fort Duquesne at the critical juncture of the three rivers known as the Forks of the Ohio. It was a bold plan made by a stern administrator, and only another bold action could maintain the balance of power in the region.

With desperation in their hearts, ministers in London began devising a strategy to eliminate the French threat in the Ohio Country. Their plan entailed politely asking the French to vacate their forts, reinforced with the threat of impending attack. The man chosen by policy makers in London to orchestrate this venture was none other than Lieutenant Governor Robert Dinwiddie of Virginia. Because Virginia was the economic and political powerhouse of British North America, he was a likely choice to take on such a task. Sealing the deal for Dinwiddie's selection were his interest in imperial success and his previous financial investments in the Ohio Company of Virginia. He was to send a delegation to the southernmost French position in the region, at that time Fort Le Boeuf, to deliver his warning. He was sent armaments and munitions to further his cause. For

Dinwiddie these supplies could only be for building a fort of his own in the Ohio Country, and the only place that would have mattered was the coveted Forks of the Ohio.

But who to send on this mission? The responsibilities and obligations of daily provincial duties answered that question for him. A year earlier, Lawrence Washington, a shareholder in the Ohio Company and prominent Virginia militiaman, died after a long struggle with tuberculosis. Upon his passing, Dinwiddie received a letter from his twenty-year-old half-brother George. In the letter, the young Washington asked for his late brother's commission in the colonial militia. With the letter sitting around for almost a year upon the recent developments of New France, Dinwiddie viewed the upstart as a natural choice. In reality there was not much harm in sending Washington on such a mission as he was a glorified mail carrier.

Glowing with pride, the freshly commissioned Major George Washington left Williamsburg on November 1, 1753. He was to meet Christopher Gist and his team at his plantation near Red Stone Fort and their mission was under way. The team arrived at Logstown on November 24 seeking out Tanacharison, the Half-King.[13]

That night, Guyasuta and George Washington, both in their twenties, would meet for the first time.

The party of men representing the colony of Virginia entered Logstown with understandable trepidation. Although the young Washington attempted to appear their leader, it was apparent to Guyasuta and the other sachems that the men were quietly being directed by the familiar Christopher Gist. Gist had held treaty with the Half-King a year earlier in this exact spot, and their return was no surprise; Logstown was an essential stop for any European delegation in the area.

As a village, Logstown had been in existence for over twenty-five years. Originally a Shawnee village, its placement on the Ohio River made it an attractive stop for interested French speculators in the region. Because of its close proximity to the Forks of the Ohio, policy makers in Montreal assigned that the relatively modest Indian post be reinforced with several European-style log cabins to attract new and powerful native clientele. As Logstown grew, and the French continued to lavish its residents

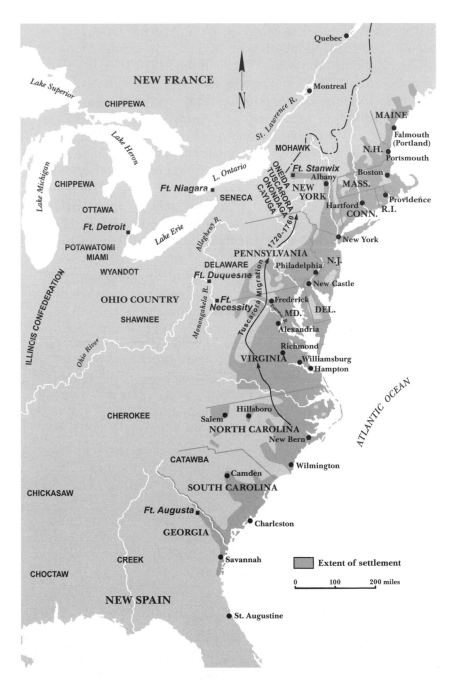

Quebec

NEW FRANCE

Lake Superior

CHIPPEWA

Lake Heron

Lake Michigan

CHIPPEWA

OTTAWA

Ft. Detroit

POTAWATOMI
MIAMI

WYANDOT

OHIO COUNTRY

SHAWNEE

ILLINOIS CONFEDERATION

Ohio River

Lake Erie

Allegheny R.

Montreal

St. Lawrence R.

MAINE

MOHAWK

N.H.

Falmouth
(Portland)

Portsmouth

L. Ontario

Ft. Niagara

SENECA

ONEIDA
TUSCARORA
ONONDAGA
CAYUGA

Ft. Stanwix

Albany

NEW
YORK

Boston

MASS.

Providence

R.I.

Hartford

CONN.

New York

1720–1760

PENNSYLVANIA

DELAWARE
Ft. Duquesne

Philadelphia

N.J.

New Castle

Monongahela R.

Ft.
Necessity

Tuscarora Migration

Frederick

MD.

DEL.

Alexandria

Richmond

VIRGINIA

Williamsburg

Hampton

CHEROKEE

Salem

Hillsboro

NORTH CAROLINA

New Bern

CATAWBA

Wilmington

CHICKASAW

Camden

SOUTH CAROLINA

Ft. Augusta

Charleston

GEORGIA

CREEK

Savannah

CHOCTAW

NEW SPAIN

ATLANTIC OCEAN

Extent of settlement

0   100   200 miles

St. Augustine

European North American Colonies in 1755.

with gifts, it became the center of the diplomatic activity in the region. Suddenly, though it was originally an insular Shawnee village, all of the prominent chiefs and diplomats from the many peoples of the Ohio Country began relocating there; even the powerful Iroquois Confederacy acknowledged that you weren't really somebody if you weren't at Logstown. Tanacharison, the Half-King, in an attempt to retain control over the many peoples of Iroquoia, was assigned permanent residence by his superiors soon after. Because of this large influx of power, Logstown was a must-see and crucial stop in the battle for the hearts and minds of the Ohio Indians. It was precisely for those reasons that the Irish trader George Croghan held a post there in 1748, the French captain Céleron de Blainville stopped there in 1749, and Washington and his men were now present in 1753.

Highlighting the diversity of the town, the Virginians were escorted into Logstown by a familiar figure to Guyasuta—the Delaware king Shingas. A traditional leader among his own people, Shingas took up residence outside of Logstown across from the Forks of the Ohio. As a Delaware, and therefore a subject of Iroquois rule, Shingas had a history of abiding by the laws of his overseers but promoting his own policies outside the watchful eyes of the Council Fire at Onondoga. As the Ohio Indians began experiencing the upswell of power and desire for autonomy that came with French intervention, Shingas gravitated to the idea of channeling his traditional influence over his people into becoming one of the renegade leaders of the New Ohio, and would become a most hated enemy of the Iroquois in the future.[14]

For Shingas, however, as for Guyasuta, there was no consensus yet in the Ohio Country that a Franco-Ohioan alliance was the correct course of action. The politics of the time were unsettled, and the Virginians hoped to catch the eyes of the prominent men of the village. Washington, upon his arrival, called for the "great men" of the village to join him in his tent where they were to "stay about an hour."[15]

The meeting held was an informal one, and Guyasuta was not invited to attend. Because of their long-standing alliance with the Iroquois and their "top-down" view of authority, the British failed to recognize the New Ohioan as a meaningful character in the same way that the Iroquois did. Because the chiefs of Logstown considered Guyasuta as merely a low-ranking Seneca and thought that the confederacy was represented by the Oneida sachem Scarouady, they believed his presence to be unnecessary. This was no slight for Guyasuta, as a young man in an old world his esteem would mature over time. Even so, it was clear that the meeting that the Virginians held on that night was unlikely to produce any meaningful results because they came for the affections of Tanacharison, who was away hunting at the time.

The next evening, when Tanacharison returned, the Virginians hosted another large gathering at Logstown. On this occasion, however, the fabric of the meeting house was more diverse than at first. Washington had intended to deliver a speech, recited by translator John Davidson, to a delegation of all peoples, not simply Iroquois. There would have been representatives of all nations present in the village at the time, but again Guyasuta was absent. Washington addressed the delegation:

> Brothers, I have called you together in Council, by Order of your Brother the Governor of Virginia, to acquaint you that I am sent, with all possible Dispatch, to visit, and deliver a Letter to the French Commandant, of very great Importance to your Brothers the English; and I dare say, to you their Friends and Allies.
>
> I was destined, brothers, by your brother, the governor, to call upon you, the sachems of the nations, to inform you of it, and to ask your advice and assistance to proceed to the nearest and best road to the French, You see, brothers, I have gotten this far on my Journey.
>
> His Honor likewise desired me to apply to you for some of your young men to conduct and provide provisions for us on our way, and be a safeguard against those French Indians who have taken up the hatchet against us. I have spoken thus particularly to you, brothers, because his Honor, our governor, treats you as good friends and allies, and holds you in great esteem. To confirm what I have said, I give you this string of wampum.[16]

Washington's request revealed the actual power that the Half-King had over the village in which he presided. The Virginian had requested the aid of the Nations present and sought an answer from Tanacharison. However, as the delegation largely consisted of representatives of the Ohio peoples, the Iroquois delegate was in no position to speak for them; he simply did not have the influence required anymore. Washington may not have known his folly, but to make such a request of Tanacharison would have been to greatly emasculate him in front of his supposed "subjects." The tide was turning at Logstown.

Tanacharison had promised Washington that he would assist him in whatever way possible, and sent his runners to fetch his wampum speech belt from his hunting cabin to the north. The following day when the critical artifact arrived, the Half-King and Scarouady both pressed Washington for the details of his mission. While the Virginian could not reveal the precise contents of his sealed message (largely because he did not know himself), he was anxious to receive any intelligence from the Iroquois. What he learned was not pleasant, and not a joy for Scarouady to repeat. News had reached Logstown that the French had held a general meeting with members of the Delaware and Shawnee at Venango, the large village to their north. At this meeting a well-known French interpreter named Joncaire informed the Indians that the next spring *la troupes de la marine* planned on occupying and fortifying the Forks, making them "masters of the Ohio."[17]

While the story reminded the Virginians that they were in a race against time to beat their enemy to the task, it rattled the Iroquois. Any meeting held in Iroquois territory should have been organized through them, and the French had bypassed their authority to go directly to the Ohio Indians. For Tanacharison it was now apparent that despite his efforts, control of the Ohio was slipping through his fingers.

If a French flag did end up flying at the Forks of the Ohio, it would be lost to the British forever.

As the next day passed Tanacharison continued his dual efforts of travel preparation and lobbying of the Ohio chieftains for support. Although he found limited success, some good news did emerge when the Delaware king Shingas, now absent from the village, sent a message pledging his support. Despite the fact that Shingas was held in high esteem in the Ohio River valley, his support would help only if the Delaware people in the surrounding areas still honored his title; in an age of such uncertainty, nothing remained set in stone.[18]

For the Half-King, regardless of his feelings toward the Virginians, French success was detrimental to the Iroquois and he promised Washington and Gist that he would deliver the sacred black and white wampum string, a symbol of war in Iroquoia, to the French garrison to their north. Finally, on November 29, Tanacharison called a general meeting of all sachems present in Logstown. The topic of discussion would be a final offer to prepare a delegation to address the French. Tanacharison, representing the Iroquois, would offer one final plea to the Ohio nations for their support. None accepted.

What developed in that cabin on that night, outside of the wondering ears of the Virginians, was a critical moment in the diplomatic history of colonial America; rather than honoring the time-honored obligations to their imperial oppressors, the Ohio Indians opted to openly abstain. Never before would a maneuver like this have been possible, and it reflected crumbling Iroquois power more than the unity and strength of the Ohioans.

The next morning, as the Virginians hoped for good news in the form of a large and determined Indian delegation, they found only disappointment. Washington was approached by just four Indians. First and foremost was the Half-King himself. Tanacharison was the highest ranking Iroquois delegate of the region and his participation was crucial. Next was another well respected Iroquois of Cayuga ancestry named Jeskakake; rounding out the delegation was the decrepit Seneca imperialist Kaghswaghtaniunt, Belt of Wampum. Joining them as a fourth was the young Seneca Guyasuta.

Guyasuta had often been left out of the conferences held at this site because of his rank in the hierarchy of those present. Kaghswaghtaniunt was the ranking Seneca, and Guyasuta would normally defer to him. But with a major diplomatic confrontation with the French on the horizon and with Iroquoia's empire at stake, Guyasuta's presence as a young aide would be welcome. While we have no definitive lists of which sachems met with Washington and which abstained, the simple fact that the Virginian describes Guyasuta only as a "Hunter" indicates that he had not interacted with him in an official capacity over the six days that he spent in Logstown. The inexperienced Washington tended to overstate the stature of any officials in his personal writings so as not to offend them, no matter how minor a figure they may have been.[19]

The delegation, though determined, was not going to alter the destiny of the Ohio Country. They were primarily Iroquois imperialists and therefore already sided with the British. On November 30 the party set out, and Guyasuta would experience his first taste of European diplomacy and the pitfalls that came with it.

For the expedition to be successful, the Iroquois believed that the Anglo-Indian force would need to work together, and Washington agreed. Many of the Virginians undoubtedly kept their distance. Much as throughout history, shared geographic landscapes of mixed cultures fostered a climate of distrust and often fear. For the modern observer, this delegation could and should be viewed as a joint venture by two equally impressive imperial bodies of coinciding interests, however for many of Gist's team it was simply not the case.

One member in particular, Gist's reliable number two Barnaby Curran, had a life of experiences to account for his pre-existing prejudices. In 1750, at the Ohioan village of Muskingum, Gist and Curran were privy to an elaborate and brutal torture and dismemberment of a female prisoner. While the Virginians watched a scene of such extreme aggression in horror, it represented a symbolic and often sacred form of violent politics to the Indian peoples involved. While Gist was shocked by the event, he understood the difference of viewpoint between the two worlds, and though he did not condone such actions he did nothing to prevent it. Curran was not so accommodating; the cruelty of the means of death and the public display of the young female's remains prompted him to remove and bury the body later that night. This form of violence was by no means unknown among the Europeans. The Half-King Tanacharison, as he marched toward his destination, likewise lived with the ghosts of his past. As a younger man the Seneca chief claimed to have witnessed his father murdered, boiled, and eaten by a French war party.[20]

For Guyasuta, the opportunity of working with the British would prove a formative experience. As a Seneca the diplomatic ties to the Crown held by his forefathers obligated him to cooperate, but his own suspicions of the men needed to be assuaged. He would have most likely known of Gist, at least in name, because of his earlier expeditions into the Ohio Country, but the six-foot-three Washington may have been an enigma. The Virginian appeared to have neither practical understanding of diplomacy, nor much experience in the elements of frontier life. He did seem to be honest enough and capable, but his age would have troubled Guyasuta. From the native perspective, respect and honor were often earned through the forge of battle and the subsequent equity of wisdom, but Washington had neither of those things. His great-grandfather John Washington did have a reputation as a conqueror a century earlier in Virginia with the nickname Conotocarius, or "destroyer of villages," but the young Seneca was not likely to have made that connection.

At twenty-one, George Washington was younger than Guyasuta and far less experienced in actual combat. Guyasuta was approximately seven years older, but a lot had happened in that seven years. Before consideration of a personal alliance with the British, Guyasuta would need to see more of their strategy unfold. The tentative plan for the delegation was to march northward at a brisk pace, despite the wintry conditions, while stopping for rest at prominent Indian villages along the way. As they were crossing the well-traveled Venango Trail, the large village that was its namesake would be their obvious destination.[21]

Venango was a large town, nearly the size of Logstown but less important in the region. Originally a Delaware village, *Venango* translates to "a mink," almost certainly a nod to its trading prowess. The village itself was mostly inhabited by Ohio Indians, and the noticeable Iroquois absence allowed European traders to gain a foothold. Venango was not unlike many of the small towns that men like George Croghan had found particularly friendly to British trade during King George's War. Much in the way that Croghan damaged the profitability of Fort

Detroit by intercepting its regular customers at Pickawillany, an Englishman named John Fraser so found success at Venango by undercutting Logstown. In 1753 when the French occupation began to overwhelm the Ohio Country, many Englishmen fled the region; John Fraser was understandably one of them.[22]

Tanacharison had his own business at Venango. While Logstown was still under his imperial jurisdiction, Venango had become something of a bastion for the rebellious Ohio Indians who were supposedly under his control. By making an appearance at the village the Half-King hoped to both confront the agitators and show that he maintained some power.

The man that both the Virginians and Iroquois sought was a familiar presence and the most vocal French ambassador in the region. Philippe-Thomas Chabert de Joncaire was born in Montreal in 1707, but spent much of his childhood with his father among the Seneca villages of New York. Because of his penchant for the language and customs of the Iroquois, Joncaire was soon given the nickname Nitachinon, which stuck for the remainder of his life. Tanacharison had met with Joncaire in the past, and the Frenchman made no apologies for his peoples' ambitions to dominate the region. If a meeting was going to occur, which was an almost unavoidable prospect, the young Guyasuta would play only a limited role in the proceedings. In the minds of his elders, Guyasuta represented the future of the Confederacy. He would need to watch and take note of the operational functions of mediation, but what none of the men realized was that the diplomacy of the future would involve not wampum strings and peace pipes but war clubs and muskets. The sachems that Guyasuta was required to respect would not survive the decade, and neither would the world that any of them knew.[23]

By all accounts the Virginians wasted little time seeking out Joncaire upon their arrival at Venango. For Washington, his experiences at this Indian village would be very different than at Logstown. Venango was now a French diplomatic stronghold in the region but did not have the sturdy cabins the Euopeans built at Logstown. It was still very much a native town built out of necessity and sustained by trade, and its proximity to the Venango Trail made it a natural gathering point for all peoples.

The French had built two forts to the north already, and they planned to construct a third at this site. The one cabin that did stand in the town was built by the recently departed English trader John Fraser, and now the French fleur-de-lis flew boldly over it. The Virginians knew that this would be the place to find Joncaire, and in Washington's mind perhaps the time to deliver the precious ultimatum of Lieutenant Governor Dinwiddie. Washington and Gist made for the cabin, and the Iroquois tended their own business in Venango.

Washington's meeting with the French is now the stuff of legend, but the Iroquois council with the Delaware the following day is often overlooked. While most historians have described Washington's dinner with Joncaire as an insight into European affairs in the Ohio Country, in reality the exchange meant very little. The men dined, wined, and Joncaire subsequently insulted both Washington and his countryman Gist. In his drunken stupor Joncaire brazenly proclaimed that the French would be victorious and there was nothing that Washington could do to stop him. The young Virginian politely excused himself and wrote of the meeting bitterly in his journal. In truth neither Washington nor Joncaire was in a position to affect European colonial affairs in any way, therefore the meeting boiled down to a night of drunken chest-thumping.

Of the events within Venango, however, the Indian council did have a dramatic impact and offered much more of a glimpse into the actual state of things. Tanacharison would for the first time realize how successful French efforts to woo the Ohio Indians had been. At the council, Tanacharison demanded that the Delaware offer their war belt, an infamous string of wampum, to the French in an official declaration of hostilities. He further legitimized his demands by stating that even Shingas gave his permission for such a maneuver. An unknown Delaware sachem rose in response, and the answer that the Half-King received was an ominous warning: "It is true King Shingiss was a great man, but he had sent no speech. . . . I cannot pretend to make a speech for a King."[24]

Tanacharison was dumbfounded. Shingas offered his support to the Half-King, but why was no word of this passed on to the Delawares of Venango? If the string was to be delivered, it should have been handled by the highest-ranking Delaware sachem in the area, Custaloga. He was not present, and neither was the war belt.

The Delaware response is a classic example of subjected peoples testing the waters of possible autonomy against their traditional masters. The Delaware sachem's answer entangled Tanacharison in two ways: the first was that the Delaware claimed that no authority had been given to them personally by the higher power of Shingas; the second was that Shingas's absence allowed them to give no answer at all. The Delaware of Venango were able to hide behind the veil of ambiguity, and Tanacharison could do little to change that. The other interesting aspect of this exchange was that even if Shingas did personally deliver the order to declare war against the French, there is little evidence to suggest that it would be noticed. The French strategy has always been to instill in the Delaware a sense of new opportunity, a way to escape the traditional chains of command that kept them suppressed. This new birth of freedom was about escaping not just the Iroquois, but their own culpable leadership as well.

After concluding the ineffective council with the Delawares, the slighted Tanacharison was determined to save face by appearing as proactive rather than reactive and went to the cabin of Joncaire to state the case of his own people. Because of the closed nature of their meeting, all three additional sachems would have joined him. Kaghswaghtaniunt, Jeskakake, and Guyasuta filed behind the Half-King into the cabin to present the monumental war string to the Frenchmen inside. For Washington, this development was very troubling.

Despite his inexperience of Indian affairs, the young major watched nervously as the Iroquois entered Joncaire's lodge. He wrote "I knew that he [Joncaire] was an interpreter, and a person of great influence among the Indians, and had lately used all possible means to draw them over to his interest; therefore I was desirous of giving him no opportunity that could be avoided."[25] He was correct.

Shortly after the sachems sat down in the cabin, the liquor began flowing freely. Though it had originally been a French custom to share a drink with their counterparts, it was quickly becoming an essential part of Indian diplomacy as the French realized that the native peoples often would drink themselves willingly into an incoherent state. Guyasuta like the others had drunk alcohol before and quickly became inebriated, but this may have been the first time that he tasted fine French wine. It was a sweetness that would prove hard to resist. Joncaire transformed the night of diplomacy into a drunken night of lavish gift-giving and reminiscing with the elder sachems about their experiences in upstate New York, and any talk of war disappeared.

The following morning, Tanacharison sluggishly made his way to the Virginians' tents to request that Washington join him in council later that night with the chiefs of the village yet again. "As I was desirous of knowing the issue of this, I agreed to stay," Washington wrote. That night the village of Venango was congregating around the Iroquois, Washington, and now Joncaire himself for the instrumental delivery of the Iroquois war belt. The Iroquois stated openly that with this black and white belt the confederacy would officially declare war on the empire of France. Joncaire, recognizing his inability to accept such a declaration, artfully dodged accepting the belt. Tanacharison again spoke and presented the sacred wampum, and Joncaire again avoided its reception. For the Ohioans in the village it was amusing to see such a once proud man reduced to such a sorry state; a "Half-King" indeed.[26]

Joncaire's refusal to accept the token was not without reason. He knew that he was not the man to accept such a proclamation, and he requested that Tanacharison take it north to Fort Le Boeuf and deliver it there. This would have been an inconvenience, but ultimately acceptable. Fort Le Boeuf was the natural destination of the Virginians anyway, so extending this delegation northward would not have been difficult. To ensure safe passage Joncaire designated that a party of French soldiers would supply the travelers and escort them personally to the next post. Tanacharison had not expected to venture so far north, but the fact that he had to further proved his ineffectiveness.

For Guyasuta, though he stood firmly beside Tanacharison, these events would likely weigh on his mind. He had been raised among the Ohioans, they were his personal friends and allies, yet his political obligations rested on his duties to the Iroquois. What occurred in Venango that night was a pathetic display of the state of Haudenosaunee power, and Washington's wide-eyed presence was almost meaningless. On the converse it was the French and Delaware that appeared the stronger of the two in almost all negotiations over the last two days, and Guyasuta would have looked on in envy. If this was what the great Iroquois Empire had been reduced to, and Washington was the best the British could provide, he would have had serious doubts about attaching himself to their side of the pending struggle for much longer.

The Anglo-Indian party of about ten men set off for Fort Le Boeuf on December 6. Two days later, they arrived at the small village of Cussewago, about fifteen miles from their destination, about a day's walk. After spending the night there, the Virginians had hoped for an early start to maximize their travel time and available daylight, but the Iroquois were hesitant to leave the small Indian village. Tanacharison had spent the morning berating and cross-examining the Delaware sachem Custaloga regarding his conspicuous absence during the last days' proceedings. Custaloga was one of the most powerful Delaware chiefs in the region, and held complete domain over two major villages—Cussewego and the aptly named Custaloga's Town. It would have been Custaloga's duty to supply the war belt of the Delaware peoples, and he made no attempt to do so. Tanacharison considered Custaloga an ally, and his inaction was likely one of the worst betrayals suffered by the Half-King thus far.[27]

By December 9 the party was feeling the effects of the long march to the fort on French Creek. It was an arduous journey and the wintry conditions began to wear on the Virginians. While Washington and Gist traveled on horseback, the Iroquois marched on foot. Washington would write often of their natural acuity for handling the terrain. As the party clashed with the elements, it would often fall on the least senior among the Indians, Guyasuta, to provide labor. During their northward trek he was often responsible for hunting, and Washington notes that he killed two buck in one outing.[28] When the party reached an impassable river it was likewise Guyasuta who fashioned a

Fort Le Boeuf as it may have appeared in 1753. (*Report of the Commission to Locate the Sites of the Frontier Forts of Pennsylvania*)

raft out of logs that he had cut himself. Though the gesture was waved off, it does offer a valuable glimpse at the man whose appearances in written sources are precious and scarce.

The next evening as the forests were beginning to darken the party was within reach of Fort Le Boeuf, and the French escorts assigned by Joncaire since Venango sent a message ahead alerting the commandant of their presence. Soon a group of French militiamen appeared from the wilderness to guide the Virginians and Iroquois north to the position. Gist wrote, "they received us with much complaisance."[29]

Fort Le Boeuf itself was a standard wilderness fortress built by the French during their campaigns of the eighteenth century. Consisting of four wooden bastions, surrounded by a larger but similarly shaped outer fence, the fort was not likely to withstand a massive British attack. And it was not meant to. While the French used the modest advanced architectural elements of the day when constructing the simple fort, Le Boeuf was designed merely to hold enough men to reinforce the positions to its south when they were completed. Inside the fort stood four barracks with enough room to sustain approximately eighty men and between the outer and inner wall of the fort was a garden for sustenance; in the cold Ohio Country winter there was little indication of that.

When the Virginians and Iroquois arrived there was little fanfare, and the meeting that Washington desired with the

Commandant became a strategic waiting game. Jacques Legardeur St. Pierre was an experienced member of the French military and a knight in the military order of St. Louis. He would have instantly recognized the inexperience of Washington and the Indians' susceptibility to persuasion. The reason given to the young major was that St. Pierre preferred to await the arrival of the commandant of Fort Presque Isle on Lake Erie before any official deliberations could begin. The Virginians had no choice but to wait, and Washington kept a close eye on the Iroquois in the meantime.

By December 13 the requested officers were present in Fort Le Boeuf and Washington presented Dinwiddie's letter. While the French deliberated in their private quarters, great efforts were taken to make the Iroquois feel welcome and all four sachems received gifts of weapons and leather goods. That night, as Washington waited anxiously for a response from the commandant, Tanacharison and his mates were continuously accommodated by the light-hearted French and the toils of the Virginians became a distant memory. Again, the elders of the Iroquois had dealt with Europeans in this fashion for most of their adult lives, but for Guyasuta the effect was magnified even greater. He was standing in a fort in the middle of wilderness, and the might of New France surrounded him in the form of almost one hundred able-bodied men with seemingly endless supplies and resources. The muskets and powder horns that he coveted in his youth or saw brandished by the Ohioans to the south appeared within his reach, available for the asking. While the Virginians had proven themselves to be clumsy, the French made every indication to Guyasuta that they were in complete control. The Half-King, Jeskakake, and Kaghswaghtaniunt could easily see through this fog of temptation, but it likely attracted the relatively inexperienced Guyasuta.

The following morning Tanacharison informed Washington that he genuinely attempted to deliver the war belt to the French, but was deflected with "many fair promises of love and friendship ... peace and trade." St. Pierre even went so far as to promise that a cache of goods would be delivered immediately to Logstown as a show of good faith. Furthering his cause, the commandant supplied the Virginians and Iroquois with canoes to speed up their return journey. Shortly after the meeting concluded, Washington approached St. Pierre to express his disgust with the commandant's advances toward the Iroquois. St. Pierre responded by stating that "the Country belong'd to them, that no Englishman had a Right to trade upon those Waters; and that he had Orders to make every Person Prisoner that attempted it on the Ohio, or the Waters of it." That night, Washington received a sealed envelope to be returned to Lieutenant Governor Dinwiddie post haste.[30]

Early the next morning the Virginians awoke to the spectacular generosity of New France when the commandant ordered a mountain of supplies be given to the party for their return journey. As his men began packing and rationing the supplies, Washington watched intently while St. Pierre continued to shower Tanacharison with affection: "He was exerting every Artifice that he could invent to set our own Indians at Variance with us, to prevent their going 'til after our Departure: Presents, Rewards, and every Thing that could be suggested by him or his Officers—I can't say that ever in my life I suffer'd so much Anxiety as I did in this Affair; I saw that every Strategem that the most fruitful Brain could invent, was practic'd, to win the Half-King to their Interest, and that leaving Him here was giving them the Opportunity they aimed at."[31]

Tanacharison approached the young Virginian to inform him that the sachems would remain at the fort for one more evening upon the request of St. Pierre. For their cooperation St. Pierre offered them a supply of state-of-the-art firearms as a token of gratitude. Incensed by this development, Washington rushed to the commandant to complain of ill treatment. He demanded that the French allow the Indians to leave on account of the delay it would cause his men. St. Pierre casually dismissed the major's grievance and promised to expedite his journey as much as possible. Washington had seen the difficult realities of French diplomacy and it seemed that the native peoples could be purchased by simply heaving gifts in their direction. What the Virginian could not see was the larger drama playing out in front of him. Tanacharison and the Iroquois would never side with New France—their allegiances were firmly with Britain—but the French paid little mind to that fact. The practice of gift giving in the Indian world was central to their concrete style of diplomacy. Not only was it a manifestation of good will, but the goods that the French had been pumping into the Ohio Country acted as the single largest stimulus to the native economy in North American history. The presence of New France in the region was a rising tide, and their regular flow of powder, weapons, and supplies lifted all the ships of the Indian populace.

Finally on December 16, the Virginians were prepared to leave the desolate French fort behind them and begin their weeks-long journey home. Washington had abided by the Half-King's wishes to remain another day, and now that he possessed a written response from the commandant to the governor, time was of the essence more than ever. Though Washington did not read the note, he was certain that it reasserted French claims to the region and that it could actually be a written declaration harsh enough to provoke open conflict. It was a war that he hoped to be a part of, and all he needed to do was deliver the message. St. Pierre and the French flattered the Iroquois more openly on this day, and when the liquor began to flow the Virginians hastily pulled their Indian companions away.

The landscape of the Ohio Country loomed as a frozen wasteland ahead of the party. French generosity meant that they need not worry about supplies, but Gist ordered several of the party to carry a good portion of the foodstuffs ahead to Venango in order to take advantage of a break in the winter weather. Because of that decision, the Virginians' group was smaller than it had been for almost six weeks, and their pace southward increased rapidly. But the Virginians moved slower than the Iroquois; the Indians maintained that if they could move ahead they could set up camp and await the Virginians' arrival; Gist agreed. When the weather changed suddenly, however, Gist decided that camping without the Indians was the best course of action.

The Virginians finally caught up with Tanacharison and the sachems the next evening. Guyasuta had earned his moniker of Hunter yet again; he shot, killed, and prepared three bears for

dinner. While for Europeans, higher rank often entails less physical labor for higher pay, from the native perspective, respect is
earned by experience and effectiveness. Though Guyasuta was a
minor sachem, his prowess in physical efforts such as hunting
would only define his power. By comparison, when Washington
returned to the comforts of Mount Vernon in Virginia, supping
before a marble-surrounded fireplace, his stories of having to
hew log rafts and cook his own food over a campfire would seem
extraordinary for a man of his standing. For Guyasuta it was
expected.

At sunrise of December 17 the Virginians continued their
southward march and the Indians remained behind at camp
while an unnamed member of their party was conspicuously
absent. Though Gist never names who this was, a likely guess
would be Kaghswaghtaniunt. Perhaps in an effort to regain the
prowess of his youth, Kaghswaghtaniunt may have taken on
some physical task himself. While the Virginians had set out
hours before, we know that Tanacharison and his sachems did
eventually catch and pass Washington and Gist by using the
canoes provided by the French. Why at that point they began to
use the crafts may give some clues as to what had delayed
Kaghswaghtaniunt. The Virginians remained unaware, but it
appeared that the elder sachem had been seriously injured days
earlier.

When the Virginians arrived at Venango on December 22,
Gist called on his team that had been sent down days earlier.
Washington went to find Tanacharison, who had arrived the
previous afternoon. As the men talked the Half-King explained
that Kaghswaghtaniunt "had hurt himself much, and was sick,
and unable to walk, therefore he was obliged to carry him down
in a canoe."[32] It was a treacherous journey for all involved, and
the fragility of the Iroquois elders only highlighted the importance of a young strong man like Guyasuta on a mission like this
one; in the months to come he would begin to replace them in
a much more profound fashion as well.

Tanacharison explained to Washington that because of the
unfortunate condition of Kaghswaghtaniunt he would remain
for the time being at Venango. The major insisted that the Half-
King stay away from the French, and Tanacharison assured him

that he knew Joncaire's tricks all too well. Tanacharison then told the Virginians that "he would order the Young Hunter to attend us, and get provisions, etc. if wanted." Guyasuta helped the men prepare their horses and collect their supplies. Because of the way Washington writes of him, never using his actual name, it is most likely the two men never spoke in their entire experience together. They said their farewells, and the Virginians turned southward alone.[33]

Guyasuta probably paid little mind to the British as they disappeared into the forest, and he was probably relieved that the mission was over. He had seen all sides of this struggle over the past several weeks, and the comparisons were obvious. British and French, Ohio and Iroquois, Indian and European; each conflict was a very real one, and each conflict had its own balance of power. Over the past month Guyusuta felt as though he had been on the losing side. The ineptitude of the British compared to the power and organization of the French was not worthy of comparison, and the feeble nature of the three sachems that he had just nearly single-handedly supplied proved that Iroquoia was not what it once was, either.

While it is not clear whether Guyasuta committed to either side, British or French, by this point, he would never be too distant from the might of New France. From what Joncaire had said earlier, the French would soon build a fort at Venango; for the time being Guyasuta would call this place home. Within hours the ties to the Virginians that he marched and camped with were a distant memory, and the young sachem had no idea that the next time he would see Washington would be at the other end of a musket barrel. The Ohio Indians that surrounded him were the people that he related to best, and the distinct lack of an Iroquois presence at Venango would allow him to set aside his old heritage and allow his new identity as a Mingo to begin to define him. As the sun began to set, Guyasuta probably headed for the cabin of Philippe-Thomas Chabert de Joncaire to partake in the many riches of New France.

TWO

Victory on the Monongahela

BRADDOCK'S DEFEAT, JULY 1755

The rushing currents of the three rivers could barely be heard over the chatter and excitement of the battle to come. Alongside the Allegheny, Monongahela, and Ohio was the extraordinary sight of Fort Duquesne, less than two years old, and a war party of nearly nine hundred men. In the fifteen months the new fort had been standing, the very fabric of the Ohio Country had changed drastically. At the Forks of the Ohio now sat a collection of Frenchmen, Canadians, Delaware, Shawnee, Mingo, and countless other Indian nations from the Great Lakes region.

The administration of New France had coveted this hallowed piece of ground for years, and Fort Duquesne was their bold statement that the French Empire would hold domain over the area, and more importantly that the French way of life would prevail over North America. The fort, though modest by today's standards, was designed in the image of the great fortifications of Europe with all the intentions of dominating the new frontier. It was small, no more than 200 feet across at any given point, but its mere presence allowed its larger mission to be accomplished. Standing at the mouth of the Ohio, Fort

Duquesne had taken command of the river that flowed directly into the Mississippi, and therefore connected an empire that reached from Canada to New Orleans and rivaled in size any in the world. Roughly the distance from Paris to Moscow, the extent of unified New France was a statement to all enemies that all-out war was a risk King Louis XV was willing to take.

It did not take long for such a challenge to be answered. En route to their position was the first legitimate attempt to capture the fort in the form of a British force of nearly thirteen hundred provincials cutting a swath through the North American wilderness that stretched over one hundred miles. At the helm of the "flying column" was General Edward Braddock, the epitome of the English martial gentleman, a man who combined the sheer force and brutality of war with all the grace befitting an officer of the British Empire. The small outpost at the Forks would face its initial great test, and for the approximately two hundred French soldiers garrisoned inside, it would be among their first tastes of open combat between Europe's two most powerful empires. On this day, though the French and Canadians stationed at the fort were outnumbered nearly seven to one, they beamed with confidence.

They would not be engaging the British alone. Congregated around Fort Duquesne was a joint Indian force of over six hundred warriors, able and hungry for action. It was the first great dividend paid for years of courtship and costly gift-giving, and the French hoped that their investment in winning the affections of North America's Indians would continue to pay off in the future. While the majority of them, nearly 90 percent by some estimates, came from the Great Lakes region, there were significant numbers of locals as well. The Ohio Indians were not numerous, and among them was Guyasuta.

For the young sachem, the two years since breaking with the Half-King at Venango had been critical in the formation of his ever-expanding reputation. Among the Mingos the thirty-year-old Guyasuta had become a key figure in their pivotal decision to participate in the coming war, and his respect and admiration was set to grow after this day. Despite the esteem among his own people, Guyasuta was something of an anonymous figure among the hundreds of warriors from the Great Lakes nations.

He had benefitted from French hospitality for two years, but he remained hesitant to make the great leap of renouncing his Iroquois roots and siding fully with New France. This impending battle would likely sway the chief one way or another, but the confidence of the Huron, Ottawas, Chippewas, and the other distant nations that greatly outnumbered him made him feel more certain of the prospects of a true French alliance.

It was July 7, shortly after sunset. Guyasuta was preparing for the coming clash, and it would be the first time that he would take the field of battle as a truly powerful war chief. The Half-King Tanacharison had died a year earlier, and though his Mingo people barely had developed a true identity of their own, they hungered for a great warrior to rally behind. As he began to paint his body in the ceremonial colors of war, he let his mind focus and body relax. Using available iron-rich ingredients and berries, Guyasuta stained his arms and body red. His face was black, caked with charcoal residue. As he gathered powder and shot provided by the French, it would have been impossible not to notice that he was surrounded by an army of others appearing just as he did. The application of war paint was a ritual to build focus and calm within the warrior, and strike fear into the hearts of his enemies.

He was a modern Indian warrior; he carried with him all the tradition and victories of his forefathers as well as the tools of the eighteenth-century world. On his shoulder was a French musket to be fired with Canadian shot and powder, at his waist was a war club or tomahawk. The firearm would be devastating at a distance and allow for a sudden approach, but the killing blow would be delivered by hand. A warrior's worth was measured by the scalps he collected and the personal bravery he displayed. Surrounding him were six hundred others with the same focus and same ambitions, and though they came from different regions of the continent and spoke different languages, their coordinated attack would break down even the most disciplined forces of the Western world. It was a system that worked, a style that combined experience of the recent world with every value of the past.

Guyasuta was unknown to most of the men around him, but his success this day would make him the heroic figure that his people needed to rally around. A victorious return by his Mingo warriors would be a critical step in legitimizing their self-determined mandate to exist. As the French began to move out south toward the Monongahela River, Fort Duquesne was soon flooded with threatening war whoops. The party began their trek to war.

Only two hundred strong, the French Regulars and Canadian Provincials were confident of their chances; approaching the fort, Guyasuta cared little for the glory of New France. He, like the hundreds of others around him wearing the war paint of their forefathers, was prepared to fight and die for his way of life.

The developments that led to one of the most disastrous engagements in British imperial history on July 7, 1755, stemmed from George Washington's fateful mission two years earlier. As Guyasuta marched through the brush and dense forest so familiar to him, yet so alien to his French allies, he probably never considered how circumstances over the last fifteen months had against the odds led to precisely that moment. The past was behind them all, and the current day's events could determine the future of a continent.

Though seemingly benign at the time, the letter that the young Virginian carried to Williamsburg in 1753 contained a brash pronouncement to all British readers that the French had no intention of leaving the Ohio Country. Furthermore, New France would expand its influence farther south to the Forks of the Ohio as soon as the spring thaw began. Although Washington did plan on carrying the message from Fort Le Boeuf personally to the lieutenant governor in Virginia's capital city, Dinwiddie was sure what the response would be even before he saw it; Washington's mission was a mere formality.[1]

Dinwiddie was aware that the French were seeking full occupation of the Ohio Country, and if he could determine a way to stifle that plot (or at least hinder it) he could derail their entire North American strategy. An evaluation of the situation revealed to policy makers in Virginia that whatever their great counterstrike would be, it would need to happen quickly. The French made the tactical error of delaying construction in the winter months, and only two of their proposed four forts had been built. While progress on the third, what would be Fort Machault at Venango, would begin at the spring thaw, Dinwiddie believed that any plan should center on the Forks of the Ohio, the nexus of strategic and diplomatic activity in the region. A concerted effort to occupy the Forks of the Ohio before his enemies could arrive would not only forestall their occupation but also, Dinwiddie believed, give the Crown an immeasurable advantage if war were to break out. Lt. Governor Dinwiddie dispatched an expedition under the command of Captain William Trent and Ensign Edward Ward to march on the vacant triangle of land and build a fort in the name of King George II.

Even before he had delivered his correspondence from St. Pierre to Dinwiddie—in fact, even before he reached Williamsburg—Washington discovered this plan. En route south back to the capital city the young Virginian, tired and worn, was passed by what he counted as no less than seventeen fully loaded pack horses in a beeline for the Ohio Country; whatever decision the major believed his letter would provoke, it appeared that things were already under way without him.

When Trent and Ward arrived at the Forks in January 1754 they were greeted by none other than Tanacharison himself. He, with his chief second Scarouady, welcomed the arrival of the Virginians. For Tanacharison, the construction of the fort at the three rivers was the lesser of two evils. In his mind, though it spoiled the grace of the region, and signaled what he hoped would be a permanent British occupation, it would also guarantee that the French would fail in their efforts to undermine his Iroquois way of life. In a show of unconditional support between the Virginia and Iroquoia, Tanacharison laid the ceremonial first log of the new fort. "[The] Fort belonged to the English and them and whoever offered to prevent the building of it they the Indians would make war against them."[2]

In the midst of a frozen Ohio Country winter the team of forty-one provincial Virginians broke ground and began the construction of Fort Prince George. Named for the future King

George III, the stockade would hardly withstand a major attack, but it was not designed to. Expediency took precedence over defensibility, and policy makers were well aware that the mere presence of a British installation was all that was needed for a larger effect to be felt. In Dinwiddie's mind the tiny fort would remind the French enemy that they were not alone in this venture of conquest, and that the British were just as anxious for a fight as they were. The Indian trade and diplomacy that would occur there were welcome developments, but they were by no means his primary purpose.

Back in Virginia, George Washington had delivered his letter and insisted on being part of the new maneuvers in the land he had just returned from. His demands also came with a requested promotion, stating erroneously that no man in Virginia knew the land better than he. Despite stumbling along the way, and nearly dying twice on his return home (both due to his own incompetence), George Washington was given the rank of lieutenant colonel. At his command would be no motley crew of Indians and frontiersmen but over one hundred and thirty provincial militiamen from the Virginia colony. His mission was to garrison the new fort built at the Forks and maintain a steady presence in the Ohio Country; Washington believed he had earned this right, but he would soon learn that his studies in the science of war were only beginning.

After almost four months of hasty construction and disorganized encampment, Fort Prince George was standing sheepishly at the mouth of the great Ohio River. It was small, yet it commanded a view of three rivers and already several Indian delegations had made their way to the site. Tanacharison used Fort Prince George as his great pitch to his subject peoples of the Ohio Country, though it did not impress them in the way that he had hoped. The elder chiefs of the Ohio Indians, those still respectful of their duties to the Iroquois, scoffed at the new outpost. They argued with the Half-King that its existence would only ensure escalation of conflict, and the French and British would rain war down on the region. If that occurred it would only be a matter of time until their young warriors would be drawn in, and that would spell disaster for all of them. The New Ohioan was a young man, hopeful for change in the future, and a war that a fort like this could create would give them the means for that change that they so desperately wanted. The Ohio sachems did not agree.

Tanacharison was dejected by these developments, but little did he know that his woes had just begun. After he was rejected time and again by men whom he had negotiated with his entire career, soon the Delaware that supplied the fort with wild game began refusing to hunt based on these objections. Tanacharison found himself a lonely man within a British fort. Finally, on April 17, 1754, the worst fears of the men stationed at the Forks of the Ohio were realized. Gliding down the Allegheny River toward them was a flotilla of over five hundred French, Canadian, and Indian allies. Floating downstream from their positions to the north, the British watched in terror as the occupation force that they feared had suddenly become an invasion force. Several dozen canoes and rafts landed on the shores of the Forks of the Ohio and quickly surrounded the fort.³

With their muskets pointed directly at the feeble Fort Prince George, the commanding officer of the French force demanded to speak with its commandant. The man leading this invasion was a savvy, experienced officer in the form of Captain Claude-Pierre Pécaudy, signeur de Contrecoeur. He was aggressive, and only months earlier had taken over for Legardeur de St. Pierre as the highest ranking official in the Ohio Country. His presence was a blunt indication of French intentions: this site would be taken by force if necessary, and when acquired it would be the new base of French power in the region. With Captain Trent absent it would fall on Ensign Edward Ward to negotiate with the French. Captian Contrecoeur offered the young Ward two options: both required giving up the fort. Only one allowed for him to leave unharmed.⁴

Ward unceremoniously surrendered Britain's greatest asset that day, and as his meager force of only forty men began to vacate the site and return southward, a deeply offended Tanacharison shouted to the French that it was he who laid the foundation of that fort. Though passionate, his admonishment largely fell on deaf ears.

Eleven days after being expelled from the Forks, Ward reached the plantation of Christopher Gist at Wills' Creek. He and his men were unharmed, but dejected. As his party had moved south, Washington's men had been marching north, and on April 25 the two groups converged at Gist's property. While Washington believed that he was marching to reinforce the existing British Fort Prince George, he was shocked to discover from Ward that the position was lost. What had been Virginia's would-be defensive garrison at the fort under Lt. Colonel Washington had suddenly become a de facto offensive force to recover the fort for the colony. Soon after these developments, the Virginians stationed at Wills' Creek received notice that Dinwiddie had rallied support from the surrounding colonies, and reinforcements in the form of North and South Carolinians, Marylanders, and New Yorkers would soon be on their way.

In the downtime, Ward took advantage of the quiet by passing on a message to Washington from the absent Half-King. It read: "We have been waiting this long time for the French to Strike Us, now we see what they design to do with Us; we are ready to strike them now, and wait your assistance. Be strong, and come as soon as possible."[5]

Though the Virginian was still green in his recent venture of military service, the Half-King's earlier experiences with the newcomer in 1753 had convinced the sachem that while he was not the ideal choice, Washington was his only option. Washington returned with a message of confidence to Tanacharison that he would arrive at the Forks with expediency.

Leaving Wills' Creek behind, Lt. Colonel Washington marched his men northward. It was a long trek, and one that he was quite familiar with, having just done it five months earlier. From his travels in the region Washington believed that his men would be best suited to attack the French from a position downriver along the Monongahela. During his march Washington regularly corresponded with Tanacharison about his progress using runners, and after a nearly fifty-mile march the Virginians made camp at a natural clearing known as Great Meadows. After days of marching through seemingly endless forested hills and valleys, it was a natural point to pause and allow his men to recover and their animals to graze. Aside from the pragmatic qualities of the site, the night before Washington had received word from his Iroquois ally that a party of fifty French and

Canadians had left the Forks seeking out Washington's men. In the Virginian's mind it could only mean an attack was imminent.[6]

What Washington did not realize was that the party mentioned by the Half-King was on a purely diplomatic mission. Led by a young ensign Coulon de Jumonville, the thirty-two French were seeking out the Virginians in order to deliver an ultimatum to retreat immediately. In reality, it was not unlike what Washington had done only six months earlier at Fort Le Boeuf. With thoughts of combat in his mind, Washington received word from Tanacharison that the French were not far from his current position. Assuming the worst, the twenty-two-year-old lieutenant colonel took a small number of militiamen in the dark of night to locate the Half-King's camp. Once there, Tanacharison supplied valuable intelligence—he knew the precise location of Jumonville's camp and acting quickly would allow their joint forces to strike first. The men agreed and marched through the dark of the early morning. What Washington was prepared to do was unprecedented in the New World. To this point there had not been a single shot fired at a British party by a French soldier in the Ohio Country, and an attack like he planned would be reason enough for any government to feel obligated to respond. It was a testament to Washington's inexperience, and Tanacharison's desperation.

At sunrise on May 28, the Half-King had delivered on his promise. As his intelligence suggested, Ensign Jumonville and his men were found encamped in a deep ravine surrounded by a sloping hill on one side and a steep cliff face on the other. It was a precarious place for an encampment, and a violation of nearly all forms of combat strategy, but the French and Canadians in the party had no intention of attacking anyone; they had no intention of being attacked themselves. While Washington and his men posted themselves around the ravine, Tanacharison took his warriors to the back flank of the French camp. While it is unknown which party actually fired first, when the French and Canadians woke up and saw Washington's men a firefight ensued.

Waving his summons in the air and through the aid of an interpreter, Ensign Jumonville desperately shouted that he was on a peaceful mission and was protected under the common convention of European war. Surrounded, some of Jumonville's men attempted to escape by retreating but were quickly intercepted by the Half-King's warriors and slain. When the firing stopped, eight to ten French Canadians lay dead in the bottom of the ravine.

Recognizing his folly, Washington approached his new prisoners and attempted to make sense of the confusion. Jumonville himself spoke no English, and by all accounts his men spoke little either, and the communication barrier only added to the disorder. Taking into account his previous actions, it may have appeared that Washington inadvertently broke a series of rules (both written and unwritten) that could lead to war. The damage however could have been minimized and written off due to miscommunication. That was until Tanacharison completed his intended mission.

As Washington and his men tried to decipher the written message from the new fort called Duquesne, the Half-King accosted the officer Jumonville with a series of rhetorical questions. The sachem tugged on the jacket of his prisoner and, according to one source *"asked if he was an Englishman."* Knowing full well what side the young man represented, the Half-King recited in perfect French, *"Tu n'es pas encore mort, mon père."*[7] Translated, the Half-King spoke "Thou are not yet dead, my father," and suddenly split Jumonville's skull open with a vicious swing of his tomahawk. Watching the scene before him in horror, Washington would have barely understood the meaning of what he was witnessing as Tanacharison wrung his hands in the brain matter of the fallen Frenchman. For over a century the empire of France had positioned itself as a friend and ally to the native peoples, but that covenant was one that Tanacharison would no longer recognize.

Neither Tanacharison, nor any Indian sachem, believed that the European ritual of signatures on parchment signified an agreement. He was from a tradition in which writing did not develop, and words on paper meant nothing to him. In his world, Jumonville represented the king of France himself, and by killing him in such a brutal display Tanacharison made the greatest diplomatic statement of his life. The Iroquois would no longer cooperate with the French, and he was now firmly allied with Washington and the British. It was a gruesome form of politics, but in the native world ink was temporary, and blood was eternal.[8]

Bewildered and unprepared for the sight before him, Washington marched his men back to Great Meadows to comprehend the scale of what had just happened; when he arrived he learned of more unexpected news. In an unusual twist of fate, a letter was delivered from Dinwiddie informing the men that a freak accident in Virginia had led to the death of a high ranking officer in the Virginia colonial militia, and as a result the young George Washington was promoted to the rank of full colonel. With this new and sudden promotion came complete control over his existing regiment, and two hundred more troops carrying artillery. With this new empowerment, Washington had decided that the only course of action was the full-scale destruction of Fort Duquesne.

In consideration of this venture, the freshly minted colonel joined his Indian allies at Wills' Creek, Gist's plantation, to discuss the possibility of military assistance. Tanacharison was present, and with him was the Delaware king Shingas. It had been over three weeks since the massacre at the glen and the repercussions were already being felt. Though the men did not know it, at the Forks Captain Contrecoeur had prepared a punitive force to find the Virginians and make them pay; to ensure its success the party was to be led by Louis Coulon de Villiers, the older brother of the slain Ensign Jumonville.[9]

Talk of retaliation had been brewing for some time at Fort Duquesne. As Washington pled his case even the Half-King was not convinced that an assault would succeed. The colonel pleaded with the men to gather their people and to begin "sharpening their hatchets in order to join and unite vigorously." Unconvinced, the Indians decided that Washington's men were in no position to attack anyone, and an incursion at the Forks could only end in disaster. The colonel offered their peoples the guarantees of protection and shelter in the event of a war, but the sachems had already decided. Before leaving Washington to his fate, the Delaware Shingas approached the colonel, the man he had only met ten months earlier, and offered what

Washington described as "strong assurances that he would assist us." With that pronouncement, the Half-King, Shingas, and their delegates marched to safety almost a hundred miles away along Aughwick Creek.[10] Washington was now abandoned, or so he thought.

Nonetheless, Washington prepared for the coming engagement against Fort Duquesne even without his Indian allies. He believed that he had the resources to not only initiate an assault but also make it a successful one. Little did he know that the battle he sought was quickly on its way to find him.

On June 28, the French Captain Villiers began his southward plunge from Fort Duquesne with over six hundred French and Canadian soldiers and approximately one hundred Indians from the Great Lakes region. Included in his party were warriors of the Ottawa, Huron, and Nipissing nations, as well as some defected Ohio sachems. Their mission was to find the Virginians responsible for the death of Ensign Jumonville and "punish them for the murder that they inflicted . . . in violating the most sacred rights of Civilized Nations." Villiers was anxious to avenge his brother's death, but his experience in the region was minimal and the only Indians in his party who were familiar with the grounds were the small number of Ohio Indians. Following their recommended paths and sending them ahead as scouts, Villiers often reported that they would return with intelligence indicating that "the English were coming in Battle formation to attack." Villiers wrote that he believed this information was intentionally misleading, and pressed his attack onward; it was not the last time that he would be given deceptively bad intelligence by the Ohio Indians.[11]

Washington, still preparing for an assault on Fort Duquesne, was caught off guard at Wills' Creek when Scarouady, Tanacharison's chief second who had stayed behind at the Forks, arrived with news of Villiers' approaching attack. Realizing that he was in grave danger, Washington sent his men on a two-day, forced backtrack to the Great Meadows to do whatever was possible to defend against impending disaster. Before he had left his army weeks earlier, the colonel had ordered the construction of a small circular fortification to be built in the center of Great Meadows. Although it was designed as a mere base of operations for his ever-growing force, it now became his last line of defense against almost a thousand hostile enemies with revenge in their hearts. The name that Washington's men gave it, Fort Necessity, was now truer than ever.

When the colonel arrived back at the fort he was without Indian allies, and after a head count he found that only three-quarters of his four hundred men were healthy enough to engage in the fight to come. Trenches were hastily dug around the position, and they soon filled with water when it began to rain. The date was July 3.

Despite the Virginian's efforts, Fort Necessity was hardly adequate. In the middle of an open field surrounded by high ground, it sat at the bottom of a bowl-shaped plot of land surrounded by dense tree cover, and was only large enough to accommodate about sixty men at a time. The rain had been persistent, and most of the Virginians' powder was now soaked and unusable. When the French arrived an hour before noon, the battle commenced as expected. It did not take Villiers long to see just how weak the enemy's position was, and he used the thick forest canopy for shelter and camouflage. With their powder dry and the Virginians trapped, the French party poured lead into their enemies. Though the battle raged all day, Washington's men felt the twinge of desperation begin, and some retreated inside their meager fort to begin drinking. By nightfall Washington tallied that thirty of his men were dead, and sixty were wounded; surrounded and battered, the Virginians were sure that the end was near. Suddenly, however, an hour before midnight a voice called to the Virginians from the forest: "Voulez-vous parler?!" The call was asking if Fort Necessity would be willing to surrender.[12]

Why the French captain called for surrender when his enemies could be so easily finished off has plagued historians for over two centuries. Washington and his men had no chance of victory, and though Villers was running low on supplies he still had enough men to overrun the position. Why call for surrender? Why then?

In much of the colonial story, giant gaps seem to invite interpretation all too often resting on fate or coincidence. Many saw the fact that Washington was spared on this date as a twist of irony in the life of a man who would go on to do great things. In history, however, there are no coincidences. We need to go beyond viewing this event as an entirely European affair; only when the role of the Indians is considered does a clearer picture develop.

Captain Villiers' call for the surrender came suddenly, and the Virginians were caught off guard. If the circumstances of the battle did not prompt the Frenchman to call for parley, then what in the status quo was altered so much that he felt compelled to do so? Villiers writes: "As we had been exposed to the rain all day long, and the Detachment was very tired, and the Indians had informed me they were leaving the next day, and it was repeated [by the Indians] continually that drum beats or cannon fire were heard in the distance, I proposed . . . that we offer to speak with the English."[13]

Villiers had been given false intelligence that "drumbeats or cannon fire" were heard in the distance. While he was low on supplies himself, that alone would not have stopped him from overwhelming the Virginians. The prospect of the enemy obtaining reinforcements, however, would change his viewpoint. The bad intelligence he received was no mistake, but a calculated effort by the Ohio Indians of his party to protect Washington. Recalling the days leading up to the battle, the Delaware Shingas promised Washington that he would "assist" the Virginians. That assistance came not in reinforcing Fort Necessity, but in misdirecting its would-be French conquerors.

Shingas directed such a tactic not however out of admiration for the young man, but rather to retain balance in the Ohio Country. Though the Ohio Indians would eventually side with the French in the Seven Years' War, by 1754 they had yet to do so. It appeared that Fort Duquesne would be at the Forks for some time, and Shingas recognized that without the British the French would be uncontested in the region. The salvation of Fort Necessity was a last gasp at neutrality by the Ohio Indians before larger circumstances forced them to choose sides.[14]

After Washington accepted the idea of surrender by waving the metaphorical white flag, it fell on Villiers to determine what to do with his prisoners. Logistically, he had to contend with a series of obstacles. To begin, Villiers had nowhere to hold his prisoners. Fort Duquesne did have a modest prison, but it could in no way contain the four hundred Virginians now before him. If he wished to capture Washington as a prisoner of war, he was limited by the obvious fact that war between France and Britain had yet to be declared; even if he did take the colonel hostage he would need to transport him to Canada for trial. With these issues in mind, Captain Villiers offered Washington surrender with what was called "the honors of war," a compliment of one officer to another that allowed the vanquished to keep their weapons, flags, and personal items.

As Washington signed the surrender, he felt sorry for himself at the loss that he had just suffered. Worse yet, as the commanding officer he would forever be associated with the defeat. Unable to read French, the colonel relied on his interpreter, a Dutchman named Jacob Van Braam, to review the terms of surrender. With Van Braam's approval Washington signed the document. What the young colonel did not realize, and would not be aware of until it was far too late, was that the document that he signed had written into its language an admittance of the assassination of Ensign Jumonville. With his signature, George Washington had confessed to the flagrant murder of a diplomatic envoy, an admission that could give the empire of France full justification for a declaration of war on Great Britain. As he and his men vacated Fort Necessity and headed back to Virginia, Washington allowed his anguish to overcome him, and he knew that the date of his surrender would haunt him for the rest of his life. It was the fourth of July.

The reactions to the events at Jumonville Glen and Great Meadows were varied, but all three peoples (British, French, and Indian) began their own processes of response. Two months after Washington's surrender, along Aughwick Creek in central Pennsylvania, Tanacharison, the Half-King, held a general conference with tribal leaders of the Ohio Country. Aughwick Creek had served as a key stopover from the frontier back to civilized English colonial society in the colony of Pennsylvania and George Croghan had profited heavily from its traffic by establishing a trading post there. While the Half-King attempted to maintain an air of civility and openness, his true intentions were poorly masked: he called the sachems together that September day to retain their pledge of loyalty to the Iroquois Confederacy.

Most of the chiefs in attendance shared his sentiments that, for the time being, the Iroquois still held their respect. The Ohioans, however, would also attest that with the presence of Fort Duquesne and with the recent developments at Great Meadows it was becoming very difficult to avoid French advances. The Iroquois had a long-standing history of good relations with the British, but for the Ohio Indians there was little in their daily lives to attest to that fact. They had respected the traditional alliance, but the colonies of Pennsylvania and Virginia were not nearly as adept at providing them with goods as the French. The whole of the Ohio Country's Indian economy was based on their ability to receive steady supplies of European goods, and the French were offering deals too sweet to set aside. They not only offered more goods to the Ohio Indians at Fort Duquesne, but they also offered them at a cheaper rate. In many ways, the Aughwick Council would be the Half-King's final attempt at retaining order, and one statement in particular has proven definitive of the night's proceedings.

Tamaqua, an increasingly powerful sachem and brother of the Delaware Shingas, rose and delivered the following address to Tanacharison: "You . . . told Us that You took Us under your Protection, and that We must not meddle with Wars. . . . We have hitherto followed your directions and lived very easy under your Protection, and no high Wind did blow to make Us uneasy; but now Things seem to take another turn, and a high Wind is rising."[15]

For all of his efforts, Tanacharison's struggle would be in vain. On this night it was clear to him that his way of life, and the order that defined it, was an old one. The Ohio Indians had made their statement that neutrality was the dream of an aging system, and the New Ohioan sought his own system away from the traditional constraints of the previous generation. They did not tell the Half-King that night that they would side with the French or the British, but if war came to the Ohio Country an alliance with one of them would be unavoidable. Tanacharison kept that message with him, and the Half-King died less than a month later outside Harrisburg.[16]

Across the Atlantic, responses to the news from the colonies had taken on a different tone. With the threat of a costly war on the horizon, policy makers in London began to divide themselves regarding which course of action would be best for the empire. Debates raged in the halls of Westminster but eventually the hawkish majority had its way. It was decided that though the potential of war would be expensive, the prospects of winning such a conflict far outweighed the costs to the imperial treasury.

Committed to stifling the French effort in North America, Parliament decided that two regiments of foot, the 48th and 44th, would be sent to Virginia under the command of the grizzled and experienced veteran General Edward Braddock. Once landed, they would be joined by two regiments already present in America and thousands of provincial colonists would be raised as well. It was an impressive fighting force, and commanding officer Braddock was soon appointed commander-in-chief of all British forces on the continent. The authority handed to Braddock would make him the single most powerful man in British North America, and his appointment was never intended to be secret. In response to the mobilization of the two British regiments, the empire of France sent three thousand infantrymen (enough to form nearly six regiments, four times the strength of Braddock's forces) to the New World. France's military expansion to keep pace with Britain had increased New France's capacity to wage war by nearly 25 percent.[17]

Before North America could truly be tamed and conquered by the Crown, the British needed to gain control of their own colonies on its eastern seaboard. For over a century the independent colonies had acted as separate entities, adopting their own policies and, in some cases, initiating their own localized wars. In 1744, during King George's War, the colony of New York acted so independently that it hardly begged permission from London at all. Each colony had its own character, and very rarely did they act in concert to accomplish much of anything. This was a troubling prospect for Britain and its interests, because a disunited attempt against the French was almost certain to fail. Only a few months earlier at a council known as the Albany Congress, delegates from seven colonies came together to discuss a host of issues ranging from Indian affairs to a potential North American union. Their interests proved to be so diverse that little was accomplished, and the meeting's defining feature, a plan to create a unified colonial entity put forward by Benjamin Franklin of Pennsylvania, was voted down easily.

By placing Braddock as commander-in-chief of all North American forces, the Crown found a practical way to circumvent the squabbles between colonial legislatures while using the backdrop of an impending war as a justification for the measure. In 1755, upon his arrival to the New World, Braddock hosted a conference in Alexandria, Virginia, to raise funds for a joint venture against New France. Those present, all colonial governors, included Robert Dinwiddie of Virginia, Horatio Sharpe of Maryland, Robert Morris of Pennsylvania, William Shirley of Massachusetts, and James DeLancey of New York.

Though the men could not agree on the figures (the governors believed the funds should come from Parliament, not within the colonies) they did devise a strategy for removing French interests from their respective spheres of influence. It was decided along the Potomac River that April day that four of New France's most vital installations would be attacked, captured, and occupied by the armies of Great Britain. Among them would be Crown Point, Fort Niagara, Fort Beausejour, and finally Fort Duquesne. Highlighting the importance of the fort at the Forks of the Ohio, Braddock proclaimed the he would lead that assault himself. After Fort Duquesne fell he planned on taking his men northward to capture the auxiliary forts leading to Lake Erie as well.[18]

By late May Braddock had amassed his invasion force at Wills' Creek; he ordered a fortification built and named it Fort Cumberland after the politician in Britain who selected him to lead this charge. Fort Duquesne was easily within reach, and from their new launch point into the Ohio Country Braddock saw little to keep him from his goal. In the days leading to his march, Braddock was flooded with all the auxiliary duties and troublesome woes of an officer preparing for an engagement, one of which was meeting with the Indians of the region. Escorted by the new Half-King, Scarouady, who had taken the mantle following Tanacharison's death, members of the Delaware and Shawnee sat with Braddock in council. Among those present was Shingas, perhaps the last hope for an Anglo-Delaware alliance. It had been almost a year since the French had taken command of the Ohio Country and by all accounts the Ohio Indians seemed anxious to help Braddock in his quest. Fort Duquesne had allowed the French to become oppressive in the minds of the sachems, and a British victory may have been the lesser of two evils. When one of the chiefs rose to ask what the status of the Indians would be in a British Ohio, Braddock's answer was stunningly honest. "No savage should inherit the land."[19]

With that proclamation the Ohio Indians promptly left Scarouady and Braddock to fend for themselves. While the French had become cumbersome, at least they recognized the Indians' right to exist. In the previous exchange Braddock revealed his great flaw—the great flaw of all imperialists—in not recognizing the necessity for collaboration with aboriginal peoples. When Benjamin Franklin, who had come to Fort Cumberland to profit off of the sale of horses and supplies, approached him and told of the need for Indian assistance, Braddock curtly replied, "Savages may indeed be a formidable enemy to your raw American militia; but upon the king's regular and disciplined troops, Sir, it is impossible they should make any impression." In his hubris Braddock had not only denied Britain a precious alliance with the Ohio Indians, but sowed the seeds of his own defeat.[20]

As Braddock left Wills' Creek on May 29, his massive army of more than two thousand stretched nearly two miles across the wilds of the Ohio Country. Their march would last over a month, and along the way Braddock hoped to carve a road into the forest that would allow easy access to the site in the future. However, as progress was found to be terribly slow, the general made the decision to split his army in two and to create a "flying column" that would move much faster toward their intended target. Left out of the flying column were some of the army's heaviest artillery. Quickly moving forward, the flying column was sixty miles ahead of the rest of the force at its greatest separation.

Braddock's march would have been an impressive sight. Consisting of twelve hundred people, the leading force consisted of British Regulars and American Provincials. In the rear were approximately two hundred and fifty men and women in support roles, bringing the food and supplies that would sustain the large army. At the front was Braddock himself, fully clothed in the regalia of the King's Regular Army. In a brilliant red jacket, Braddock maintained the appearance and might of the British Empire. With him was a who's who of up-and-coming officers, including George Washington, now one of the general's primary aides-de-camp. Washington, who now fancied himself a genuine military man, bought into the image of Braddock as the great conqueror. He marveled at his poise and confidence and for the month-long march gushed over the parcels of wisdom that the general bestowed on him. By July 9 General Braddock's flying column had begun to cross the Monongahela River just nine miles south of Fort Duquesne.

Little is known of how much the French at Fort Duquesne knew of Braddock's force before it arrived. By July 6, Captain Contrecoeur seemed to have received word of the army bearing down on him, but reports indicate that he had no accurate sense of its size. Although Braddock only had twelve hundred in his advance guard, Contrecoeur was dealing with intelligence from Indian scouts that he had as many as four thousand. The captain's garrison at Fort Duquesne was a formidable two hundred French and Canadians, but nothing compared to those numbers. For the French to find victory he knew that he would have to act first, and he was in desperate need of Indian allies.

With rumors circulating around the Forks that Braddock's goliath army was coming, there was much debate among the Indian peoples present over whether engaging it was the best course of action. Many nations, particularly the prominent Great Lakes peoples, appeared anxious for the fight, yet others had their doubts. In all there were nearly seven hundred warriors at Fort Duquesne, and the politics between them was every bit as complex as anything mustered in the palaces of Europe. Contrecoeur needed a figure that could bring together and rally the Indians to his disposal, as he himself had not been successful to that point. The man he turned to was a recently appointed underling named Daniel Hyacinthe Marie Lienard de Beaujeu.[21]

Beaujeu was a young hopeful in the French military and a valuable asset to the captain as he was born and raised in Canada. Beaujeu had extensive experience with the native peoples, and like the British Americans, he was affected by his interactions on a deeply cultural and sociological level. He could deal with the Indians in a way that a man of France could never understand. Living in North America, for a provincial, was not the same as living in Paris or London. Although they flew the same flag, it was truly a new world. As much as Beaujeu would have been transformed by Indian interactions, the Indians were equally altered by his people and these two societies developing side by side influenced one another immensely.

On July 8 Beaujeu spoke passionately to the hundreds of Indian warriors but failed to convince them to join his cause. Many were swayed by his speech, but some nations, like the Potawatomi, remained hesitant. It was agreed that if some of the warriors held back, none would join the French. That evening, a group of Ohioans approached Contrecoeur and Beaujeu to discuss their willingness to engage Braddock. While no names are given, it is indicated that the men were representatives of the Shawnee and Iroquois nations of the valley itself. While the French likely had not yet noticed a people as separate from the Iroquois, this was likely the Mingo. If it was the Mingo, then Guyasuta would have been speaking for his people on that night. To Guyasuta, such a pronouncement would have been monumental, as he was outnumbered nearly ten to one by Great Lakes warriors who were long-time allies of the French. For him to offer the open support of his people would have spoken volumes to Contrecoeur regarding the state of the Ohio Country. Aside from the obvious outcome of this meeting it also would have made Guyasuta recognizable as the leader of this new Mingo people, and the French would know to seek him out for future considerations.[22]

The following day Beaujeu began his rally cry again, and dressed in full war paint, the Canadian whipped the nearly seven hundred warriors into a frenzy. Whatever impassioned speech the Canadian gave dissolved enough of the doubt among the Indians to mobilize for the defense of Fort Duquesne. They and about two hundred Candians and French soldiers began their march at approximately eight o'clock in the morning.

The plan of attack was a simple one. As the French and Indians did not know the true strength of Braddock's force, they believed an ambush as he crossed the Monongahela River would be the most effective course of action. Yet, knowing his army was nearby but not exactly where, and taking into consideration the lateness of their march, there was very real concern that the force of nearly one thousand men would not reach the river in time to set the trap. Only expediency would win the day and the two hundred French and Canadians and six hundred Indian warriors pushed southward in search of their quarry.

The two forces destined for collision pressed onward in the July heat. The British believed that Fort Duquesne would be an easy conquest, while the French thought they were taking on an impossibly large force. When Braddock reached the Monongahela River, the last obstacle of his great conquest would be faced. If he was going to be attacked, Braddock believed, an ambush while his army was at its most vulnerable while fording the river was the most likely scenario. As his two-mile train of soldiers and supplies began to emerge on the other side of the river, however, it appeared that the French had missed their lone chance of stopping him.

Guyasuta and the warriors around him set the pace of approach realizing this fact. Though Contrecoeur had hoped for an ambush, both the Indians and the French believed their window of opportunity was closing quickly; they did not realize that they had missed it all together. Pressing hastily forward with the Indians was Beaujeu, shirtless and painted like the warriors around him. It seemed like a trivial gesture, but the young provincial was earning their respect with every stride toward battle. Guyasuta was surrounded by hundreds of young men of different peoples from hundreds of miles around, and although they would work together, Indians fought as a group of individuals seeking individual success. When the trap was sprung, every warrior would rush the enemy in pursuit of personal glory. If the natives won the day, they would be six hundred champions rather than one victorious army.[23]

Braddock's army had moved much more quickly than expected, and as the long trail continued to climb out of the river, victory appeared to be assured. Those yet to cross the

Monongahela River were as much as two miles behind those in the front of the column, but once fully landed the force would have been on a speedy march to Fort Duquesne. Yet from the front of the line, those in back heard shouting followed by gunshots. The forces of twelve hundred British troops and nine hundred French and Indians had collided head on. In their rush to establish the ambush, the Indian warriors and Canadian militiamen had run unknowingly into the front end of Braddock's flying column. The first reaction was confusion, followed shortly by total chaos. Surrounded by dense forest, and recognizing the enemy before them the British under Thomas Gage unloaded a disorganized volley of musket fire. In mid-stride Daniel Beaujeu fell dead.[24]

By this time both armies had turned initially in retreat: the British out of surprise, and the French, unaware of how large an army awaited them, out of fear. But in the midst of the confusion between the armies of the two most powerful empires of Europe, the Indians began their assault without need of direction. In a flash the natives split into two massive parties and dissolved into the forest. Using the bright red coats of their enemies as a focal point, the warriors formed in dual columns parallel to Braddock's thin line and attacked from the both sides.[25]

It was a complete breakdown of the rules of war, an utterly disorganized melee, and therein lay the strength of the Indian attack; their strike was a model of order and efficiency disguised as mindless savagery. As the British tried to make sense of the situation evolving around them the Indians to their left and right began to fire into the column. Recognizing how the Europeans behaved in war, the natives targeted the mounted officers of Braddock's force. One by one the supervisors on their horses dropped, leaving behind a rabble of redcoats with no one to direct them. To escape the madness, the front of Braddock's stretched out column turned in retreat only to crash head on into their own reinforcements moving toward them. In this now infamous showdown, much was to be learned about the fighting style of the English compared to that of the Americans. Although Braddock's Regulars did their best to retain their discipline while attempting to survive, many of the American Provincials took to the cover of the trees. They were familiar

"Defeat and Death of General Braddock in North America," a nineteenth century engraving. The French and Canadians fired from the woods like the Indians, and did not form a line of battle. (*New York Public Library*)

with Indian warfare, and they knew that the European methods of war had to be adapted to the frontier to contain the chaotic fighting style of the warriors around them. The battle raged for nearly three hours, and Indians retained their advantage, cutting down the British before them.[26] The results were staggering.

Braddock's army was decimated by the Indian warriors and supporting French and Canadians; more than two-thirds of the column were killed or wounded and sixty of the eighty-six officers present were dead. Among the wounded was General Edward Braddock himself. During the battle he boldly stayed mounted on horseback to direct his men, but was struck in the back by a musketball. Thrown from his horse as a result, he was perhaps the single greatest casualty of the battle. Though he survived the melee, Braddock would die less than a week later. His lone uninjured aide-de-camp, George Washington learned a powerful lesson. In the span of the three hours of engagement, Washington had two horses shot out from underneath him. Never leaving Braddock's side, he had multiple bullets rip through his coat, but miraculously he was never hit.[27]

As the British fled the field of battle out of sheer panic at the thought of a further Indian attack, the warriors that wrought so much damage did little to pursue. For them the victory had been achieved, and going after a retreating enemy enticed them little. Their reward was not a captured flag or a piece of territory—it was the spoils. From the Indian perspective, possession of land carried no weight, but artifacts of dominance in battle were their prize. Guyasuta joined the frenzy of warriors basking in the glories of their hard-fought victory. The plunder taken was immense; the wounded abandoned by their British brethren were quickly scalped, each grisly trophy a symbol of the individual warrior's achievement. The weapons and foodstuffs left behind were gathered as well. Some reports indicate that over two hundred gallons of rum were among the first rewards to be collected. The scene was one of both gore and celebration, and the warriors marched back to Fort Duquesne in triumph. The Indians whooped and cheered as they counted and compared their loot, and the French stood victoriously at the Forks of the Ohio.[28]

This was the great turning point in the early struggle for the Ohio Country. While the French had gained the favor of the Ohio Indians with years of trade and flattery, the utter devastation wrought over the British at what would be known as the Battle of the Monongahela cemented the alliance. Guyasuta and the other chiefs of the region had wrestled with the idea of declaring independence from, and therefore war against, their Iroquois oppressors, with the only inhibition being an inability to withstand the backlash. But, after smashing Braddock, supposedly the most able man in the British military, the upswell of pride and confidence was palpable among the native peoples. New France had always been more generous to the Ohioans, and now it was obvious its army was superior to its British counterparts. If the Mingo, Delaware, and Shawnee truly wanted to win their freedom from the Iroquois Confederacy, an alliance with France was the best option, for the success of one was directly entwined with the fortunes of the other.

One week later at Great Meadows, Washington had the painful duty of burying his fallen hero. To ensure that Braddock's body would not be dug up and disgraced, he was interred in the center of the road so as to disguise his final resting place. Washington wrote of his battle experience: "We were attacked by a party of French and Indians, whose number, I am persuaded, did not exceed three hundred men; while ours consisted of about one thousand three hundred well-armed troops, chiefly regular soldiers, who were struck with such a panic that they behaved with more cowardice than it is possible to conceive."[29]

Over thirty miles away, Guyasuta was firmly entrenched at Fort Duquesne enjoying the fruits of his victory. It was an air of joy at the Forks of the Ohio as the French believed their way of life had been proven victorious. The Ohio Indians likewise believed that destiny was as much in their own hands as ever. Since the battle had ended, the French post now had a much larger presence of Ohioans, and the Great Lakes peoples had begun their long return home to their native lands.[30]

New additions were arriving at Fort Duquense every day, and the shared empowerment made it the uncontested center of diplomacy and trade in the region. One of the faces that Guyasuta recognized immediately was that of Phillip-Thomas Chabert de Joncaire, the boisterous trader and interpreter he had known from Venango two years earlier. As the representative of his people, a now recognizable Mingo people, Guyasuta would have been duty bound to discuss the week's events with his former acquaintance. While they drank and spoke lightly at their first meeting in 1753, the tone of this night's discussion would be very different. What Guyasuta and Joncaire negotiated was an official alliance between New France and the Mingo people. Following the events at the Monongahela, all parties involved knew that a deadly conflagration was about to ignite. The kings of France and Great Britain were preparing soldiers for war on five continents to determine the great fate of empire across the globe, and the Ohio Country would be a key component. The great war ahead would bring down an empire, and make the winner an unchallenged global power.

THREE

Uncertain Alliances

THE SEVEN YEARS' WAR, 1756–1763

That autumn Guyasuta, Joncaire, and several Mingo sachems made the long trek north to the heart of New France; their destination was Montreal. To some, Montreal appeared more as a fort than a city. Surrounded by over 3,500 meters of stonework, this emerging and influential city of New France stood as a bold testament to modern engineering and imperial strength. The outer walls of Montreal stood a daunting six meters high, and its curtained wall created no less than fourteen formidable defensive fronts. The stonework was made of hand-hewn black limestone and across the perimeter of the walls were eight entrances, many equipped with drawbridges. In many ways this imposing fortified city was the brainchild of Gaspard-Joseph Caussegros de Léry. As the king's chief engineer of New France he had designed and constructed defenses for Quebec City, Fort Niagara, and Fort Saint-Frederic, but Montreal was his crowning achievement.

Caussegros de Léry's vision of Montréal combined power and grace, strength and majesty. Though the outer walls sent a daunting message to its enemies in North America, what was inside was even more precious. As the center of New France, Montreal contained some of the most exquisite structures on the continent, and those inside felt all the security and comfort of living as citizens of one of the world's greatest empires. Caussegros de Léry was assigned the task of defending the city within a year of his appointment, and after twenty-seven years it had proven to be a priceless bastion of calm in a very unstable new world.

Its fortifications aside, Montreal occupied a strategic position in New France. Nestled alongside the St. Lawrence River, the city took full advantage of the waterway that was the lifeblood of the colony. Along its shore, Montreal was lined with a massive stone construction of gun sites and steep sloping banks. In this way a symbiotic relationship with the St. Lawrence developed; its currents fed and supplied the city, and if an enemy invaded the river, Montreal would be its protector.

The people of Montreal were as unique as the city itself. With over four hundred houses within its walls, Montreal sheltered soldiers, settlers, and members of religious orders simultaneously. Its streets were landscaped with gardens, and its buildings exemplified the finest architectural elements of Paris. At the heart of the city was the stunningly beautiful Church of Notre Dame, proving that Montreal was as much a Catholic power-base as a political one; in the French world the line between the two was often too blurred to recognize.

It was in this city that Guyasuta had found a new home for the last few winter months of 1756. The previous fall he had come to the city, and it was everything that Joncaire had described to him before his arrival. Following the Battle of the Monongahela Guyasuta had ventured to the site with twenty of the Mingo peoples' most respected sachems, and he had the honor of being the chief orator of his people during their long stay. They had met some of the most influential military officers of the French Troupes de la Marines, and were even able to hold council with the Governor-General of New France himself. Pierre de Rigaud de Vaudreuil de Cavagnial, formerly the executive of Louisiana, had assumed control of the whole of the continent less than a year earlier, and he was pleased to form an alliance with Guyasuta's Mingo people. After Braddock's defeat the Iroquois Confederacy reasserted neutrality to Vaudreuil, and the presence of this new group of renegade defectors reassured the policy makers in Montreal that the Haudenosaunee were growing more powerless by the day. Montreal had seen many delegations of natives passing in and out of the city, and the council with the Mingo certainly meant more to Guyasuta than to Vaudreuil.

The harsh Canadian winter had forced Guyasuta and his sachems to remain at Montreal for the winter months of 1755 and early 1756, during which time the warrior chief grew accustomed to French ways. He had seen the way that his people could benefit, and when compared to his past experiences with the British he was sure that his decision was the right one. In spite of these recent developments Guyasuta desired a return to his homeland in the Ohio Country, a region torn apart by the scourge of war. In his meetings at Montreal Guyasuta formulated a clear strategy of attack for his people, working alongside the French war effort, to devastate British ambitions in the region. His plan of calculated ambush and a campaign of terroristic propaganda would require cooperation between the warriors of his own nation as well as the Delaware and the Shawnee; he knew that thousands would die, including many by his own hand. Fort Duquesne would be his base of operations, and his effectiveness would be measured only by the fear he could spread and the scalps that he could compile. It had been a very long winter, and at the first great thaw of spring he and his sachems would return south to deliver the message of alliance to the Ohio Indians.

The St. Lawrence River was now rising, and the season of war was set to begin.

By the summer of 1756, the Seven Years' War, the great imperial struggle between France and Great Britain, would be fought on five continents and embroil their traditional allies in heated conflict around the globe. The Ohio Country, only one of dozens of theaters of the war, had become a drastically different world.

The frontier, once teeming with Indian and European settlements alike, was now again a desolate wilderness. The agreement between the French and Indians of the Ohio Country was a complex arrangement, largely supported by promises that would never be fulfilled. From the perspective of the local natives, if the French defeated their English nemesis their lives would improve dramatically. They would receive trade goods directly with no interference from the Iroquois Confederacy, and for the first time in over a century they would implement their own policies on their own terms. It was a lofty prospect, and for those new freedoms the Ohioans took up the war hatchet alongside their French "fathers."[1]

While the armies of New France conducted their war on British fortifications around the continent, the natives took on a familiar role as a key component of French imperial strategy. They would sometimes join their French allies on the field of battle, but most often their greatest effect was on the Ohio Country frontier itself. In many ways the Seven Years' War was a battle of worldviews. All parties involved believed that they were fighting for the supremacy of their own way of life, and to vanquish their enemy was to see those practices blessed and inspired by God himself. While the Europeans often decided the outcome of their wars by capturing a hill or planting their flags triumphantly on a piece of enemy territory, no such tradition existed in the Indian world. As no man owned the land, at least not in a way that was meaningful to the Indians, the land was not a commodity—it was simply a battleground.

For the Indians to be successful their war would not be waged on the idea of Britain, but on the British themselves; the only meaningful expressions of English presence in the Ohio Country were the settlements established by the colonists themselves. By attacking and destroying those settlements and trading posts inhabited by the British, the Indians saw a practical and effective way of removing both the settlers and their worldview once and for all. Therefore, while the armed forces of New France performed disciplined, orderly maneuvers against strategic military positions, the Indians would simply pillage and plunder on the frontier. It was in this combination of managed assaults and seemingly chaotic raids that the French found their first true formula for success against their British opponents early in the war.[2]

For much of the summer and fall of 1756, Guyasuta and his Mingo warriors moved undetected across the frontier ambushing the homesteads and trading posts of English settlers and American Provincials with devastating efficiency. Day after day across the region, French-allied Indians swiftly attacked settlements in full war paint, spreading fear throughout the frontier. Although the raids appeared chaotic and savage, Guyasuta and his warriors had a keen understanding of psychological warfare. By assaulting and killing one family in an often gruesome and visible way, the Ohioans quickly realized that hundreds more would flee for their lives. In many cases the warriors would massacre one or more victims in extraordinary ways, such as dismemberment, and display them openly in the middle of a heavily trafficked road. When later settlers would discover the gruesome scene, panic would sweep across the countryside to inhabitants of all places that relied on that road. Therefore, while dozens were massacred in the summer of 1756, thousands more abandoned their settlements and became refugees in response.

What developed in the early stages of the war was a brilliantly applied form of strategic violence that made the frontier a completely undesirable place for would-be pioneers seeking to expand the English world. Guyasuta and the Ohioans used their unique brand of extreme violence and aggression to give the Ohio Country a reputation for savagery that became renowned throughout New France. In the east, reports like the following from an Englishman only perpetuated the intended fear desired by the Ohioans: "Our tender Infants hath their brains dashed out our wives big with child hath their bellies ript open those killed within their houses are mostly burnt with them . . . if thay flie into the woods or hideth in the hedges the murderers soon finds them & plunges their hatchets either into their brest or skull . . . their once sweet cheeks & lips now stained with dust & blood & their bosom filled with clotted gore."[3]

The effectiveness of the Ohioans on the frontier, coupled with French successes that summer, were ominous indicators to the people of Great Britain that they were losing the war. In March, French forces led a successful attack on Fort Bull near present-day Rome, New York; overseas in the Mediterranean the French took control of the key British stronghold of Minorca that May. Finally, in August of 1756, Fort Oswego fell in New York. All across the colonies of Great Britain it seemed that the ineptitude of leadership in London coupled with the momentum of the French would lead to the greatest defeat the empire had ever seen.[4]

Meanwhile, as war was officially declared in Europe, the frontier had continued its rapid descent into madness. The Indians took to their role in the larger military strategy well and became a vital component of New France's efforts in the Ohio Country. By targeting strategic points of British power on the frontier, the Franco-Indian alliance had proven itself to be quite effective. One particular endeavor stood out as a turning point that highlighted the destructive capability of the Ohio Indians. On the morning of August 2, Louis Coulon de Villiers, the same man who defeated Washington at Great Meadows, led a strategic raid on Fort Granville, an enemy position on the Juniata River that supplied all other forts to its west. Primarily designed to protect settlers from the dangers of the frontier, the post represented a major concentration of British power that the French believed needed to be eliminated.[5]

Villiers enlisted the assistance of the Delaware sachem known as Captain Jacobs, and with his warriors in tow they began their assault on the modest position with stunning efficiency. As fate would have it, when the attack began most of the garrison was spread throughout the surrounding countryside patrolling for renegade Indian bands, only magnifying the effectiveness of the assault. Throughout the night Fort Granville was besieged; with the employment of fire arrows it quickly was engulfed in flames. The commandant of the post was killed, and by the next morning his second-in-command John Turner was forced to surrender. Turner was tortured and killed by the Indians as a statement of their total war strategy, and the dozens of civilians inside were soon taken prisoner.[6]

In the wake of these events, the Quaker-dominated legislature of Pennsylvania raised funds to form an expedition to punish the Delaware and Captain Jacobs for their role in the slaughter. It was determined that the man to lead the force was Lt. Colonel John Armstrong, the brother of the slain commandant of Fort Granville. Their target would be the village of

Kittanning; a hub of Delaware activity in the region, it was also the home of Captain Jacobs and Shingas. Since the war had begun, both men had become instrumental in applying the Indian strategy of mass terror on the frontier, and each had a seven-hundred-dollar bounty on his head. They were considered by many as the faces of terror in the Ohio Country. Kittanning sat in the Allegheny River valley less than thirty miles from Fort Duquesne, and estimates placed nearly one hundred white prisoners at the site. In Philadelphia it was believed that to destroy Kittanning was to deliver a decisive blow to the Delawares' reign of terror in the west.

As Armstrong's three hundred Pennsylvanians initiated their attack on the position, many of the village residents who were noncombatants fled; Shingas, who most surmised was across the river, escaped. For Captain Jacobs, however, it would be his last stand. After he holed himself up in his cabin, Armstrong's force set fire to the building. The Delaware chief defiantly claimed that he could "eat fire," until a powder barrel exploded, killing him and his family. Witnesses said that the blast was so great that body parts were scattered yards away as a result.[7]

While the victory at Kittanning was a point of pride in the British war effort, it was the lone bright spot in the first two years of the war. Though Armstrong was lauded for his bravery, his raid produced mixed results. Though Captain Jacobs was dead, the Pennsylvanians suffered more casualties than they inflicted, and the warriors that escaped Kittanning took most of their hostages with them. At any rate, the resounding success of Armstrong's forces that fall was celebrated throughout the colonies, but for the Ohio Indians it was denounced as a massacre. Across the frontier for the remainder of the year hundreds of white settlers would die in brutal and torturous acts of retaliation.

The struggle continued to rage on the frontier throughout the spring and summer of 1757, and after two years of combat the British came to call the opening phase of the Seven Years' War "the Years of Defeat." Policy makers in London believed that they were losing the war, but stern examinations of the French and Indian combat strategy revealed some telling secrets. First, the Indians were a most effective distraction. By acting on their own and striking at random intervals, the Indian war never allowed the colonies of North America to focus on making organized counterstrikes at New France. The best they could muster were singular attempts at punishing individual peoples, such as Pennsylvania's foray at Kittanning. Second, although the Indian raids were effective, the French had little control over them. The Indians attacked wherever and whenever they wanted. As long as the Indians continued the fight, the French would only benefit. For this reason Vaudreuil ordered that weapons, liquor, and supplies be made available to the warriors at all times at the many forts of New France, Fort Duquesne among them.

Another glimmer of hope for Great Britain was the rift that appeared to be growing between the Ohioan warriors and the French army officers. In August 1757 Daniel Webb, the commandant of Fort William Henry, was forced to surrender after a successful siege by French general Louis-Joseph de Montcalm. The terms of the capitulation followed the tradition of a European war, and both parties agreed that all 2,300 persons stationed inside would be escorted out of the fort by a French guard to ensure their safety. Montcalm instructed the warriors attached to them to leave the surrendered persons alone according to the stipulations agreed upon by the French—a terrible affront to the native peoples. Believing that they were responsible for the victory, the Indians expected all the spoils of war. At five o'clock in the morning the next day, the Indian forces attacked the marching column of unsuspecting British detainees; killing nearly two hundred. One of the harsh realities of an alliance with an Indian nation during a time of war had always been that the battles rarely ended on European terms and never under European rules.[8]

Like the year before it, 1757 had ended in disaster for the British cause. While there was plenty to go around, most of the blame fell on the policy makers in London. It was generally believed that the current officials were too incompetent to organize such a massive war effort. In 1758, however, many in the City hoped their fortunes would change with the rise to power of William Pitt, the Earl of Chatham, now secretary of state.[9]

The traditional role of secretary of state was often limited in the British monarchy; however, due to the extraordinary circumstances of multi-theater war, the office was expanded to an extent never before seen. Pitt, ambitious and shrewd, was given control of not just the diplomatic arm of the empire, but also Britain's army and naval forces. With these resources at hand it was his responsibility to formulate Britain's new strategy to defeat the French empire. In short, he was given the unenviable position to fix the mess that his predecessors had wrought over the previous three years.

William Pitt (the Elder), the Earl of Chatham, led Britain through the Seven Years' War. (*Library of Congress*)

Pitt developed what he called in personal letters a "system" that addressed many serious issues at once. Generally, an examination of his policies would leave historians scratching their heads; they were a scattered lot of recommendations directed around the planet. The nature of the war had changed, and a global conflict made traditional practices a thing of the past. Only when the entire strategy was seen in operation could his tactics be appreciated. The plan that Pitt had devised was complex, but could be boiled down to a few basic points. The first would be to strip France of its most valuable colonies through the use of naval blockade and eventual invasion. By striking at key locations in French territory, such as Fort Duquesne in the Ohio Country, Pitt hoped that its weak grasp of the region would likewise end. To ensure that all of these maneuvers would be successful, Pitt added that only British Regulars should lead such attacks. He had felt that ample evidence was available that Provincials were not disciplined or experienced enough see the job done. The Americans, in his view, were still welcome to serve, but only in support of the Regulars themselves.[10]

The man selected to lead the charge against Fort Duquesne in 1758 was a stubborn and intelligent Scot named John Forbes. As a former physician, Forbes had proven himself to be a careful and steady man; the importance of the expedition would require such a figure to be successful. His plan was a simple reconstruction of what the French had done so well five years earlier. Fort Duquesne was reinforced with three forts directly to its north, and these three forts would serve as a line of communication back to Montreal. If Fort Duquesne would ever fall under attack, the presence of the northern posts would guarantee that the armies of New France could easily reinforce the position. Forbes would mimic this strategy by creating his own line of fortifications across southern Pennsylvania. He would march his men out of Carlisle, and slowly grind his way toward the Forks of the Ohio, building a road and several auxiliary forts along the way. It would take much longer than Braddock's march three years earlier, but it would remedy all the problems that prompted Braddock's failure.[11]

The obstacles to such a cumbersome expedition required that Forbes begin his march prepared, the weight of his task dictated that failure could not be an option. In the spring of 1758 Forbes launched from Carlisle into the great wilds of the Ohio Country, working as he moved. For every step taken toward Fort Duquesne, hundreds of workers toiled to tear up the virgin ground and carve out a wide road for later supplies to travel. As the men camped night after night, small posts were built to fortify the road, and at widely spaced intervals construction began on much larger forts that would stand as the backbone of the expedition.

By June, Forbes's campaign had reached the frontier outpost at Fort Loudon. Before the construction of what would be later called "the Forbes Road," Fort Loudon was terribly isolated. With the completion of the pass now in front of it, it became a hub of activity. The councils at Loudon that June were directed at gaining the alliance of nations who were not affiliated with the French and had little connection to the Ohio Country. At the center of this tricky diplomacy were the Cherokee. Forbes wrote, "the Cherokees are of such consequence that I have done everything in my power to provide them in their necessaries." To gain such an ally would bolster the British cause, and potentially turn the momentum of the war in their favor. The proceedings were challenging, and most of the oration from Forbes's side came from his second-in-command, Colonel Henry Bouquet. A mercenary of Swiss origins, Bouquet had fought in battles across

Europe, and he had proven himself as a capable leader in this wild country. The results had been mixed, but the young officer was hopeful nevertheless.[12]

Perhaps one of the most anxious onlookers attached to Forbes's massive force was Colonel George Washington. Though Washington only joined at Fort Loudon, he proved to be a valuable asset to Forbes as he led units of Virginians in a surveying capacity for the campaign. He would be one of the first men to find the best possible routes, and his history at their destination in the Ohio Country would make him one of the few officers that had actually been in the area. He had seen the Forks of the Ohio before any fort stood on its flats five years earlier, and to see Fort Duquesne fall would have held a special significance in his heart.

The march was long and slow, but by September construction had begun on a new fort called Bedford. Soon after, an advanced guard moved farther west to begin building Fort Ligonier at Loyalhanna Creek. From their current position, still over fifty miles from the Forks, Colonel Bouquet wrote to Major James Grant. The orders passed on by the colonel that night involved Grant, a Scotsman himself, leading approximately eight hundred Scottish Highlanders and American Provincials on a reconnaissance mission to survey Fort Duquesne. Upon arriving at the Forks, Grant was to record with as much detail as possible the position and situation of the fort, and return post haste to present the intelligence to Bouquet. When Grant's Highlanders left the site of Fort Ligonier they, like Forbes's entire column, anticipated victory in the months to come. What awaited them at Fort Duquesne, however, would reveal the brutality of Indian war.

On September 13, after two full days of marching, Major James Grant's reconnaissance force approached Fort Duquesne. To that point they had moved unnoticed, and Grant's primary objective of surveying the size and strength of the garrison at the position seemed easily within reach. Before he had left the post at Loyalhanna, Grant received a memo from Bouquet indicating that there were likely as many as five hundred French and three hundred Indians at the site. He dissuaded Grant from attempting to engage the fort at all, for with those numbers defeat seemed assured. As Grant surveyed the position, he was not so certain that his enemies were as strong as originally suspected.[13]

From his vantage point in the hills around the Forks, Grant estimated that there were probably no more than two hundred soldiers in the garrison. By those figures, even though the major despised American Provincials and thought little of their capability in battle, he figured even they should be able to overrun the position. Therefore, with no permission from his commanding officer, Major James Grant began strategizing his impromptu attack on Fort Duquesne. Considering his forces, Grant had at his disposal approximately eight hundred able-bodied men; more than half were Regulars. With those odds, Grant was quite confident that victory awaited him. That night his scouts located and burned a vital storehouse for Fort Duquesne located two miles from the Forks.

The next morning Grant deployed his troops into the formation that he planned the evening before. Using his best soldiers in front, Grant marched a company of Highlanders from the 77th Regiment of Foot directly toward Fort Duquesne itself. This maneuver would serve as a diversion to draw the enemy out and allow the second component of his attack to begin. After the French engaged the decoy company, Grant planned to unleash an ambush of provincial militia under the command of the Virginian Andrew Lewis. With the numerical advantage Grant believed he had, and the added element of surprise, the attack seemed foolproof.[14]

The morning of September 14, Guyasuta awoke at Fort Duquesne expecting little to develop. Since the inception of the war he had been well-supplied by the garrison and its new commandant, François-Marie Le Marchand de Lignery. When the warriors were not raiding the backcountry, they would often remain at Fort Duquesne to engage in lively diplomacy and consume seemingly endless quantities of liquor. The relationship that was formed between the two powers, Mingo and French, seemed to be benefiting everyone. It would have been a peaceful morning, and the rivers calmed by the coming coolness of fall.

Whatever Guyasuta had been doing was interrupted by the whining of bagpipes in the distance. It is not known whether the Ohioans at the Forks had ever heard bagpipes before, but the reaction of the French told them quickly that danger was at hand. Grant's decoy had gotten the attention of the French and Indians inside and around the fort as intended, but it acted more as an alarm than as a distraction.

Indians burning their prisoners from a title page. Accounts of Indian atrocities were a popular subject throughout the eighteenth century. (*Library of Congress*)

The warriors were caught off guard, but their erratic and responsive style of war dictated they were rarely unprepared. As Grant's company of Highlanders readied for battle, they were quickly overrun by the nearly five hundred Indian warriors that spilled forth from Fort Duquesne. In the chaos, Andrew Lewis's ambush contingent was spotted and soon engaged as well. The speed of the natives shocked Grant's force, and their ability to disappear into the surrounding wood line made fighting them in any orderly fashion nearly impossible. When Lewis attempted to rally the Virginians to support the overwhelmed Highlanders before them, they too were routed as the Ohioan warriors assumed the high ground above them, forcing a retreat. One soldier recalled that because the Indians were "concealed by a thick foliage, their heavy and destructive fire could not be returned with any effect."[15]

While Lewis's Virginians were left with no option but to run for their lives back to Loyalhanna, the Highlanders, including Grant himself, suffered the wrath of the victorious warriors. In total 342 casualties were inflicted on the British force, over 230 from the Highlanders of the 77th. Both Grant and Lewis were taken as hostages in the exchange and, protected by the French, were set aside for deportation to Canada as prisoners of war. The remainder of the wounded and captured, those deemed as low-value targets by the French, were given over to warriors as prizes to be collected. The dead and wounded were scalped, the survivors tortured. The Highlanders' screams filled the valleys around Fort Duquesne for the next several nights and haunted the imprisoned officers; some were burned alive, others brutally dismembered. Some of Forbes's scouts later reported that the road toward Fort Duquesne was lined with pikes holding the severed heads of the Highlanders as a grim reminder of what lay ahead.[16]

From his position as prisoner, Major Grant wrote a lengthy account of the day's events to General Forbes. In this letter he writes:

> I could not help saying to him that I was undone. However, though there was a little or rather no hopes left, I was resolved to do the best I could, and whenever I could get anybody to stay with me made a stand, sometimes with 100 and sometimes with 50, just as the men thought proper, for orders were to no purpose. Fear had then got the better of every other passion, and I hope I shall never see again such a panic among troops—till then I had no conception of it . . . I may have committed mistakes without knowing them, but if I was sensible of them I most certainly should tell you in what I thought I had done wrong. I am willing to flatter myself that my being a prisoner will be no detriment to my promotion in case vacancies should happen in the army, and it is to be hoped that the proper steps will be taken to get me exchanged as soon as possible.[17]

When news of the slaughter at the Battle of Fort Duquesne arrived fifty miles eastward at Fort Ligonier, Forbes's expedition was shocked. They had sent the troops under Grant's command on a relatively benign intelligence mission, and the result was a catastrophe. Aside from the obvious loss of men, Forbes's main force had not been fully detected by his enemy, and the knowledge that they were now within striking distance of Fort Duquesne was now made apparent to them. Bouquet did, however, gain the necessary intelligence on the size of the French fort's garrison, but the cost greatly outweighed the benefit.

For the next month, the French and Indians at Fort Duquesne and the British at Loyalhanna found themselves in opposite mindsets. Bouquet and his men, well advanced of the majority of Forbes's expedition, were continuing construction of Fort Ligonier as their winter quarters. They were well supplied from the east, and the long, slow construction of the new road was already paying dividends. At the Forks of the Ohio the scene was very different. Since the new British strategy of William Pitt had been implemented, a number of key links in New France's chain of North American forts had been severed. One of them, Fort Frontenac, two months earlier, had been depleted, effectively cutting off the vital supply chain to Fort Duquesne. Starving and desperate to reverse his fortunes, the French commandant François-Marie Le Marchand de Lignery planned a daring raid on Bouquet's encampment.[18]

While he was not certain of the speed of the British force, he was aware that they were close by. Due to the diligence of his Indian scouts, de Lignery also knew that Bouquet had dug in at the Loyalhanna Creek. Although there were nearly fifteen hundred able-bodied men at Fort Ligonier, the French commandant estimated that deploying his four hundred *troupes de la marine* and nearly one hundred fifty Indian warriors would be sufficient to overwhelm them. Led by Captain Charles Phillipe Aubry, it would be the largest French force ever mobilized in the Ohio Country. He expected to add a third rout to Braddock's and Grant's defeats, as the British had done little to convince him otherwise.

The size of his force, which used every Frenchman at his disposal, gives an interesting insight into just how desperate Fort Duquesne's situation had become. Although they crushed Grant's Highlanders and Provincials a month earlier, the victory may have been more of a last stand than a great triumph. The plan of attack would be to stifle Bouquet's progress, but more important to raid the camp's plentiful stores of supplies. De Lignery had a good sense of what the British could muster if he did initiate an attack, and his Indian allies had proven invaluable by picking at the position over the last month at random intervals. Whatever the outcome of an ambush of his enemies, the commandant knew that he would get nowhere without the Ohioan warriors.

As the French and Indian force—likely counting Guyasuta among its number—began to march eastward toward

Loyalhanna, Henry Bouquet was no longer at the site of Fort Ligonier. Because he was at the head of a long column, the Swiss mercenary would routinely venture back and forth along the new road to communicate intelligence to his superiors. In his stead was the surly yet inexperienced Pennsylvania colonel James Burd. Although Pitt's new strategy dictated that Provincial militiamen be given limited positions of command, Bouquet assumed that Burd would have little trouble outside of the occasional Indian encounter. While Burd was very much a secondary character in the long history of the Ohio Country, his background was a testimony to the diversity of colonial America. Though he served the Pennsylvania militia, Burd was born and raised in Scotland. He had come to the American colonies in 1748 and elected to serve the Crown in his new colonial home. In Bouquet's absence, things had been quiet and slow.

For Burd as well as Bouquet, leading an advanced force at the head of a much larger column was a logistical nightmare. In addition to the soldiers of the party, there were often just as many auxiliary forces to maintain livestock and supplies of the army. Because those items were so precious to the success of any expedition, it was essential they be protected. From Bouquet and Burd's perspective they had to not only lead the soldiers but also supervise construction of a fort *and* guard their rations. Therefore on October 12, as was the case in many other days at the camp, Burd had instructed that many of their soldiers spend the day in the countryside around the fort to guard the vital livestock from enemy attack.

It stood as a testament to the ingenuity and adaptability of the Ohioan warriors that Burd would use such a large percentage of his men for such a secondary assignment. Since the encampment had begun a month earlier, the warriors out of Fort Duquesne often targeted the cattle of Fort Ligonier as easy and effective ways to terrorize their enemies; often they were not even seen.[19]

For those sentries on cattle duty (generally the most inexperienced of Bouquet's force), the days were long and uneventful. Situated as far as a mile and a half from camp, the men would often be lulled to sleep by the monotony, but when action did heat up it often occurred in a flash with devastating consequences. On this day the peace and quiet was shattered by war whoops, followed unexpectedly by orders shouted in French. While the sentries anticipated a minor exchange with an Indian party, none believed that they would be attacked by de Lignery's great assault. The sentries were quickly overrun and killed.

By the time Colonel Burd at Ligonier heard the waves of gunfire, the French and Indians were already bearing down on his position. He dispatched two hundred Marylanders toward the commotion, but they were soon repelled, and Burd witnessed them turning back in a chaotic rout. Thinking quickly, Burd rallied the full garrison of the camp into action, and nearly all of the two thousand stationed there were prepared to meet their attackers with muskets loaded.

Viewing the British holed up in the partially constructed Fort Ligonier, Guyasuta and his warriors disappeared into the tree line. Their French allies were not far behind. Throughout the war the French had adjusted readily to the Indian style of war, and though it was unconventional, it did have its benefits. The British, knowing that their enemy was only out of sight yet still very present, waited patiently and even received reinforcements that afternoon. Still in the tree line, the French and Indians found themselves in a stalemate—if they attacked they would be gunned down by the defending force; if they stayed in place their window for success would all but disappear. In the midst of the battle, Colonel Burd wrote:

> This day, at 11 a.m., the enemy fired 12 guns to the southwest of us, upon which I sent two partys to surround them; but instantly the firing increased, upon which I sent out a larger party of 500 men. They were forced to the camp, and immediately a regular attack ensued, which lasted a long time; I think about two hours. But we had the pleasure to do that honour to his Majesty's arms, to keep his camp at Loyal Hannon. I can't inform you of our loss, nor that of the enemy. But must refer for the particulars to Lieut. Col. Lloyd. One of their soldiers, which we have mortally wounded, says they were 1200 strong and 200 Indians, but I can ascertain nothing of this further, I have drove them off the field; but I don't doubt of a second attack. If they do I am ready.[20]

As the sun dipped behind the peaks of the Laurel Highlands, Burd and his resupplied garrison kept a careful watch for their hidden enemies. At nine o'clock that night the attack came on one of Fort Ligonier's redoubts built alongside the fort itself. The attack was ferocious, but the supply line again proved to be decisive. The artillery of the British tore through the forests and sufficiently damaged the Franco-Ohioan force enough to allow an orderly retreat. Although the Indians remained behind to kill and capture almost two hundred British horses throughout the night, de Lignery's final gasp was a losing one.[21]

As the British celebrated, the French and Indians slunk back to Fort Duquesne. They had been defeated, and their prospects for the future were anything but promising. For Guyasuta the defeat at the Battle of Loyalhanna produced a startling revelation; while the French cause had empowered his Ohioans, it had become clear that it was wholly dependent on the warriors' success. Likewise, the war appeared to be changing before his eyes. Whereas the Redcoats, the British Regulars, remained easy prey for the warriors, the American Provincials were growing increasingly adept at adapting the European style of combat to wilderness warfare; the Indians had even gone so far as to label the Virginians specifically as Ashalecoa, or the Great Knife. When they returned to the Forks he saw the post in a different light. Surrounded by high ground and water, Fort Duquesne could be easily captured if a force was close enough to do so. To that point, Braddock was only able to come as close as nine miles away, but Grant had marched within firing distance. If Forbes's expedition moved as quickly as it seemed it would, Fort Duquesne would collapse whether Guyasuta and his warriors were present or not. Without them, it was destined to fail. This notion was not lost on the administration of New France; in the papers of the governor-general himself was this passage, now translated:

> Fort Duquesne, in its present condition, could not offer any resistance to the enemy; 'tis too small to lodge the garrison necessary on such an occasion. A single shell would be sufficient to get it so on fire, too, that 'twould be impossible to extinguish it because the houses are close. The garrison would

then find itself under the painful necessity of abandoning that fort. Besides, 'tis so near the confluence of the Beautiful river with the Malangaillee [Monongahela], that it is always exposed to be entirely submerged by the overflowing of the rivers. M. de Ligneris is having such repairs done to that fort as it is susceptible of, regard being had to its bad situation; but that will not enable us to dispense with the erection of a new fort.[22]

Following nights of council, Guyasuta would have discussed with the other Mingo sachems the possibility of abandoning Fort Duquesne and their allies of the past three years. The Mingo cause was never the same as that of the French, but the French had been the chosen vehicle to achieve their goals. Now, with Forbes's seven thousand marching toward the Forks, the only thing that a perpetual French alliance would produce was total defeat. Aside from the war effort, the warriors also had to deal with the reality that it was hunting season, and their wives and children at home relied on them for provisions. Guyasuta likely informed de Lignery bluntly of their intentions, and walked away from the Forks of the Ohio well beyond the reach of the man they called "Iron Head," John Forbes.

Almost three hundred miles to the east at Easton, Pennsylvania, the remainder of the Ohio nations made their peace with Great Britain on October 26. In a great council with the colonies of Pennsylvanian and New Jersey, a bargain was made between the Shawnee, Delaware, British, and Iroquois nations that would secure the peace that followed the war. Among the provisions were that in future political engagements the British would deal directly with the Delaware without first consulting the Iroquois. This effectively ended any hopes for the Haudenosaunee that their previous power would be fully restored. Also included in the Treaty of Easton was the return of recently taken Iroquois land, and most impressively a promise that no white settlers would be legally able to settle the lands of the Ohio Country.

Although the council of Mingo sachems at Fort Duquesne and
the negotiations among the British, Iroquois, and other Ohio
peoples at Easton were very different, they led to the same
result.[23] While Governor-General Vaudreuil rested peacefully in
Quebec that night, he had no idea that the true fate of the
French empire in the Ohio Country had been settled.

On November 23 François-Marie Le Marchand de Lignery
was forced to make a decision that would not only affect the rest
of his life, but possibly determine the outcome of a world war.
In the middle of the cold winter, he had only three hundred
Canadians garrisoned at Fort Duquesne with almost nothing to
eat. Many were sick, some dying slowly, and the greatest force to
ever march through the Ohio Country was bearing down on his
position. Fort Duquesne would fall, and the question that the
commandant faced was whether it would by his terms or by his
enemies'.[24]

After moving the valuable cannon and artillery onto barges
for floatation to far off French settlements, de Lignery ordered
that the powder stores that he had relied desperately on for the
last year be ignited. With his men on board rafts, the commandant watched as Fort Duquesne burned to the ground. With its
walls crumbled, and now a useless, smoking wreckage, de
Lignery and his men paddled northward against the current of
the Allegheny River to Fort Machault. Perhaps he believed he
would return with troops that spring to reclaim the site, perhaps
not. Whatever the case may be, de Lignery had to live with the
decision to surrender the Forks, and in his mind it was still the
best one for his men.[25]

Encamped nine miles away, the advance guard of the Forbes
campaign heard the sound of the exploding powder at Fort
Duquesne and were momentarily rattled. Though the general
himself was still almost a hundred miles away at Bedford, the
soldiers and officers were overjoyed when they realized what
they had just heard. The explosion was far too erratic to be
artillery, and too large to be from any weapon; Fort Duquesne
must have been abandoned.

On November 24 the advance party of Forbes's expedition
marched triumphantly to the Forks of the Ohio to capture Fort
Duquesne. Their scouts had told them a day earlier that they

had seen smoke at the site, and the small British force that day only stood to verify it. Their commanding officer had led the forward scouts throughout the campaign, and to return to the Forks under these circumstances would likely make his career. In triumph, Colonel George Washington rallied his men and waved the flag of Great Britain again and again before planting it near the smoking ruins of the fort. It was the greatest victory he had known in his young career, and his loyalty to King George was never stronger.

Over the next several days more and more of Forbes's campaign trickled onto the Forks of the Ohio to survey the fruits of their labor. It had been nearly seven months since they initially set out on their mission to dig, cut, build, and conquer, and after too much of the former they finally sampled the sweet taste of the latter. Bouquet and his men arrived shortly after Washington and the general himself days later. For Forbes it was a bittersweet moment; although he did accomplish his mission and would be celebrated throughout the colonies, he was painfully slipping into the final stages of cancer. The disease had left him confined to a flat board that was carried by two aides for he could no longer walk. He had arrived last, but his men greeted him with all the cheers of a conquering Caesar.

He proudly called this new place Pittsburgh, after his visionary secretary of state who organized the campaign. As a Scotsman, he would have pronounced the site "Pitts-boro" after his ancestral capital of Edinburgh, or "Edin-boro." The fort that would be built there would also bear the Earl of Chatham's name, Fort Pitt.

Constructing Fort Pitt would be a logistical nightmare, but the mere thought of its existence represented a great change in the Ohio Country. Unlike Fort Duquesne it would not be a temporary position that was inherently weak; the French fort relied on the chain of smaller forts to its north for both strength and substance. This new fort, an English fort, would be a permanent, bold statement of the power and grace of Great Britain. It would be the largest of the entire British North American frontier, and dominate not just the immediate area but potentially the entire Ohio Country and beyond. It sat at the mouth of the Ohio River, and any vessel wishing to venture to the

Mississippi River from the northeast would have to first pass its fortified position. Once built, the presence of Fort Pitt would send a message to both the native population and other Europeans as much as it would protect the region.[26]

It did not take long for construction to get under way, and in the meantime a tiny post along the Monongahela River would serve as a placeholder until the larger fortification could be completed. It was left under the command of Lieutenant Colonel Hugh Mercer, chief second to Washington's column during the campaign. With him were less than three hundred men, and instructions that under no circumstances could he allow the Forks to be retaken by the French. Time was of the essence, and in the cold December of 1758 Britain's great triumph felt like the loneliest site in the New World.

As the spring thaw began, construction on Fort Pitt was nearly at a standstill. Aside from the fact that the fort had to be constructed entirely of local materials, both labor and capital had moved slowly to the position during the winter. When the weather turned warmer, however, Mercer felt more and more in control. His fort would outdo its French predecessor in every way: Fort Pitt would be nearly three times larger than Fort Duquesne and hold more than four times the garrison. While Fort Duquesne was built in less than a year, it would take almost three full years to complete the British post. It would hold more provisions, support more civilians, and encourage the spread of British life in a way that the French never could. It would also function as a major site for Indian diplomacy, and there was much to be done after such a traumatic series of events in the Ohio Country.[27]

Though the war was far from over, removing the French from the region had all but quelled the internal fighting among the British and former Indian allies. The Treaty of Easton cemented that peace, and all that remained was to inform those sachems not present when the agreement was signed what the new changes represented. While it was the Ohioans that fought the war, their great war chiefs were largely left out of the October proceedings, and the deal that was brokered made their struggles instantly illegitimate. While men like Guyasuta and Shingas led the charge of fire in the Ohio Country, the peace was settled

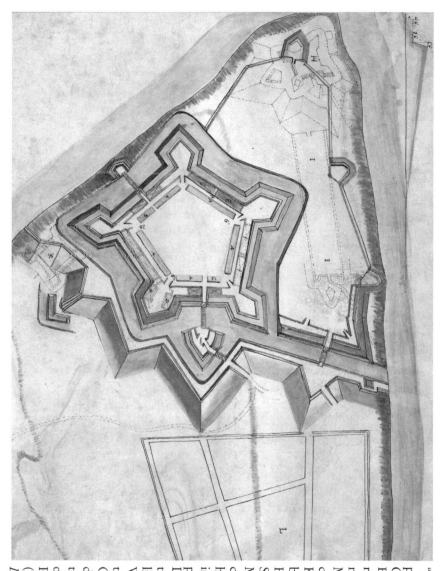

"Plan of Fort Pitt and parts adjacent. . . ." Originally drafted by Bernard Ratzer in 1761, redrawn from the original in the British Museum in 1882, and copied here in 1903. Key: A. Barracks already built. B. Commandant's House not built. C. Store House. D. Powder Magazines. E. Casemate completed. F. Store house for flour. G. Wells in two of which are pumps. H. Fort Duquesne ruined (dotted line indicates the earlier fort's footprint). I. Where stockade covered the French barracks. K. Old English fort destroyed (also with dotted lines indicating the original structure). L. Public gardens. (*Darlington Digital Library*)

with others who were less involved. The Mingo had no representation at Easton, and the Delaware representative on hand was Teedyuscung, a peace chief. Teedyuscung's involvement highlights the divisions even among the Delaware between east and west. Shingas and Teedyuscung shared the same lineage, but their common ground ended there.

On July 5, 1759, Mercer held his first critical meeting at the Forks of the Ohio; though small, the council would set the tone for British policy in the region. In the four years that Fort Duquesne stood it had become the absolute center of Indian diplomacy in the Ohio Country, and the French style of mediation had proven very favorable to the native peoples. Now, representing the only European power left in the region, Mercer had to present the British as being not just *equally* competent as the French, but superior in every way.

For Mercer this was no easy task. Born in Scotland, Mercer had been at Braddock's defeat as a medic three years earlier, and saw firsthand the terrible consequences of an Indian engagement. He counted the dead and counseled the wounded, and ever since he was so enraged by the scenes of violence that he dedicated his life to military service. He was not equipped to deal with these peoples, whom he had just battled, by himself. Joining him was the most experienced British Indian trader of the region, George Croghan, a familiar face to the Ohio sachems. If anyone could ease the transition from war to peace it was him.

Joining Mercer and Croghan was Captain William Trent, the man who established Fort Prince George before the French captured and overtook the Forks five years earlier. The sachems in attendance were a who's who of war chiefs in the Ohio Country. Representing the Delaware nation was Shingas, who two years earlier was considered the most wanted fugitive of the entire frontier. He was joined by his brother Tamaqua (called King Beaver) and two other sachems, Killbuck and Captain Pipe. The Shawnee were not in attendance because of their united presence at Easton. Finally, the sole representative of the Mingo was Guyasuta.[28]

Most of these men, either in the past or in the future, would battle against the British as enemies; for that day, however, they met peacefully. Unbeknownst to the officers seated with them at the time, these figures would all play major roles in the future history of the fort which was expected to be built at the Forks. Following the obligatory ceremonies to begin the council, Croghan began to explain the new agreements of the Treaty of Easton through his interpreter Andrew Montour. Montour had already made a powerful name for himself in the Ohio Country, and his esteem was set to grow. As the son of a woman of native and French ancestry, Montour spoke several languages including Shawnee, Delaware, French, and English. His father was a chief of the Oneida, so his ties to the Iroquois Confederacy were equally legitimized. He was one of the few natives who marched with Braddock, and also accompanied Washington at Fort Necessity. He was not trusted by the Ohioan sachems, and the French had even placed a bounty on his head for his service to Great Britain.

The council was chaotic; neither party was certain how to proceed and what exactly was to be accomplished. Tamaqua stood and vented his frustration: "The Beaver (Tamaqua) then got up and desired to know when they might Expect the Peace to be confirmed, as the Deputies from the Several Nations had fixed a time for their return. Colonel Mercer and Captain Croghan appointed a private meeting next morning to fix on the time."[29]

The council met again on July 7, 8, and 9; during those meetings many topics arose including land ownership, fur prices, and relationships with the French. The discussions soon turned to prisoner exchange and remedying the hardships that war had imposed on the region. Through the vast majority of these exchanges Croghan took the lead as the voice of the British world until finally, on July 9, Tamaqua spoke to Mercer directly: "When I was here in the fall, I desired our People might have Liquor, but sparingly; but now I desire the Bung may be knocked out of the Keg, and when the Liquor comes, we may have Liberty to purchase, and then returned thanks for the Speeches we had made them, which he said he believed come from our Hearts."[30]

Immediately following this request Mercer obliged by offering the Delaware chief equal rights to purchase what little alcohol was at the site, "Then returned thanks for the Speeches they had made us, and the Colonel gave the whole an invitation to dine with him next Day." It seemed to him a trivial matter, but the Ohioan delegation had many different voices to consider in their diverse and uncertain constituency. Guyasuta was not likely silent in this meeting, but the fact that the British in attendance do not mention his participation indicates a strong distrust that was not likely to go away because of a treaty that he personally never agreed to. The men concluded their session on good terms, and the first post-French council held in the Ohio Country appeared to be a success. For Mercer, he hoped that the amicable terms that they discussed on that hot July day would be permanent; peace though, unfortunately, was nowhere in sight.[31]

Guyasuta was placed in a precarious situation that no other Ohioan sachem could comprehend. For the previous three years he had abandoned his Iroquoian roots to lead a rebellion against his ancestral fathers. The Iroquois viewed the Delaware and Shawnee as having participated in a rebellion of opportunity, and as these groups were their subjects, the Iroquois hoped they would be contrite and their obedience recovered. The Mingo, however, were not merely rebels, but traitors. When Guyasuta took up the hatchet against the British, he turned his back on his obligations and traditions as an Iroquois chief to form his own renegade way of life. Now that the French had been removed from the Ohio Country, Guyasuta was faced with the choice of both accepting defeat and pleading with the Iroquois for clemency or continuing his struggle for freedom and autonomy. The French alliance was merely a means of achieving independence, but French rule was never independence itself. His next move would be a monumental one, and the only certainty was that to align himself with the British was to once again accept traditional Iroquois supremacy.

If the struggle of the New Ohioan was a just cause in principle, then the continuation of the fight despite the changing political circumstances around him would be justified as well. What he was contemplating was nothing less than full-scale rebellion against both British and Iroquois rule, but a measure so extreme would need many more than the handful of warriors that his Mingo band could produce. The Delaware and Shawnee had made their peace with Great Britain at Easton, and they would be reluctant to join him. For success on a scale of this magnitude, he would need the cooperation of hundreds of warriors, and that meant leaving the relatively tame confines of the Ohio Country. He would need on his side entire nations that, because of the decline of New France, would feel the same sense of hopelessness and defeat as the Mingo had suffered. He would need a people that, with the loss of French input, felt the same twinges of abandonment and frustration that they did. Guyasuta and his warriors would need to look west to the Great Lakes.

The future that Guyasuta and the native peoples of North America would find themselves a part of was quickly becoming a British one. In 1759 the war continued to rage, and one by one the strategic positions of New France fell to their English foes. After the fall of Fort Ticonderoga, British forces besieged and overran their French enemies at the Plains of Abraham. A subsequent victory at Fort Niagara in 1760 cut off New France's vital supply line to the west. The defeat in North America was made official when a massive British naval force under the command of John Byron surrounded Montreal and effectively captured the city.

In September of that same year Governor-General Pierre de Rigaud, Marquis de Vaudreuil-Cavagnal negotiated the surrender of New France to General Jeffery Amherst. The surrender of Montreal was a crushing blow to the war effort of the French empire, and though the Seven Years' War would continue for three more years, all of King Louis's North American holdings were lost. As a last request Vaudreuil petitioned Amherst that any French citizens who wished to remain on the continent be allowed to worship and live as they pleased. Amherst relented, offering that any soldier that had fought against Great Britain return to France never to serve again in any still-active theater of combat. Seemingly overnight the size of King George's American colonies more than tripled in size. For his efforts, Amherst was promoted to governor general of British North America.

Although the British way of life had prevailed seemingly once and for all, there remained thousands of men, women, and children left behind at the close of the conflict. The native peoples of North America experienced widely differing outcomes at the cessation of hostilities; for the Iroquois, their strategic decision to remain steadfast and loyal to the British appeared to have paid off. Although they would never regain the power and influence that they had before the war, they believed themselves in the best position possible to regain it. The heretofore French-allied peoples of the Ohio Country and the Great Lakes were left with little option but to accept English domination. The French had convinced them that an alliance with their side would empower them as never before, but now all that remained was anger and disappointment. Questions began to spread throughout the native communities of North America regarding where their supplies would come from, and how their economy, which was almost completely sustained by French goods, would survive.

From the British perspective, whatever grievances the Indians had could be dealt with in due time; they still had a war to fight. While the battle for North America may have been all but settled, the Seven Years' War raged, and the French and their allies were still very present in other parts of the Western Hemisphere, as well as elsewhere around the globe, threatening British interests.

FOUR

Fire on the Frontier

THE INDIAN INSURGENCY OF 1763

I n September 1761, Fort Detroit was a very different place than it had been only two years earlier. Since the fall of New France, British forces had occupied the site and taken full command of the position. While its wooden palisades stood the same as they had for decades, the fortified heart of the French frontier now flew the king's colors proudly overhead. The native peoples that had camped in and around the post were reluctant to leave, and since hostilities on the continent had ceased in 1760 there was little indication as to what role they would play in the future.

Outside the walls of Fort Detroit the usual frenzy of activity had continued. Traders and trappers openly displayed their recent acquisitions, and foot traffic had increased when a large council fire was announced days earlier. Though the British were victorious, the stipulations of the surrender of New France did not force existing French colonists to abandon the region. As a result, the Great Lakes remained home to a diverse population of French, British, Canadian, Irish, Dutch, and Indian settlers, all seeking the same fortune that the colonial frontier offered so readily.[1]

The Great Lakes region was home to some of the most powerful nations on the North American continent. For years the

Huron, Ojibwa, Potawatomie, Ottawa, and Miamis maintained a fragile balance of power, and since the construction of Fort Detroit in 1701 they had all found a friendly ally in His Most Christian Majesty. Their support had made victory in the Seven Years' War a realistic possibility for France, and their now uncertain future could potentially determine the outcome of British expansion into the region.

Since the summer began, tribal representatives from around the continent had flocked to the site to acquire a sense of how their new British tenants would honor their agreements vacated by their fallen French allies. With the threat of war gone from the region, British policy makers, most notably the recently appointed governor of North America Jeffery Amherst, had done little to assure the native peoples that any economic subsidies would be provided. In the months prior, Amherst assigned the responsibility of Indian affairs to his trusted advisor Sir William Johnson, and when it was announced that he would be at Fort Detroit, it became a hub of activity; familiar faces were present including the ever-ready George Croghan. As superintendent of Indian affairs, Johnson was to maintain the alliances with North America's Indian nations at all costs.

What brought Johnson to Fort Detroit on this September day was discussion of a potential Indian rebellion brewing in the Great Lakes. While he was uncertain as to which party was responsible, the deputized Croghan kept his supervisor informed. He wrote to Johnson, "the Six Nations look on themselves to be ill Treated by the English General [Amherst]. . . . Traders are not suffered to go among them . . . and the General is giving away their Country to be settled. . . . These steps they say appears to them as if the English had a mind to Cut them off the face of the Earth."[2]

The accusations that Croghan relayed had been the efforts not of the Iroquois, as he erroneously specified, but the singular efforts of Guyasuta and his fellow Mingo sachems, including his longtime ally Tahaiadoris. An interesting collaborator in the emerging independence movement, Tahaiadoris was the son of a former commandant of Fort Niagara, and the half-brother of Guyasuta's old ally Joncaire of Venango. For the previous two months the two sachems had held many councils in the Great Lakes region and openly presented a large, red belt of war to the sachems of its resident nations in hopes of gaining allies in their potential uprising against Great Britain. While he was met with mixed responses, Guyasuta's plan was, in theory, a sound one. By unifying, he believed that a pan-tribal alliance could upset the strength of their European oppressors by strategically isolating Britain's individual forts of the frontier. His case was made stronger by referencing Europe's precarious style of regional command. He argued that by disabling Fort Detroit, the Great Lakes peoples would force the British to flee the region altogether, and by doing the same to the recently completed Fort Pitt, the Ohio Country would be free as well.

Guyasuta and Tahaiadoris persuaded the chiefs for days, even claiming that they "were but one people & had but one voice." This idea had actually taken hold in the Ohio Country, and many of the western Delaware, still angry from the sudden French defeat, joined Guyasuta's cause, but it would have been completely alien to the chiefs at Fort Detroit. The Indian peoples of North America had always considered themselves as separate nations; the Mingo and Ottawa were as different as the British and French. This new notion of a unified Indian identity was ahead of its time, and Guyasuta failed in his efforts to rally support for his militant cause.[3]

Therefore, well aware that the unnamed perpetrators of this seditious act were present but not gaining support, Sir William Johnson appeared at Fort Detroit to nullify any thoughts of uprising and reaffirm His Majesty's promises and warmest regards. On September 9, in front of a delegation of scores of sachems from dozens of nations, Johnson delivered the following speech:

> It gives me great pleasure to meet so many Nations assembled here on my summons, and as I am come A long journey to see, and talk with you, on matters relative to your interest, in order to prepare you to hear the same I do agreable to the Custom of our Ancestors, wipe away those Tears from your Eyes which were shed for the losses you sustained during the War in which you were imprudently engaged against the

English, that you may clearly discern your present interest & look with a Chearfull and friendly countenance when you speak with, or are spoke to by your brethren the English.[4]

In a lengthy discourse, Johnson spoke on all subjects that his office considered priorities. From the delivery of captives taken during the Seven Years' War to the availability of trade goods, Johnson proved his adeptness by following all of the traditional protocols, notably presentations of wampum strings, as the night continued. During his oration with Croghan at his side, Johnson strongly denounced those nations responsible for circulating the war string, careful not to mention Guyasuta by name. As usual during a council of such magnitude, Johnson understood that it would take many nights to accomplish his intended goal.

The following evening the delegation of peoples came together again to issue a prepared response to Johnson. Delivering the message of his people was Chief Anaiasa of the Huron. After a number of displays of gratitude and the obligatory pleasantries, the Huron made a startling revelation: "We are now to answer your demand concerning the belt sent to us, the motives for their so doing who were the cause thereof we know not but here is the Man now present who was one of the Messengers, he best can inform you, and we hope our proceedings thereon with which you are well acquainted, will convince you —of our disapprobation thereof."

When Anaiasa acknowledged the chiefs responsible for the rebellious activities, he pointed his finger directly at Guyasuta; Johnson and Croghan looked on disapprovingly. The Huron then finalized the betrayal:

> You desire to know the people who sent the bad Bird lately Among us, to stir us up against our Brethren—It is certain such bad Birds have been among us, but we should look upon ourselves as a very unhappy people if we payed any attention to such disturbers of peace whom we shall always despise for attempting to put such evil thoughts into our ears, who are all determined as one Man to hold fast by the Covenant Chain for ever—But if you would know who this bird is, Cast your Eyes to Kayashota [Guyasuta] & you will see him.[5]

Guyasuta had been foiled in his plans that year in Fort Detroit. He had not only failed to gain support for his rebellion; he had also suffered the indignation of being singled out personally by a fellow sachem whom he had spent weeks trying to persuade. The council that night in front of the highest-ranking Indian officials in British North America had unraveled an entire summer's worth of work, and single-handedly placed him at the center of a conspiracy of the gravest order. Johnson and Croghan recognized that Guyasuta's efforts had been in vain, and left Fort Detroit making no efforts to censure him; if he had no allies, he had no rebellion. If he had no rebellion then he was simply not a threat.

The speech delivered by the Huron Anaiasa represented the conservative views of an aging chief, anxious for peace after years of war, but it did not represent the entire delegation's feelings toward Guyasuta's efforts. Many responded encouragingly to the Mingo sachem; however, the greater Indian world that he courted was not prepared for what he was proposing. Guyasuta's revolution was ahead of its time.

The Mingo chiefs returned to their families in the Ohio Country that fall, likely feeling the pain and embarrassment of public reprimand and betrayal. Though they had been victorious in unifying the Ohio Indians in the east, it seemed that his passionate cry had fallen on deaf ears at Fort Detroit. What he was not aware of was that some members of delegation *were* paying attention, and one man would deeply consider his message in the coming months. His name was Pontiac, and in two years he and Guyasuta would bring British North America to its knees.

With the prospect of his rebellion lost, Guyasuta sent one of his sons to Philadelphia. In the colonial capital, the sachem hoped that his child would learn to master the English language and have a future as a guide in this ever-changing world.

The events at Fort Detroit that summer were of little concern in London. The North American portion of fighting, soon to be renamed the French and Indian War, had ended, but Great Britain was still battling France and her allies around the world.

The Seven Years' War had been a world war, and after the fall of New France it became a much more diverse one. In 1762 Britain declared war on Spain, and the long-standing Franco-Spanish Bourbon alliance resulted in a new empire joining the fight. Sensing opportunity against its new enemy, British forces initiated a concentrated attack from its Caribbean possessions to capture Havana, Spain's primary naval station in the Western Hemisphere. Cuba was besieged by British forces for two full months, until it was forced to surrender on August 13.[6]

One month later, British forces under William Amherst much farther north found success against an old enemy. Earlier that same year French forces were able to muster a last victory by capturing the city of St. John's, Newfoundland, in an unexpected attack. In anticipation of a counterattack the Comte d'Haussonville fortified a position known as Signal Hill. By September 13 a force of two hundred Redcoats landed just north of the site at Torbay, and three days later they reclaimed the position. Open combat had been a rare thing in North America after the capture of Montreal, and this venture in Newfoundland, and another out of Florida, were the final major combat seen on the continent for the remainder of the war.[7]

When the warring parties met in February 1763 to end the planet's first truly world war, they did so with much at stake. In Paris delegations of Great Britain, France, Portugal, and Spain decided the fate of empire in the Western world with hours of deliberations and a few well-placed signatures. For the British, their victories in battle had given them distinct advantages when it came to dictating the terms of the agreement. Since the war began almost a decade earlier, Britain had been able to conquer and claim Canada, Gorée, the Senegal River settlements in West Africa, and major trading posts in India from the French. Much more valuable, however, were the Caribbean sugar giants taken from the French in the islands of Martinique, Saint Lucia, Grenada, Saint Vincent, Dominica, Tobago, and the Grenadines. From the Spanish, though late to the war, were taken Havana, Cuba, and Manila in the Philippines. France did capture the Mediterranean hub of Minorca early in the war and some trading posts in Sumatra, but their hopes of continued empire lay almost entirely on the generosity of the British.

As the defeated parties, the French and Spanish were obliged to return their minor conquests to their victorious counterparts. In exchange, Britain also returned Havana and Manila to the Spanish, and many of the Caribbean and West African holdings to France. What was gained, however, would change the face of empire forever; the Treaty of Paris gave Great Britain all of Canada, many profitable Caribbean islands, and the entire eastern half of Louisiana from the Mississippi River valley to the Appalachians. Spain would hand over Florida. The stipulations of that agreement had given Britain the true spoils of war—a massive collection of the Western Hemisphere's most profitable colonial holdings, all pumping out a fortune worth of raw materials every day to make London the economic capital of the Western world.[8]

With that kind of wealth falling into their hands seemingly overnight, policy makers in London had some serious financial evaluations to consider. How much debt had the war accrued? What could they afford? How much did they stand to profit? The year 1763 would prove to be a formative one in the identity of the new British Empire, and an age of *pax Britannica* appeared set to begin. While they tallied their newfound riches, what those in London did not account for was the true cost of expanded empire; that was a figure measured not in pounds sterling, but body counts.

All empires eventually fail. To gauge the success of an imperial venture, the historian seeks out not whether an empire survived, but "for how long?" They all fail, and many fail for the same reasons. Whether it is the difficulties of assimilating foreign societies into a new worldview or the sheer financial expense of maintaining such a large body, the life of an empire is filled with pitfalls and failures. Britain had the benefit of using history as its ally in 1763; it could look to the weaknesses of previous empires like the Assyrians of the eighth century B.C.E. and Alexander's great Hellenistic world to see how to avoid the terrible mistakes of the past. Unfortunately, the empire that they now found themselves controlling was larger and more diverse than almost any other before it, and as time passed it felt more like an experiment than the final product of five thousand years of imperial trial and error.

Empire is never gained without significant investment, and the investment is almost always long and terrible wars. Although they viewed themselves with all the arrogance and pride of a modern entity sneering at the foolishness of the past, the British knew outright that they were not immune to this. If they truly believed that the war was just a means and not an end, all they had to do was count the deficits in the royal treasury to be reminded. At the start of the war British debt was nearly £74.4 million, and by the end it had reached over £122 million. While they did stand to make a substantial fortune out of the new colonies that they had recently acquired, that would likely take years to accrue in any meaningful way. The British were now dealing with the single largest economy that the world had ever seen with mouths to feed on five continents; there was no handbook for how to negotiate that kind of gargantuan power.[9]

The problems that Britain faced were both modern and ancient. While many empires in the past had ruled over different continents simultaneously, none of the ancient world ever crossed a void the size of the Atlantic. As a general rule empires need to grow, but it is often that very expansion that serves as the first chink in the armor to bring the giant down. In the imperial world, every inch the border expands is one more inch that needs to maintained, reinforced, and protected. That kind of presence requires a large and diverse military, and to truly entrench those men in position costs millions; therein lies the great foil of empire. To create an empire that truly rules the world it begins with an almost impossible initial investment, and collecting fully mature dividends requires the one thing that cannot be afforded—more spending.

This is the position that Great Britain found itself in during the year 1763. The debt had increased tremendously from fighting the Seven Years' War, and before true profit could be realized London had to decrease the size of the debt. That they learned from the past is obvious and reflected in the measures they would employ. Their sheer hubris, however, in thinking that their empire was immune to the failings of those of the past ensured demise. If the British had attempted to adapt and allow their colonies more autonomy, survival was possible, but by staying the course it cemented its own failure at truly maintain-

ing a peaceful world. Great Britain is an island, and a tiny one
at that. The stance that a geographic area so small could dominate the world was unlikely; trying to do it while highlighting
that fact was impossible.

The course of action taken by the palace of Westminster was
a simple one: balance the imperial budget with the mechanisms
they most easily controlled. After days of deliberation
Parliament decided that through the calculated application of
revenue increases and austerity measures the debt accrued during the Seven Years' War could be slowly but safely neutralized.
Its decision to raise taxes and cut spending was not an easy one,
but when the course of action was agreed upon, the next question became: who would be taxed?

Because Britain's European allies handled most of the fighting in the European theater, the likely population to carry the
weight of the tax load would be the regions in which the most
money was spent. Without question the bulk of British forces
and financial investment fell to North America, and because
those colonies benefitted most from the war effort it only made
sense they should pay for it. It was a startling revelation for
North America's colonists, but hardly a burden. The effective tax
for living in London in 1763 was approximately £26 per year; the
new tax placed on America's colonists amounted to the equiva-
lent of £1 per year. Despite all of the anxieties expressed over the
now infamous Stamp Act, revolution was still a distant dream.
The fact remains that when the tax was repealed after only two
years, statues of King George III and Secretary of State William
Pitt were erected in New York City to honor the occasion.

The taxation proposed by Parliament was not popular, but in
many ways it was the easy part. The difficult measures to be
taken would be the cuts to spending. Austerity is never easy, in
either the twenty-first century or the eighteenth, and it often
leaves many of the most wanting members of a given society
feeling abandoned. The determination of where to cut, and
often how much, was not entirely decided by Parliament but
passed down to the colonial leadership; many of the toughest
choices would fall to Governor-General Jeffery Amherst.[10]

Amherst was instrumental in defeating the French at Quebec,
Louisbourg, and Montreal; now with an entire continent under

his control the general would place Indian relations near the bottom of his tasks at hand. For Amherst, who had spent much of the prior decade battling the French and their many Indian allies, engaging what was in his opinion an inferior race was not something that he considered as necessary or prudent. As it was, however, maintaining good relations with the tribal nations of North America would be essential for continued peace. Amherst was instrumental in fashioning Britain's policy toward the native peoples; because of his inherent prejudices toward Indians they proved to be an easy target for the first major cuts to be enacted. Gift-giving, which was a vital aspect of regular diplomacy for the native peoples of the eighteenth century, was a policy that Amherst stopped following the expulsion of the French. Though Amherst had little face-to-face contact with the many Indian groups of the continent, he passed on his wishes to Secretary of Indian Affairs Sir William Johnson, who would further instruct his deputies. They would suffer most of the diplomatic backlash as a result.

For Amherst, the regular practice of giving gifts was nothing more than a bribe at worst, and a costly nuisance at best. When small pockets of resistance began to develop in the southern colonies, Amherst wrote, "Purchasing the good behavior either of Indians, or any Others, is what I do not understand; when men of what race so ever behave ill, they must be punished but not bribed."[11]

This would have been a crushing blow to the economies of the Ohio Country and the Great Lakes region. Out of necessity the French incursions into the continent a century earlier had formed a mixed economy, and after four to five generations of regular European presence the Indian village subsisted almost completely on foreign goods. Therefore when the regular and plentiful supply officially disappeared, the initial shock among the tribal leaders of the frontier soon turned to rage. George Croghan highlights the misgivings and grievances among the people by writing: "since the English has Conquered the French they insult (the Indians), and won't let them travel thro' their own Country, they are forbid the Communication. . . . Powder and Lead is prohibited being sold to them . . . which the King of England Promised to secure for their use."[12]

Governor-General Jeffery Amherst, left, was also commander-in-chief of the British Army in North America. Sir William Johnson, right, was superintendent of Indian affairs for the northern colonies. (*Library of Congress*)

The changes that brought about the great anxiety among America's native villages were not new and were all too predictable for some. For these reasons Guyasuta made his initial foray to Fort Detroit two years earlier. The Mingo sachem warned the tribal delegates of the region that his people's dependence on foreign goods had weakened their situation. Guyasuta's foreshadowing was not received well by those peoples because it lacked a tangible element that the average Indian man could grasp; certainly their situation gave the British the upper hand, but until the powder and supplies *did* stop, it was nothing more than unfounded panic. Once Amherst's policies took hold across the frontier, though, the fallout was immense.[13]

The economy of the Indian world crumbled almost instantly; without European goods, the trade-based market all but disappeared. Furthermore, a massive depression followed in Indian villages when muskets and especially powder and lead stopped flowing into the frontier. Men, who had always maintained their traditional role as hunters, quickly realized that without ammunition for their firearms they could not provide basic food for their families. Some had retained their proficiency with the bow and arrow, but many had come to rely completely on European weapons for sustenance. As with economic downturns in all parts of the world, alcoholism rates began to skyrocket and productivity plummeted.

One of the curious antecedents of depressions on this scale however has always been an increased level of religious fervor. Left without results and little evidence of hope, people have been turning to organized religion for centuries. Aside from the therapeutic benefits of meeting regularly with people in similar circumstances, faith-based communities often provide their adherents with an internal peace where none was to be found otherwise. While many gain a feeling of hope, some of the best medicine that the spirit of the divine can provide is simply acceptance of one's own failings. In this cycle of self-repair eventually the believer finds grace in being thankful for what they still have instead of incessantly seeking more. The depression that resulted from Amherst's policies produced its own religious revival among the native peoples of the frontier, and it would prove deadly when combined with the political ambitions of zealots like Guyasuta.

Beginning in 1761 a movement of spiritual resistance fostered by the economic downturn of the period emerged among the native peoples on the American frontier that centered around the teachings of a Delaware prophet called Neolin. While a scarcity of details regarding his early life make him one of the most shadowy figures in Native American history, the impact that he had following the Seven Years' War makes him a vital cog in the complex machine of the Revolutionary Era. In Neolin the downtrodden Indian society of North America would find a central figure that unified an intense anti-European opposition, and his radical teachings would sow the seeds of rebellion.[14]

Following long periods of fasting and self-deprivation, Neolin was said to have received a vision from the monotheistic Master of Life. During his exhausted state, the Delaware claimed that his sacred deity provided him with a specific and clear message with the potential to change the lives of Indians across the continent. The message that was passed to him was that of an Indian Utopia, a world past that was devoid of any European settlers and in his mind a perfected paradise. Neolin spoke a message of confidence that emphasized the strength of the Indian and the majesty in his unspoiled way of life. The

Indian, Neolin claimed, was not backward and not defeated, but simply misguided by overindulgence in European goods. By spurning the things that they had grown dependent on, the very goods that Amherst had cut away, the Indian could reclaim his traditional ways and grow closer to his ancestral roots. By 1762 the prophet was speaking regularly to hundreds of desperate warriors and their families in village councils across the frontier.

The goods that he scorned were not just those that he believed to be non-Indian, but also the ones most dangerous to any communities in times of woe. Neolin had watched as hundreds of men and women around him grew addicted to alcohol, and in the deadly drink he found his first great vice to attack. He saw that his people could live without alcohol on a daily basis, but when large shipments came to their villages they would drink to excess and be taken advantage of by predatory traders seeking unfair prices. By eliminating alcohol altogether, Neolin claimed, the personal failings of the individual would disappear as well. Only when the soul was recalibrated could the warrior realize the value of throwing down his musket to reclaim his bow and arrow. Likewise, Neolin believed that the adoption of European fashion also needed to go; if a person did not dress like an Indian, how could he possibly feel like one? Interestingly, while Indians began dressing more and more like their white counterparts, settlers on the frontier had regularly donned the buckskin because of its own practical uses. Across the frontier native men and women participated in a massive purge of whatever trade goods remained, including the use of a vile black substance known as the "black drink" which induced vomiting. The practice, encouraged by the prophet, was to eliminate totally any traces of non-Indian materials inside the body; its use became so widespread that one village was pejoratively called "Vomit Town" by white traders. The Neolin movement became well known in the east, and he soon began describing the British as "the Imposter"; this great leap into the political realm fueled his religious revival on the shared animosity that many placed on Amherst's foreign policy. The prophet is quoted as saying: "If you suffer the English among you . . . you are dead men. Sickness, smallpox, and their poison [alcohol] will destroy you entirely."15

While Neolin and his followers had no written language, the cultural impact of centuries of Indian-European relations was profoundly evident in his teachings. Though he never converted to Christianity, as a Delaware he would have had regular discussions with missionaries in his village as a young man. He would have seen Europeans waving their holy book at him incessantly, and while the Indians did believe in a monotheistic god of their own, the idea of a connection to a written book was likely a strange one. The Master of Life was all around them in nature and in person, and the notion that divine inspiration could come from symbols on paper would have been completely alien. With years of regular religious discourse in that manner, it is no surprise that Neolin's movement soon produced a holy document of its own. Called "the Great Book of Writing," Neolin's complex, wordless map traced the route that a person's soul would need to take to find Heaven. It was not in any way a book, but its very existence highlights the unique exchange of ideas and cultural diffusion brought forth in colonial America.[16]

While the Indian theology of self-determinism that Neolin promoted began to take hold, it was only when it was applied to political logic that the movement produced earthshaking results. Neolin was now a recognizable figure on the American frontier, and when his teachings were interjected into the discourses of men like Guyasuta they became a powerful weapon. Two years earlier, Guyasuta found little support in his independence movement, but when discussed in accord with Neolin's teaching, the notion of open rebellion became not only reasonable but nearly unavoidable.

One such movement that attached Neolin's ideology to a political agenda emerged in the spring of 1763 in the Great Lakes region led by the Ottawa chief Pontiac, who developed a pronounced brand of peace through bloody resistance. Pontiac stands as one of the most fascinating characters in American history, and his life is a testament to the connectivity of the Indian world. Like Guyasuta, Pontiac was born in approximately 1725 and very similarly threw his affections to the French throughout the Seven Years' War. While Guyasuta likely had not noticed, speculation even puts Pontiac at Braddock's defeat fighting alongside him. With the fall of New France, Pontiac too felt the pains of British rule and as an experienced man of nearly forty years old he would be considered a prime candidate to lead a massive resistance force.[17]

On April 27, 1763, Pontiac began to put his plans into motion by holding a council along the Ecorse, a tributary of the Detroit River. At the meeting the Ottawa sachem presented a plan to attack Fort Detroit with enough force to sufficiently end Britain's presence in the Great Lakes regions. Four days later, Pontiac and fifty other Ottawa sachems marched into Fort Detroit to assess the current strength of the site; the British inside had no idea of his plans, and viewed their arrival as inconsequential at best. After his reconnaissance, Pontiac held another council and confidently proclaimed that victory would be easily achieved—all that he needed was the manpower: "It is important for us, my brothers, that we exterminate from our lands this nation which seeks only to destroy us. You see as well as I that we can no longer supply our needs, as we have done from our brothers, the French. . . . Therefore, my brothers, we must all swear their destruction and wait no longer. Nothing prevents us; they are few in numbers, and we can accomplish it."[18]

Pontiac's plan was a simple one: by besieging and overtaking Fort Detroit and its surrounding posts, Britain would lose its primary foothold in the region. Although the might of the British military could easily overrun the warriors, Pontiac correctly estimated that they were not likely to send an entire army into the wilds of the Great Lakes. Like all insurgent wars the guerrillas had the benefit of not having to win the war, just outlast their more powerful opponents. Eventually fighting the rebellion would become too expensive, and the larger body would surrender the post rather than spend more to keep it. Considering that this was the exact plan of attack put forth by Guyasuta two years earlier, and that Pontiac was in attendance at his council, Pontiac may have been putting Guyasuta's Ohio model into practice at Fort Detroit.

Six days after his great speech, Pontiac approached Fort Detroit under the outward appearance of a peaceful delegation with three hundred sachems and warriors from all nations of the Great Lakes. The plan entailed surprise followed by total shock and devastation. As the party approached the fort, each man carried a pre-loaded musket under his clothes, and when inside they would unleash a major volley to capture the post. Henry Gladwin, the commandant of Fort Detroit, had caught wind of the coup days earlier from friendly Indian informants, and his armed garrison was fully prepared for the ambush. Following a firefight Pontiac and his warriors abandoned the fort and took up positions outside of its walls; the siege of Fort Detroit had begun.

Throughout the spring months of 1763 the same tension that had boiled over at Fort Detroit had entangled the Ohio Country. Guyasuta's efforts had served as a catalyst for the Mingo and their fellow nations of the region; they had laid the plans for a unified Indian identity, and only the fires of combat could truly forge them into a cohesive group. Upon hearing of Pontiac's actions against the British, many of the region's Indian sachems met in council with the warriors of the Ohio Country to deliver belts of war. Unlike the terms two years before, this time Guyasuta's prompts were received with little resistance.

Just as Fort Detroit had been the primary target of Pontiac's warriors, in the Ohio Country the bold statement of British power was the massive and powerful Fort Pitt. Finished just a year earlier, Fort Pitt was made of the earth itself. Designed with five bastions, the fort at the Forks sat in the shape of a large star and offered full command of all three rivers. Its walls stood over fifteen feet tall, and it was surrounded on three sides by a large trench that would become a defensive moat as the river flooded. It was one of the single most fortified positions in North America, and many policy makers in London believed it would be the fort that would allow the British Empire into the great unknown of the North American west. Around the fort were the beginnings of a town, since 1759 called Pittsburgh. It was a rabble of small cabins and trading posts and generally inhabited by settlers and their families. Since the fall of Fort Duquesne five years earlier Fort Pitt had become the center of all Indian diplo-

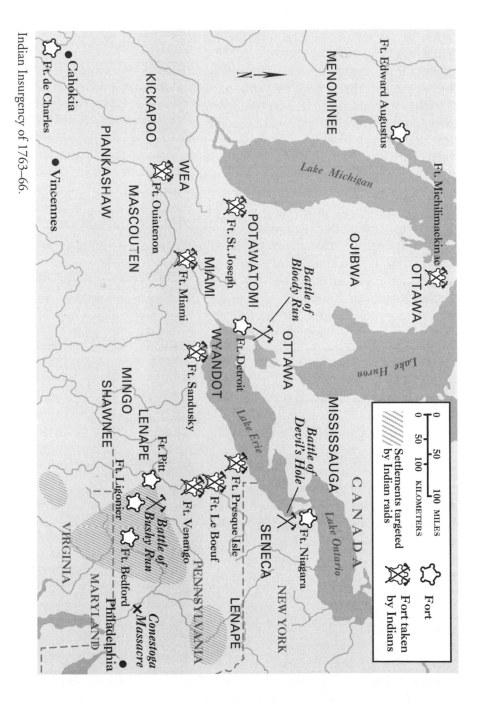

macy in the region, and the chiefs who now plotted against it knew it all too well.[19]

Fort Pitt's strength came in its strategic position. Surrounded by water on three sides, it was naturally defended by the Allegheny, Monongahela, and Ohio rivers. The sides of the fort that faced those waterways were covered in sod, as there was no fear of an attack from a European enemy. On the side facing the land, Fort Pitt was reinforced with a formidable stone and brick face that stared directly down the Forbes Road. The Indians knew that Fort Pitt was well placed to fend off a French attack, as its design and construction took place entirely during the Seven Years' War, but they also knew that its greatest strength would likewise reveal its greatest weakness. If a coordinated Indian assault surrounded the position, and most important severed its connection with the vital lifeline to the east that was Forbes Road, Fort Pitt would wither and die. The only way that necessary goods could reach the fort was if they came from Fort Ligonier, fifty miles away; by blocking that road Fort Pitt would be stranded and forced to surrender.[20]

When the violence that began in the Great Lakes region spilled over into the Ohio Country, it did so in measurable fashion. Within the same month that the siege of Fort Detroit began, the cries of war had begun three hundred miles to its east. The attack on Fort Pitt would only be part of the campaign that Guyasuta and his allies designed; for the effort to truly expel the British they would need to rid the area of all British forts. Since the beginning of the Seven Years' War, the American colonies had developed a distinct fear of Indian war. Its atrocities had become a very real fear for settlers in the region, and the extraordinary brand of violence that it required had become the stuff of legend. The warriors who prepared to banish their enemies knew that no quarter could be given; entire families, if necessary, would need to be killed in brutal fashion. Like their British counterparts, the Indians knew the price of peace was the terrible investment of war. From Fort Detroit to the Ohio Country, tensions and hostilities were mounting more with each passing day.

On May 29, a horse driver by the name of Daniel Collier arrived at Fort Pitt in a state of shock. Earlier that day to the north, the young Collier was a member of a British trading party that was approached by the Delaware sachem Tamaqua. A long-time peace advocate, Tamaqua was at the councils and was aware of the terror that the coming rebellion was sure to bring. The chief instructed the men "to depart immediately with all the whites that he could take." The team promptly heeded Tamaqua's warning and returned south toward Fort Pitt. En route they were attacked by a party of Ohio Indians; Collier escaped, but he claimed that he heard "seven or eight death cries" and assumed that the rest of his men were killed on the spot. Along with this terrifying news, Collier relayed a message from Tamaqua that British-held Fort Sandusky, in present-day Ohio, had been captured and its commanding officer was taken prisoner. Fort Sandusky had played a vital role in connecting the American frontier since the fall of New France. Like Fort Pitt, it was built as a result of conquest and positioned strategically along the southern coastline of Lake Erie at Sandusky Bay. While it was always a small post, the fort was the vital link in the line of communication that joined Fort Detroit and Fort Pitt; its destruction was a startling indicator that the insurrection was no regional phenomenon. The Indian rebellion against British posts was moving east at a blinding speed, and Fort Pitt was next in its path.[21]

Later that day, the small outpost at Pittsburgh was shaken by news that there was a pair of murders only a few hundred yards from the walls of Fort Pitt. Two craftsmen had been working diligently at the fort's sawmill when they were attacked by a party of Ohioan warriors and killed. The location was only a stone's throw across the Monongahela from Fort Pitt; the bodies of the two craftsmen had been terribly mutilated and scalped. The orientation of the men indicated that they were caught off guard and killed without warning. It was to stand as the first of a long-list of atrocities on the frontier by the Ohio Indians.

Guyasuta now had the rebellion that he had sought for almost three years. On May 16, Fort Sandusky was overrun when a group of Wyandots entered the post under the pretense of a council. Once inside, unlike at Fort Detroit, the Wyandots kidnapped the commandant and killed everyone else inside. The fort was then burned down. With the fall of Fort Sandusky, it had become clear to colonial administrators that the Indians found success not by besieging the large, central fortifications but by utterly destroying the forts that supplied them.

On May 25 Fort St. Joseph was captured in the Great Lakes region and its entire garrison was killed. Two days later Fort Miami to its south would fall as well. To lure its commandant out, one of his native mistresses coaxed him into the open and he was gunned down by a group of warriors in waiting. On June 1 Fort Ouiatenon further west was taken in a bloodless capture. On June 2, however, the fourth and final fortification that supported Fort Detroit was taken after Fort Michilimackinac's garrison was lured outside its walls by the promise of a friendly game of lacrosse; half of the soldiers were tortured and killed as a result.[22] By June 22, the two largest fortifications in British North America were fully under siege. While Fort Detroit had been under attack by Pontiac and his allies for over a month, Fort Pitt had fallen to the unified nations of the Ohio Country.

In the Ohio Country, Guyasuta and his Mingo along with their Shawnee and Delaware allies fared equally well. While the Ohio Indians started their campaign weeks after their Great Lakes counterparts, the damage was equally devastating. On June 16 a Mingo party captured Fort Venango, eighty miles north of Fort Pitt. After killing the twelve men inside, the Mingo kept its commandant alive long enough to pen a document listing their grievances. Upon completion of the letter he was roasted alive on a wooden stake over an open fire. On June 18 that same party ambushed and burned Fort Le Boeuf to the north; although the damage to the fort was catastrophic, the garrison escaped to Fort Pitt. Finally, the last of the three French forts built a decade earlier was taken when over two hundred fifty Ottawa, Ojibwa, Wyandot, and Ohio Indians besieged and captured Fort Presque Isle on Lake Erie. Although the men inside negotiated the surrender, the majority of them were killed upon leaving the safety of the fort.

To view these actions as a coordinated effort would be erroneous, yet to say that they were unrelated would be absurd. While the conflict is generally called Pontiac's Rebellion, it is much more complex than one war chief mobilizing an entire continent of people. While it is easy to assume that all of North America's Indians were working together in a uniform fashion in 1763, it must be remembered that each nation acted on its own, and many more abstained from participating in the violence altogether. Most historians conclude that the efforts of the Great Lakes peoples motivated others in neighboring regions to join the insurgency; their joint economic hardships and similar grievances created the appearance of one monolithic response. Though the Ohio Country nations all participated in the war, it was the young Delaware warrior Keekyuscung that led his people's charge. Shortly after Forbes's campaign captured Fort Duquesne five years earlier, it was Keekyuscung that delivered the following ill-fated message to the conquering British: "If the English would draw back over the mountain, they would get all other nations into their interest; but if they staid and settled there, all the nations would be against them; and . . . it would be a great war, and never come to peace again."[23]

After sufficiently razing the support positions north of Fort Pitt, Guyasuta and the Ohio Indians resumed their attack on the Forks itself. The Indians largely stayed out of sight most days, but nights would hold terror for the huddled masses of men, women, and children inside Fort Pitt. Since the siege began, the village of Pittsburgh moved fearfully into the fort. The Ohioan warriors knew full well that the citizens trapped inside the post would require the most support in the form of food and supplies. Therefore, when the sun would rise and the sentries would survey the land outside of Fort Pitt's walls, the warriors would often kill livestock openly so as to increase panic inside the post. When time was of the essence, the faster that fort surrendered the sooner the insurrection could end.

Inside Fort Pitt the desperation of its residents was growing by the day. The daily journal of Captain William Trent, the original builder of Fort Prince George who was writing inside the fort, contains a fascinating account of just how bad things had become, "Out of our regard to them we gave them [the Indians] two blankets and an handkerchief out of the Small Pox Hospital. I hope it will have the desired effect." What Trent had written of was the presentation of two blankets taken from Fort Pitt's isolated smallpox quarters to the Indians in the hopes of infecting their attackers. While it is often a minor footnote in the siege of the fort, many historians agree that this devious gift stands as the first example of biological warfare in North American history.[24]

Unbeknownst to the Indian warriors and the people of Fort Pitt, colonial administrators were preparing to address the Indian uprising with deadly force. Governor-General Amherst wrote on June 6, "I am fully convinced the only true Method of treating those Savages, is to keep them in proper Subjection & punish, without Exception, the Transgressors." In his next order,he refers to Fort Pitt once again as a vital possession of the British Empire. "If the Indians have really Cutt off any of our Garrisons, no time must be Lost in Retaking the Posts, & securing them." Earlier in the summer, Amherst had kept reserves of Highlanders (the 42nd and 77th Regiments) and light infantry (the 17th Regiment of Foot) stationed at Staten Island, and when hostilities erupted in Pittsburgh the commanding general of North America promptly put them into action. From Staten Island, Amherst ordered the units to march not west toward the Forks, but south toward Philadelphia. In a letter to Colonel Henry Bouquet dated June 12 Amherst writes: "You will Dispose of these two Companys, according to the Advices You may Receive from Above, without Waiting for further Orders from me, which might be Attended with Unnecessary Delays; And if you think it Necessary, You will Yourself Proceed toward Fort Pitt. . . . You may be better Enabled to put in Execution . . . Securing the Communication, & Reducing the Indians to Reason."[25]

Bouquet responded two days later: "I propose to march these two Companies to Fort Pitt." In this simple declaration Bouquet would initiate a forced march out of Philadelphia with five hundred Highlanders to break the siege at the Forks of the Ohio. Their journey would take nearly two months of hard trekking over rough terrain, and though they did not know it at the time their arrival would drastically alter the face of the Ohio Country forever.[26]

Fighting finally subsided on August 1 at Fort Pitt. The night before, some Indians had used the cover of darkness to infiltrate the trench that surrounded the post; the garrison promptly eliminated that threat by throwing grenades into the fosse. Curiously enough, Captain Trent writes, the Indians that surrounded them mysteriously abandoned their positions and disappeared into the forest "with their baggage."

The following day, one described as "all quiet," a Cayuga Indian and a white captive approached Fort Pitt with hopes of meeting with its commandant. The Cayuga, a member of the Six Nation Iroquois Confederacy, introduced himself with the Christian name of John Hudson. Hudson clarified that his intentions were friendly and that Colonel Bouquet had sent him to deliver three letters, but because of an attack he could only deliver one. According to Hudson, he had been captured by a warrior party and his correspondences ripped open. Though the white man who accompanied Hudson is not named, it would have been his job to translate Bouquet's letters for his captors. The letters, now lost to history, would have claimed that the colonel was well on his way to Fort Pitt and would arrive shortly.

With this new information in hand, the Ottawa members of the Ohio delegation proclaimed that "they would not make peace while one of them was alive." The Mingo, Shawnee, Huron, and some Delaware soon agreed. It was a telling armistice in the terrible fighting that had raged for over a month; the Delaware had been largely divided over aggressive action toward the English for some time. Tamaqua, a long-time ally of the British, was one of the primary Delaware voices advocating for peace. The Ottawa, however, was the nation of Pontiac himself. This meeting underscores the divisiveness that existed on the American frontier among native groups during the summer of 1763.

While those inside of Fort Pitt were unaware exactly why the incessant firing and taunting had stopped that day, they would have welcomed the respite. For the last month and a half Henry Bouquet and his Highlanders had snaked their away along the Forbes Road in the hopes of liberating Fort Pitt; those inside knew this and could hardly await his arrival. They had no idea though that the Ohioans had intercepted intelligence alerting them to his progress. It was for this reason that fighting seemed to end on August 1; Guyasuta and the other warriors were hoping to meet Bouquet and his column head on.

On August 5, the five hundred Highlanders and Redcoats who marched through the forests of western Pennsylvania were growing tired, yet their leader propelled them forward with a potent mixture of enthusiasm and duty. Henry Bouquet and his men had left Fort Ligonier two days earlier, and Fort Pitt was still twenty-five miles ahead of them. Bouquet had promised his men that they would stop to drink and rest at Bushy Run Station, the halfway point along the Forbes Road between Loyalhanna and the Forks of the Ohio. The site was never fortified, but since 1758 a former sergeant named Andrew Byerly maintained a post near Bushy Run Creek, and any party traveling the Forbes path would have stopped there. Since the Indian insurgency had begun, Bushy Run had been all but abandoned by its British caretakers; the arrival of the Highlanders and Redcoats would be about reclamation as much as rehydration. Because of the rebellious state of the area the colonel knew that hostile Indians could be awaiting him, and much of the column's provisions were left behind at Fort Ligonier to expedite his march.

By early afternoon, Bouquet's column of men was over half a mile long, with the Royal American Redcoats in the front, joined by the Highlanders, and followed by a motley crew of civilians, beasts of burden, and supplies. Due to the logistics of feeding and moving over five hundred men, plus transporting provisions to a besieged Fort Pitt, Bouquet's small army was quite literally a mobile supply depot. The march had begun to drag as morning ended, and the colonel planned to make good on his promise to rest at Bushy Run; their scheduled stop was only a mile to their west. To suggest that Bouquet anticipated an attack is misleading, but his previous correspondence did indicate that an engagement would benefit his overall mission by drawing Ohioan warriors away from Fort Pitt.[27]

As the lumbering column crawled ahead, with Bouquet in the back, the force found itself rolling simultaneously over two large hills, one to the front and another to the back. The line began to slow while climbing and descending the terrain, and at approximately one o'clock the peaceful silence of the forest was split by the cracking of musket fire and the unmistakable war whoops of the Ohio Indians. The ambush unleashed at that moment was a textbook example of frontier Indian warfare. The Shawnee, Delaware, Mingo, Huron, and Ottawa warriors caught Bouquet's tired and weary men completely by surprise. While the colonel himself was in the back away from the firing, Lieutenant James Dow of the Royal American Regiment commanded the front. Surveying the damage but holding his position, Dow ordered his men to fire; Dow killed two warriors himself in the counterattack.[28]

From the rear, Bouquet assessed the strength of the Indian ambush as formidable. Using their knowledge of the terrain to their advantage, Guyasuta and the Ohioans initiated their attack from the highest ground in the area. Recognizing the importance of this hill, Bouquet ordered two light infantry of Highlanders, the vaunted Black Watch, to rush the position and claim the high ground. As a tribal people themselves, the Scottish Highlanders had proven an invaluable addition to Britain's overall war strategy. They were surlier than Britain's Regulars but more disciplined than the American Provincials; they took the hill with ease. Although it appeared to be a minor victory, the position held little actual value to the native warriors. Coveting a hill or a parcel of ground was a strictly European ideal, and only when one organized force faces another does it carry any strategic value. The Indians, however, fought not as one unit but as countless individuals; they shared an understanding that they had strength in numbers, but it was this lack of order that most often shattered the lines of structured, European armies. The Indians played by their own rules, and in that style of war they found success.

As in Braddock's defeat, the Indians gave way on the hill and quickly enveloped Bouquet's men. The colonel wrote, "as soon as they were driven from one Post, they appeared on another." Just as at the Monongahela, the chaos that the British fell victim to was actually a well-organized maneuver. The day was turning against Bouquet's column, but the resilience of the Highlanders and an innovation by Bouquet that allowed them to survive the day. During the combat, Bouquet ordered that the long supply train of flour sacks be unloaded and piled into a makeshift fortification. Within this ring of flour Bouquet kept his wounded, and as the sun began to set it would serve as a temporary command. When the fighting subsided and it seemed that Bouquet's column had survived the first day, he established a defensive perimeter and strategized for the next day. The Ohioans and Guyasuta shouted jabs throughout the night, reminding the British that only death awaited them the next morning.[29]

The following day the Indian attack resumed with a declaration by the Delaware sachem Keekyuscung. He is said to have called to Bouquet himself, according to the recollection of a Robert Kirk, and shouted that "they would have his scalp before night." After seven years of war and months of diplomacy, the men squaring off on both sides knew each other all too well. Many of the insults were shouted in perfect English, making Bushy Run one of the most compelling battles of the entire rebellion. Realizing the value of the Highlanders' ability to bend the rules of traditional British combat, a quality shared by Bouquet himself, the colonel devised a strategy for day two to not only escape with their lives but also defeat the Ohioans altogether.[30]

Using the terrain and his meager flour fort to his advantage, Bouquet instructed his officers to engage the warriors for a time, and feign retreat. By running toward and around the pile of flour sacks, Bouquet hoped to lure the Ohio Indians into an ambush of his own. After engaging the warriors that morning, the Redcoats did as instructed and turned in retreat. For Guyasuta and the Ohioans, seeing retreating British forces was something that they were fully accustomed to during the Seven Years' War; as usual they shouted their intimidating war whoops in an attempt to overrun their foes. As they ran, many discarded their firearms and grabbed their knives to collect the scalps of their fleeing enemies, letting their guard down as they did so.

According to Bouquet's initial plan, the Indians fell directly into a trap. While the provincials fled, the focused Indians ran into the arms of the waiting Highlanders. The Scotsmen shouted with rage, many remembering the horrible massacre of their people at Grant's defeat, and tore at the surprised warriors with their bayonets. Caught entirely off guard, the natives broke and ran. Although Indian war dictated a well-understood approach for attack, it offered almost no method for an orderly retreat. The Ohioans ran through the forest around them, leaving their

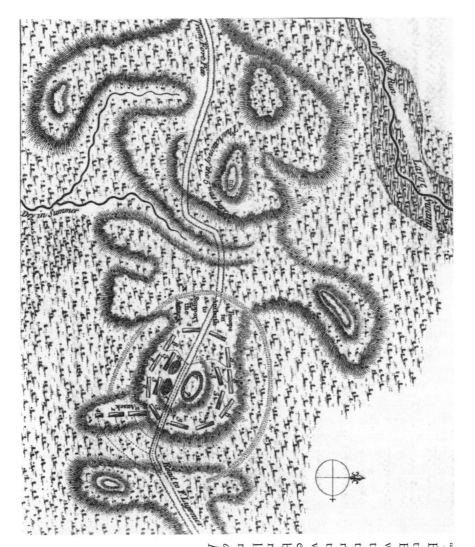

"A rendering of the Battle of Bushy Run." Bushy Run is at the top left. Col. Henry Bouquet's camp can be seen with his men formed around the wounded in the circle in the center. His troops feigned retreat drawing the Indians toward the camp, where they were then ambushed and routed by the troops indicated below the main camp. The road leads to Fort Pitt to the left and Fort Ligonier to the right. (*A General Topography of North America and the West Indies, 1768*)

A depiction of the British Highlanders' vicious repulse of the Ohio Indians' attack at Bushy Run in 1763. The ferocity of the Highlanders had been stoked by earlier Indian atrocities. (*Library of Congress*)

wounded comrades behind; North America was still a tribal world, and on August 6 the Scots proved themselves to be the most dominant of all.

Bouquet's men hollered with delight in the forest that day with no regard for stealth as there was no enemy left to attack them. For the first time, and the last time, a British force had completely defeated that of an Indian enemy on the field of battle. Guyasuta was among the survivors, and the Delaware Keekyuscung among the dead. In all, fifty British soldiers, both Highlander and Royal American, had been killed at the Battle of Bushy Run; sixty more were wounded. Bouquet estimated that at least as many Indians had died as well. That night, lighted by the fires of his tired men, Bouquet wrote to Amherst: "the Behaviour of the Troops on this Occasion Speaks for itself So Strongly, that for me to attempt their Eulogium would but detract from their merit."[31]

As gallant as Colonel Bouquet's victory was, it did not end the insurrection on the frontier that had left hundreds dead and thousands without homes. In the far reaches of the North American west the Indian rebels of Pontiac had made significant gains, and the killing would continue for another three years.

After Bushy Run, the most capable warriors of the Ohio Indians were either disillusioned or dead. Although many of the warriors would return to Fort Pitt, they could never again rally the strength or zeal to continue their exhaustive efforts to besiege the post. Fort Pitt had been designed to take on the full force of the French empire; the greatest challenge it would ever confront though was not a three-day bombardment of cannon fire, but a terrifying summer of Indian rebellion. The war with France had ended, and King George was now confident that he could expand his reign across all of North America with the battle-tested fort at the Forks of the Ohio anchoring the charge.

While the general insurgency was far from over, the magnitude of the victory by Bouquet at Bushy Run cannot be stressed enough. By defeating the Ohio Indians in battle, the triumph had two distinct effects. The first was the obvious logistical benefit; by defeating the warriors, and therefore crushing the Ohio Indians' capabilities to wage war, the British military could successfully strengthen remaining positions and potentially build new ones to solidify their hold on the region. Also, by marching directly through the line of assault, Bouquet had reconnected the vital communication from the east in Philadelphia and allowed Forts Littleton, Bedford, and Ligonier to once again flourish. With this crucial road now reopened, goods, information, and reinforcements lost during the summer of 1763 could easily be transferred to Pittsburgh with limited danger.

The second effect was much more difficult to quantify. The triumph at Bushy Run greatly demoralized the Ohio Indians, therefore quashing the ambitions of many more potential rebels who might have taken up arms in the future. Likewise, though the news of defeat was devastating for the natives of the region, it came as a desperately need morale boost for white settlers. After crushing the Indian force so completely, Bouquet gained fame that quickly spread from the outpost at Pittsburgh to London itself. He had done something that few or no commanders had yet accomplished in the New World: defeat an Indian force completely in a head-to-head battle. From Fort Ligonier, Lieutenant Archibald Blane congratulated the colonel on "being the first Person that has ever thoroughly convinced these Rascals of their inability to cope with us." Since the outbreak of violence had begun, average settlers were forced to flee east and south into Pennsylvania and Virginia for fear of their and their families' lives. Until the Battle of Bushy Run they had little hope that the British military could do anything to protect them.[32]

On a personal level for Guyasuta, that hot August day represented a major turning point in his nearly forty-year life. The Battle of Bushy Run has been described as a battle of familiars; the Ohio Indians engaged a British force that they knew all too well for the very last time. They had grown accustomed to viewing the Redcoats as their enemies for almost a decade, and their engagement with the Highlanders on that day represented the end of an era for the native warriors involved. With Bouquet's victory came hope for the white settler of the frontier; it also signaled the end for the New Ohioan. During the Seven Years' War the Delaware, Shawnee, and Mingo peoples had put their full faith in the French to relieve them of their Iroquois oppressors; that shift created the New Ohioan. When the French were forced out of the region, the Ohio Indians were left without an ally. The insurgency of 1763 represented their last attempt at escaping their old way of life. It was an exhaustive effort, and though the Battle of Bushy Run did not end the rebellion continent-wide it did signal the beginning of a new age in the Ohio Country.

For Guyasuta the defeat was heartbreaking. His undying defiance of foreign powers made him a well-respected and popular war chief, yet he lost much more than a battle at Bushy Run. He had gained admiration among the new nations of the Ohio for his position as leader of a resistance movement, but after Bouquet's victory the movement seemed destined for failure. When Guyasuta and his warriors retreated that day, in many ways his new identity died as well.

FIVE

Dream of His Fathers

POSTWAR DIPLOMACY IN BRITISH NORTH AMERICA

F ew rivers in North America are more impressive than the
Ohio. Translating to "the beautiful river" in Iroquoian, it
has stood the test of time as one of the most vital waterways in
history. Its creation is one of peace, formed by the tranquil collision of the Allegheny and Monongahela rivers; its life story
though has been one of division, violence, and war. At nearly
one thousand miles long, the Ohio River has factored into the
designs of no less than three world superpowers. At its widest
point it is a mile across, and the impassability of its waters has
physically separated unique and conflicting cultures for over
three hundred years.

In the colonial period, the Ohio River was viewed as the great
passageway to the west. Beginning at the Forks of the Ohio, its
currents would take settlers deep into the heart of the continent
before joining with the mighty Mississippi. At this meeting
point at Cairo, Illinois, the Ohio River appears its most expan-
sive, and its more famous counterpart seems meager in comparison. From a strictly hydrological perspective, the Ohio is the
main stream feeding the entire southern Mississippi River system; why the Ohio River is not considered to flow all the way to
the Gulf of Mexico is one of the great injustices of geography.

Thomas Jefferson once wrote that "the Ohio is the most beautiful river on earth. Its current gentle, waters clear, and bosom smooth and unbroken by rocks and rapids, a single instance only excepted." When America only stretched as far as the Mississippi, the river stood as more of a boundary to the west than as a gateway. Jefferson's words are magnified by that fact; he was writing of the natural beauty of his soon-to-be independent country and the Ohio was the first image in his mind.[1]

Perhaps the river's true meaning could only be recognized from the perspective of a stranger. In 1831 when the French political philosopher Alexis de Tocqueville published *Democracy in America,* he included a description of the Ohio River. Tocqueville found himself straddling two worlds, one free and one slave. His words resonate:

> Thus the traveller who floats down the current of the Ohio to the spot where that river falls into the Mississippi, may be said to sail between liberty and servitude; and a transient inspection of the surrounding objects will convince him as to which of the two is most favorable to mankind. Upon the left bank of the stream the population is rare; from time to time one descries a troop of slaves loitering in the half-desert fields; the primaeval forest recurs at every turn; society seems to be asleep, man to be idle, and nature alone offers a scene of activity and of life. From the right bank, on the contrary, a confused hum is heard which proclaims the presence of industry; the fields are covered with abundant harvests, the elegance of the dwellings announces the taste and activity of the laborer, and man appears to be in the enjoyment of that wealth and contentment which is the reward of labor.[2]

The Ohio River was more than just a waterway. While North and South, slave and free, were separated by the widely acknowledged but invisible Mason-Dixon line in the east, the Ohio formed a very real western border between the two. When the nation raced to Civil War in 1861, the currents of this river divided the Blue from the Gray.

Almost sixty years after Jefferson's description, another would-be president in the form of the young Abraham Lincoln paid homage to this selfless giant in his 1838 Lyceum Address:

"At what point shall we expect the approach of danger? By what means shall we fortify against it?—Shall we expect some transatlantic military giant, to step the Ocean, and crush us at a blow? Never!—All the armies of Europe, Asia and Africa combined, with all the treasure of the earth (our own excepted) in their military chest; with a Buonaparte for a commander, could not by force, take a drink from the Ohio."[3]

Lincoln identifies the Ohio not as a mere tributary, but as the quintessential American river. The Mississippi was sought for so long by so many because it connected America with the world. When valuable trade goods would be collected in the interior of the continent, moving them to the major ports of Boston, New York, or Charleston was not always feasible. The Mississippi provided a direct link to the markets of Europe from the frontier. In that way the Mississippi was western America's link with the world. From time to time foreign navies traversed the great river, and some even controlled it, but the Ohio though remained in American hands. As Lincoln had stated, no enemy had ever dominated the Ohio River and no enemy ever would. For those back east wanting to reach the Mississippi, the only way to get there was by first sailing down the Ohio; the Ohio River was truly America's river.

But long before the United States of America existed, the Ohio River played a very different role. After the Seven Years' War it stood as a potent symbol of possibility for the British world. Its direct navigational link with the Mississippi was not yet fully realized, but there was no doubt that fortunes were to be made. With the British Empire alone to its east, the lands to the west were destined to be explored. Therefore, as peace fell across the continent, the Ohio River became one of the most active rivers in North America.

It was on banks of this river where Guyasuta and his hunting party sat in October 1770. The Indian rebellion for him had ended seven years earlier at Bushy Run and he, like all willing parties, was benefiting from the prosperity that came with peace. Since the fighting had ended, Guyasuta had learned to conform to the changing norms of colonial America, and he had become a productive member of this new society as a diplomat, trader, and guide. He had earned the respect of his people through combat, and now through his recent political efforts he had also garnered the admiration of many within the British world as well.

Since the end of the rebellion, Guyasuta had to reconsider his life. He valued his position as a Mingo chief, but he reconnected with his original Seneca roots. When peace was regained, the British-Iroquois alliance began to reclaim its traditional power, and he found that returning to the Iroquois Confederacy would be his most prudent decision. His past as a Mingo was never forgotten, and many still resided in the Ohio Country, but Guyasuta would now embrace his Iroquoian heritage openly and proudly. After all, in this new British North America it would have been foolish not to.

He had seen much over the previous seven years, and much had changed in his own world. The lands that he used to call home, the Ohio Country, were now lost to the unstoppable waves of white settlement. His Indian brethren remained in the region, but life was a constant losing struggle with migrants from the east looking to establish their own way of life. For two years Guyasuta had found himself staying deeper in the recesses of the Ohio River valley, from present-day West Virginia to Kentucky, and it was his prerogative to do so.

Even though he was far removed from Fort Pitt, that beacon of British power that so disrupted his world, he still encountered travelers from its immediate vicinity. For them, reaching the Mississippi was as easy as hopping in a canoe and floating downstream. It was a tense reality for the many Indian peoples around him; two years earlier the British signed an agreement stating that the valley belonged exclusively to the Indians. Guyasuta was never ill-taken by the encounters with the settlers though, and he had even found that leading them as a guide could be quite profitable.

As the sun set on that October 1770 day, Guyasuta and his Indian comrades settled for the night at the meeting place of the Hocking and Ohio rivers. While the men gathered around their fire, the bubbling currents of the waters carefully rolled onto the rock shores. They were surrounded by seemingly endless mountains of green. Several miles away there were Indian villages, but the sounds of carriages or blacksmiths' hammers were absent.

The sounds of colonial settlements were gone, and all that was left was nature as it stood; they were truly in a world of their own.

Suddenly, from around the river's bend came the slight echoes of voices. As the men around Guyasuta reached for their weapons, he did not. At forty-five years old the sachem had long outlived the days of his rebellious and fiery youth. He no longer jumped to confrontation, and his experience taught him that it was always better to assume peace; sound diplomacy was smart diplomacy.

There came toward him a small group of vessels indicating a simple surveying party. Generally one of the small boats carried the men of the voyage, and the remainder floated the supplies. Since the Ohio Valley had been rid of any French presence a decade earlier, the British saw its untapped resources as pure profit; these were the spoils of victory. While the Indian party lined up on the shore to inspect their alien visitors, its apparent leader stood up to greet them as it docked. Rising out of the boat, standing at nearly six foot three inches tall, was a figure that Guyasuta had not seen in almost twenty years: George Washington.

In this barren wilderness, hundreds of miles from the splendors of Virginia and the ruins of Fort Le Boeuf, where the two men had first met in 1753, they were face to face yet again. Although they had only been yards apart at Braddock's defeat, it was almost certain that neither of them were aware of one another. On this day, however, there was no doubt. Washington wrote: "When encamped opposite the mouth of the Great Hockhocking we found Kiasutha and his hunting party encamped. Here we were under a necessity of paying our compliments, as this person was one of the Six Nations chiefs and the head of those upon this River. In the person of Kiasutha I found an old acquaintance, he being of the Indians that went with me to the French in 1753."[4]

It was a joyous occasion. Washington had been surveying the Ohio Valley for over a month in an attempt to buy land and extend his fortunes. In the meantime he had ventured to Fort Pitt, surveying the fruits of his 1758 triumphs, and met with prominent individuals along the way. Since leaving Pittsburgh he had snaked down the Ohio River, never expecting to find a familiar face in such an ancient and empty place. With warmth in their hearts the two parties camped together that night, and supped on the buffalo that Guyasuta and his hunters had killed earlier that day.

It is not known what the two men discussed, but there would have been much to talk about. Since their last official meeting in 1753, they had each become much more than they were as young men in their twenties. Washington was a commissioned colonel, but in the *pax Britannica* he had become a wealthy and powerful member of Virginia's gentry class. He was a land owner, a slave owner, and one of the most respected men in North America's premier British colony. Guyasuta had grown in his own right. Seven years older than Washington, he too had become one of the most powerful Indian sachems in the entire Ohio Country. They likely shared their war stories and compared their proverbial battle scars; it was an unusual meeting for the two men whose careers were defined by battling the ideological fortunes of the other. The next morning, Washington and his party continued downriver. It would be the last time he and Guyasuta would meet.

The radical change that allowed for Guyasuta and George Washington's peaceful reunion in 1770 would not have been possible without the seven years of trial and tribulation that came before it.[5]

The month following Bouquet's clash with Guyasuta's Ohioans in 1763, the promise of peace brought forth by the victory quickly disappeared. On September 14, a party of nearly five hundred Seneca warriors sat in ambush at a strategic pass linking Fort Schlosser and the high-value position of Fort Niagara on Lake Ontario. A vital supply route, the trail in which they sat had historically been dominated by the natives, but since the end of the Seven Years' War the British had taken control of the pass. While the Seneca warriors sat in waiting, a large wagon train bumped and bustled unknowingly through the

The site of the "Devil's Hole Massacre" near the Niagara Gorge. This bloody encounter highlighted the violent uncertainty of the Indian insurgency of 1763. (*Author*)

pass. Using the sheer drop to their advantage, the Indian ambush broke the supply line down into sheer chaos. As the animals were cut loose, the beasts and their packs plummeted clumsily into the Niagara River gorge below.[6]

With news of the attack two units of the 80th Regiment of Light Armed Foot rushed to the scene, only to be attacked by the Seneca a mile from their destination. The warriors rushed in with tomahawk and knife and decimated the British force, killing eighty-one men and wounding nine. The event became known as the Devil's Hole Massacre, and it was the single worst defeat that the British would suffer throughout the length of the rebellion.

With these developments the American frontier cried to the Crown for support. As subjects of the British Empire, and recently victorious ones at that, the American Provincials believed that they deserved all the protection that King George had to offer. What they received, however, was less than adequate support. As their families were murdered and their homes raided, they felt betrayed by their imperial brethren and called desperately for action. By the end of 1763 hundreds of women and children had been taken captive, and many deaths had followed. Therefore, on October 7, Parliament's hand was forced; the result nearly sent the American frontier into a frenzy.[7]

King George issued the Royal Proclamation of 1763, which he hoped would appease all sides of the North American conflict. Among many stipulations he wrote:

> And whereas it is just and reasonable, and essential to our Interest, and the Security of our Colonies, that the several Nations or Tribes of Indians with whom We are connected, and who live under our Protection, should not be molested or disturbed in the Possession of such Parts of Our Dominions and Territories as, not having been ceded to or purchased by Us, are reserved to them, or any of them, as their Hunting Grounds. . . . And We do further strictly enjoin and require all Persons whatever who have either wilfully or inadvertently seated themselves upon any Lands within the Countries above described or upon any other Lands which, not having been ceded to or purchased by Us, are still reserved to the said Indians as aforesaid, forthwith to remove themselves from such Settlements.

The Proclamation of 1763 effectively stated that no British citizen was to establish a settlement west of the Appalachian Mountains; if they did so, they would be liable under the penalty of law. While the white settlers of the frontier clamored for protection from the Indian insurgency, the remedy of the British Empire was to place blame squarely on them. As a result of the proclamation many settlers did withdraw from the frontier, but those that stayed behind did so at their own risk.

This pronouncement was ill-received by many in the American colonies. For the frontiersmen it was an ultimate act of betrayal, effectively bypassing their protections of equality under the law as full citizens. For those in the east, however, it was viewed differently, though with similar distaste. Following the French defeat, Britain's expansion into the west appeared its destiny, and the wealthy investors seeking to purchase and sell land saw the proclamation as an obstacle to their perceived capitalistic rights. For the investment companies in New York, Boston, Philadelphia, and Virginia, the king's pronouncement

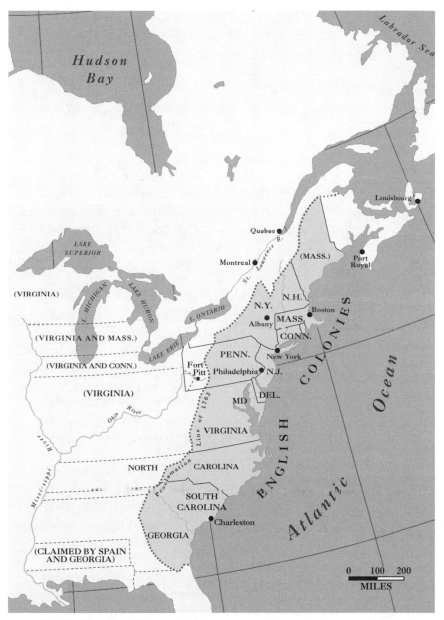

The Proclamation Line of 1763.

was a gross overreach of his royal power. America was the financial bedrock of the British Empire, and the balance of power was shifting; suddenly the empire appeared more reliant on North America than the other way around.[8]

While the proclamation was discussed in taverns across the American colonies, the terror and destruction wrought by the Indian rebellion was having a transformative effect on the frontier. In the wake of the massive refugee crisis that followed, many border areas between long-settled lands and the wilderness of the Allegheny Mountains became political battlegrounds. As in most cases in history, political instability leads to radical response; that response could either be reconsideration or rebellion. The Indian insurrection is a testament to how perceived minor economic tweaks could lead to bloodshed; it also reveals how similar situations left unchecked could cause further retaliatory actions.

Known as the "Fighting Parson," the Reverend John Elder had found himself in a suddenly powerful position. Elder had a small church in Paxtang, a settlement near Harrisburg, Pennsylvania; though it was far from the frontier, the Indian experience was not. The people of his region coexisted with Indians over the previous century, and the native peoples who lived nearby were largely anglicized—many were even Christian converts. Though actual Indian attacks were many miles away, Elder was forced to deal with his congregation's irrational fear that they would be raided next.

Elder could have done his best to justify peace through the Good Book itself, but instead, like so many political commentators, he only further aroused the suspicions. Not unlike partisans in the twenty-first century, Elder discovered that by delivering fiery sermons that spread both fear and dependence, he had become one of the most influential men in Pennsylvania. He spoke of the savagery of the Indian, and the futility of the Crown to manage it. Political discussions in America in the eighteenth century were generally reserved for prominent gathering places, almost always the tavern and the church. The "Fighting Parson" had turned his pulpit into a battle cry: to justify his heated rhetoric, Elder never shied away from interweaving his message of hate with Old Testament wisdom. From 1

Samuel 15:3 he is said to have recited, "Now go, attack the Amalekites and totally destroy everything that belongs to them. Do not spare them; put to death men and women, children and infants, cattle and sheep, camels and donkeys."[9]

It did not take long for Elder's ideological message to become a martial one. Soon after he began preaching, a group of primarily Scots-Irish immigrants rallied together to form a rough militia known as the Paxton Boys. Their misguided message was to protect themselves and their families by preventing Indian raids, and they selected Elder as one of their fearless leaders. While their ambitions were simple, they were often inspired by rash, irrational logic. Much of their fear mongering was spread by the misguided belief that all Indians, whether residing on the frontier or in the colony of Pennsylvania, were essentially the same. The reality could not have been further from the truth; William Penn had founded his proprietary under the pretense that all peoples would be treated as equals. It was in this "Peaceable Kingdom" that Penn had found many nations willing to cooperate in his egalitarian dream world, notably the Conestoga. Although some natives had balked at the idea, and notwithstanding the insurrection in the west, Indian America remained a diverse patchwork of peoples.[10]

What the Paxton Boys failed to realize was that their native neighbors were as divided as they themselves were. Pennsylvania had become a home to many different European ethnic groups because of its favorable policies, and Irish, English, French, and Germans all coexisted within its boundaries. While many of them did not interact due to old prejudices, and their conflicting example of Protestantism was almost militant in some cases, to say that all Europeans were a monolithic block would have been laughable to the Paxtonians. Their basic ignorance reveals the true tragedy of the Paxton Boys' Rebellion.

On December 14, 1763, the Paxton Boys marched angrily into the village of Conestoga Town with vengeance and fear in their hearts. In their heated rage the militia killed six adult members of the Conestoga and eight children; they waved their scalps triumphantly in the air. The Conestoga were a peaceful people who never engaged in any Indian rebellion. They were largely Christianized, and had a long history of friendly trade and cooperation with Pennsylvania and its European residents.[11]

The result was political upheaval across Pennsylvania. As governor of the colony, John Penn was coerced into declaring the killings to be murders, and the Paxton Boys to be criminals. He placed a bounty on their heads, and to protect the remaining Conestogas had them locked away in protective custody nearby at Lancaster. His efforts to quell the emerging conflict failed. Thirteen days after their initial attack the Paxton Boys marched on the jail that held the remaining Conestogas, pulled them into the street, and massacred them in brutal fashion. It was one of the single most horrifying scenes of the entire insurgency, and it set a new standard for savagery. One account details the entire scope of the massacre:

> I saw a number of people running down street towards the gaol, which enticed me and other lads to follow them. At about sixty or eighty yards from the gaol, we met from twenty-five to thirty men, well mounted on horses, and with rifles, tomahawks, and scalping knives, equipped for murder. I ran into the prison yard, and there, O what a horrid sight presented itself to my view! Near the back door of the prison, lay an old Indian and his squaw (wife), particularly well known and esteemed by the people of the town, on account of his placid and friendly conduct. His name was Will Sock; across him and his squaw lay two children, of about the age of three years, whose heads were split with the tomahawk, and their scalps all taken off. Towards the middle of the gaol yard, along the west side of the wall, lay a stout Indian, whom I particularly noticed to have been shot in the breast, his legs were chopped with the tomahawk, his hands cut off, and finally a rifle ball discharged in his mouth; so that his head was blown to atoms, and the brains were splashed against, and yet hanging to the wall, for three or four feet around. This man's hands and feet had also been chopped off with a tomahawk. In this manner lay the whole of them, men, women and children, spread about the prison yard: shot-scalped-hacked-and cut to pieces.[12]

What had resulted were reactive and uninhibited examples of dual ethnic cleansing; the violence brought forth by the Indian rebels of the frontier was now matched by a dualistic counterre-

Violence along the Pennsylvania frontier inspired this 1763 cartoon showing how the Quaker leadership's support of the Indians threatened the lives of German and Irish immigrants. (*Historical Society of Pennsylvania*)

bellion by the Paxton Boys. The militia had sent their message to John Penn, and after the killings they even attempted to march on Philadelphia in open revolt. A delegation sent by the colonial legislature intercepted them and turned them away through peaceful negotiation. Among the primary negotiators on behalf of Pennsylvania was Benjamin Franklin, whose persuasive efforts halted the rioters. Nonetheless, Britain's inability to pacify the Indians had enabled all of these terrible acts of violence.

Perhaps the single worst occurrence in the long and bloody frontier rebellion came in July 1764. As the war had dragged on, many settlers east of the Appalachians had become startlingly aware of how unsafe they were. The Royal Proclamation had dictated that any persons living west of the mountain chain were there illegally, and the conventional wisdom was that moving closer to Carlisle, on the eastern side, meant that the chance of Indian attack would decrease dramatically. If one could relocate closer still to Philadelphia, one would be out of harm's way altogether.[13]

Frontier war, however, was never predictable, and over a decade of insurgent warfare abroad in the twenty-first century has created a new awareness of just how a single, random act of violence could cause unrest for hundreds of miles around. Such was the case in the summer of 1764. If a strike occurred in an area known to be peaceful, the rebels could upend an entire region. Though the heat of the rebellion remained in the west, Indian attacks on Forts Ligonier and Bedford caused great alarm as far east as the Susquehanna River valley.

On July 27, 1764, the colony of Pennsylvania was upended by a terroristic ambush designed to suit just that purpose. In his one-room schoolhouse in south central Pennsylvania a schoolmaster named Enoch Brown was midway through his lecture when he and his twelve students were disrupted by a series of howls outside in the forest. Befuddled by the sound, Brown was soon fully aware of what he was hearing when four Delaware warriors burst into the cabin. His students ran in panic, but the small space was overwhelmed quickly. Two of the warriors guarded the exit as Brown begged for his attackers to kill him and spare the children; the warriors promptly shot him in the chest and scalped him as he died. The same tragic fate also befell the pupils inside, most of whom were under the age of twelve. As a group of farmers ran to the site upon hearing of the ambush, which became known as the Enoch Brown Schoolhouse Massacre, they found ten children dead and scalped. One child, Archie McCullough, was crawling blindly on the floor still alive despite being attacked. Another small girl was in a nearby creek, trying frantically to wash the blood from her dress.

Only a short distance from the site of the massacre, the same Delaware war party struck again, this time against a young woman named Susan King Cunningham. Like many women of the frontier, Susan was a strong and resilient worker, doing her regular chores despite being over five months pregnant. Shortly after the Enoch Brown episode, Susan King Cunningham was discovered by the Delawares as she was walking to visit a neighbor. The warriors proceeded to club her to death and disembowel her where she lay. They placed the extricated fetus beside her lifeless body and fled the scene. These shocking events rattled Pennsylvania's countryside, and the sight of a dead Enoch Brown still clutching the Bible would live forever as a reminder of just what horrors were possible when the problems of the frontier spilled over into the "civilized" world.[14]

In these attacks one can estimate the true terror of Indian war and yet the response of the attackers' communities reveals how divided the natives of the region were. When the warriors responsible for the killings returned to their villages along the Muskingum River in modern-day Ohio, they proudly displayed the scalps that they had collected in the process. At this point, sources say, they were met with mixed reactions, and one of the most senior sachems of the village, named Night Walker, publicly scorned them as cowards. This side of the story was rarely, if ever, heard by the families in the east. While the Delawares on that day hoped to spread fear, what they had achieved was to spread hatred.[15]

In London, news of the terrible unrest on the American frontier drove policy makers into action. The frontier had been a vital supply for them over the last century, both economically and militarily. In many ways the Seven Years' War had begun over hostilities to control the difficult, forested regions on the perceived edge of society. If they were to lose control of the frontier, they very well could lose control of all of their settlers in North America. In the months leading up to the Royal Proclamation of 1763, that great stop-gap that would prove a failure, King George and his advisors wrestled with notions of how to quell the Indian rebellion in the American wilderness; the proclamation, as it turned out, was not the last offering in a fruitless struggle.

The king's Privy Council had played a tremendous role in British royal politics for over two hundred years. Its wealthy noblemen swayed the king in any number of directions, and had become known in London as the great puppet masters that pulled the strings of the empire behind closed doors. Before they decided that the Proclamation of 1763 was their only alternative, they had first opted for a general housecleaning of administrators in North America. No position was safe in the British Empire; all high-ranking offices were appointed by the king with no required qualifications and no tenure of office. For a colonial governor or general to be promoted, climbing the political ladder was as easy as attaining the signature of the king. By the same token, it was equally easy to be removed from power. In August 1763 it was believed that the proverbial fish rotted from the head down, and Governor-General Jeffery Amherst was relieved of his command over British North America.[16]

The man that replaced him was no stranger to Indian warfare on the frontier. At forty-three, General Thomas Gage appeared destined for great things in the armed services of the king. He had been born in East Sussex and was the son of an Irish nobleman. Like many who one day hoped to take advantage of the English peerage system, Gage joined the military to serve his empire and earn the respect that only a martial gentleman could enjoy. He had marched alongside Braddock at the Monongahela and displayed true virtue as a capable leader in the midst of the chaos of the now infamous battle. Following the defeat of the French in 1760, Gage was appointed as military governor of Montreal, and his promotion to the rank of governor-general, commander-in-chief of all British forces in North America, was a natural stepping-stone in his ambitious career.

Like many political leaders that assumed power during a crisis throughout history, Gage made use of his office quickly in the midst of the Indian rebellion. He was under pressure from London to do so; after all, it was Amherst's perceived lack of initiative that sent him packing. In the spring of 1764 Gage had prepared a three-pronged offensive to subdue and eliminate the Indian uprising in a disciplined and orderly fashion. The first part of the strategy would be to employ the diplomatic efforts of Sir William Johnson to negotiate peace with the tribal leaders near Fort Niagara, most importantly any renegade Iroquois. Johnson was to both secure vital supply routes and convince the eastern nations to detach themselves from the conflict that Gage would portray as a dying one.

The remaining path to suppression was where Gage placed his full confidence. Two expeditions would march simultaneously to crush the remaining insurrection with pure force. One would be led by Colonel John Bradstreet, who was to sail across Lake Erie and relieve Fort Detroit. The other would be led by none other than Colonel Henry Bouquet, the star of Bushy

Run, to march out of Fort Pitt in an all-out sweep of the Ohio Country. In Gage's mind, if anyone could tame that restless region it was Bouquet—he had done it once before. Although Johnson's diplomatic efforts would be monumental, as a military officer the governor-general placed more faith in the persuasive power of a musket than that of a quill pen.[17]

The first part of Gage's plan was to dispatch Johnson to Fort Niagara, situated directly at the meeting point of Lake Ontario and the Niagara River. Protected by thick stone walls, Fort Niagara had been built and maintained by the French until the fall of New France in 1760. It commanded both bodies of water equally well, and the massively constructed commandant's quarters stood as one of the most impressive buildings in all of North America, and certainly the most luxurious structure in any of its frontier forts. It was two stories tall with over a dozen rooms, and for Johnson it would be home until his proceedings were completed. His plan was a multi-tiered one; knowing the complexity of North America's Indian peoples and the tenuous nature of their alliances, Johnson was the best possible man for such an immense job as negotiating peace. He knew that it would take not one but many negotiations to end the rebellion, but if done correctly the first one could buy much-needed time.

Johnson held a special position among the tribal leaders that he dealt with regularly, and they called him Warraghiyagey, or Doer of Great Things of Business. From Johnson's perspective, the treaty that Gage assigned to him would actually be many small treaties with many different peoples. As secretary of Indian affairs, Johnson had made a rare misstep in bypassing the Iroquois Confederacy to deal directly with their subjected peoples; in the process he had effectively leveled the playing field for a host of nations that in accordance with the Iroquois Covenant Chain should have never spoken with him. Of those groups the Delaware seemed to have gained the most favor. If Johnson was to regain order in the east, his mission would need to restore and reaffirm power to the Iroquois; the New Ohioan in many ways was a direct result of Johnson's misguided empowerment of subjugated Indians.[18]

In addition to restructuring the Indian hierarchy of the region, Johnson knew that he would need to subdue the renegade Seneca nation and rein them back into the Iroquois

Confederacy. As the subjected nations of the Confederacy had gravitated toward independence, the westernmost Iroquois nation of Seneca had begun acting independently of the council fire at Onondaga. From the Seneca were born the Mingo, the most radical product of this independence.

Johnson's struggles were long and difficult, and over a period of weeks he accomplished his goal. It took hours of council with many different peoples, but his creative diplomacy paid off. He treated the Seneca as obstinate children; when their sachems sent wampum strings he denied them, and when their delegations entered Fort Niagara he refused to see them. Because of their role in the Devil's Hole Massacre, when they finally relented, it was on Johnson's terms. He required that before negotiations would begin they would return any prisoners they held and, most important, hand over control of the Niagara portage route. The Seneca had now been brought back into the Iroquois fold, and what remained to be dealt with were the remaining remnants of the New Ohioan.

With the Covenant Chain seemingly restored, Johnson treated with the Iroquois and devised a strategy to eliminate the threat of the Ohioan nations. Since the siege of Fort Pitt had ended, Guyasuta and his Mingos, as well as the Delawares and Shawnees, had been encamped along the Muskingum River. Though distant, this camp had become the heart of the remaining insurgency in the Ohio Country. For the Iroquois, delivering a crushing blow to these people was more of a pleasure than a duty. The Ohioans had traditionally been subjects of the Iroquois alone, and in the Iroquois traditional mindset it was their responsibility to punish the Ohioans for their disobedience. While Johnson wrote to Gage to inform him of his plan to mobilize the Iroquois against the Ohioans, there seemed to be no objection from the governor-general.[19]

As Johnson concluded his deliberations with the Seneca and other Indian peoples who were tired of rebellion, Colonel John Bradstreet set out to fulfill his mission on August 8. While he was unsure of what lay ahead of him, Bradstreet followed his instructions to sail through the Great Lakes to Fort Detroit where he would subdue whatever was left of the Indian force that besieged the post. At his disposal was a massive force of over twelve hundred men including two hundred and fifty native warriors arranged by Sir William Johnson himself. Bradstreet was an experienced officer; he was passionately British, but North America was the only home he had ever known.

Born in Nova Scotia, Bradstreet served in many different capacities during his military career. He was captured as a prisoner of war during King George's War in the 1740s, and later went on to build a reputation as a studious and competent officer in the Seven Years' War. During that spell he had participated in the attack on Fort Carillon, and later headed up an enormous effort of over three thousand men that captured Fort Frontenac. Like most Americans, he believed that the victory over the French was an affirmation of his own existence, and he viewed the Indian uprising that he now faced in a similar fashion. By the time that Bradstreet had mobilized his men, however, the situation at Fort Detroit for Pontiac's warriors had begun to deteriorate. The siege had lasted for months, and while Pontiac and his Ottawas promised a fast victory, they had delivered little in the way of results. The unified force that he had amassed months earlier had disintegrated, many turning their backs on the movement altogether. Even Pontiac himself was conspicuously absent at Fort Detroit as he had ventured into the untamed Illinois Country to find more support from a new population of warriors. He even made attempts with a French officer to draw them into his new war against the British.[20]

Bradstreet was no fool. He could potentially face an Indian war party of thousands at Detroit, and while the crisis had already begun to pass, he was prepared for the worst. He had seen the horrors of frontier combat, and if he could avoid a confrontation and spare the lives of his twelve hundred men he was determined to do so. On August 12, as Bradstreet and his men sailed westward across Lake Erie toward their destination, a powerful gale had suddenly kicked up. Sensing danger, Bradstreet docked his ships at a point a short distance away from the burned ruins of Fort Presque Isle.

While Bradstreet and his men waited out the conditions, he was approached by a party of ten Indians claiming to be from the Scioto region of the Ohio Country. They spoke with him in confidence, stating they were representatives of the Shawnee,

Delaware, Huron, and Mingo peoples. With the apparent graces of opportunity knocking, Bradstreet began an impromptu council with the Ohioans. The discussion was both apologetic and worrisome for the Indians; they informed Bradstreet that they had gotten word of an impending strike on their encampments, and whether they were referring to Bouquet's planned march or that of Johnson's Iroquois, they were right to be concerned.

Bradstreet and his men were skeptical of this delegation. There was no doubt that they had heard of Sir William Johnson's meetings at Fort Niagara, and he was technically the only representative of the Crown licensed to negotiate peace. The delegation claimed that they had not attended out of ignorance, unaware that such a conference had begun. Bradstreet saw through the façade, however, because they had earlier claimed to know the results of his councils. Negotiating from a position of power, Bradstreet greatly superseded his own authority by offering to negotiate a peace treaty with the Ohioans himself. He not only had no justification for such an action, but he was explicitly violating the orders of his commander Gage by not pressing directly to his intended destination.

The terms that Bradstreet dictated were of the utmost seriousness, and his naivite seemed evident as he named his requests. He offered that the Ohioans could have peace and avoid a larger attack only if they would release all the hostages they had taken and held at the camps. While their encampments on the Scioto and Muskingum were several miles away, he gave them the freedom to meet him days later at Sandusky with their prisoners in hand. Along with this pronouncement Bradstreet stipulated that the Ohioans release and vacate all the forts that they had taken over the course of the rebellion. Finally, Bradstreet demanded that any warriors that had participated in an attack of any sort against a white person should be handed over as criminals to be punished with the full force of the law. The Ohioans agreed, and left for their villages. While there is little more than hearsay to suggest this, it is likely that Guyasuta may have been present at the meeting on Lake Erie that week. While Pontiac was faltering in the west, the Ohio Country rebellion was still very much in the hands of Guyasuta.[21]

When Bradstreet arrived at Sandusky Bay days later, he was met with no hostages and only a limited number of Ohioan sachems. They asked for more time, and the gullible Bradstreet accepted. He believed that his own simplistic form of diplomacy had worked; in reality it was playing directly into the hands of the Ohioans. He was so confident in his own abilities that he even invited the sachems of the Illinois Country, people that he had no experience with, to meet him at Fort Detroit and join the peace negotiations. To build good will he sent a delegation of his own men under Thomas Morris to deliver his gifts to the chiefs personally. On their journey his Indian guides led Morris and his men into a trap where they were captured and taken to meet with Pontiac himself. Through the help of a moderate Miami chief, Morris was able to escape and trekked over two hundred and forty miles to meet with Bradstreet's party at Fort Detroit.[22]

Although Bradstreet confidently arrived at Fort Detroit with his supplies and reinforcements in tow, he had no idea that in the east his actions had created a maelstrom of anger among his superior officers. When Thomas Gage received word of Bradstreet's Presque Isle treaty, he viewed it as nothing short of insubordination. Only weeks earlier he had specifically laid out the colonel's duties and mission; making ad hoc treaties along the way was not part of the job. Even Henry Bouquet, himself preparing to march into the Ohio Country, was astounded by the news of Bradstreet's false peace agreement. "The Terms he gives them are such as fill me with Astonishment. After the massacres of our Officers and Garrisons, and our Traders & Inhabitants, in Time of a profound Peace: After the Immense Expence of the Crown, and some of the Provinces to punish those infamous Murderers, not the least Satisfaction is obtained . . . Had Col: Bradstreet . . . recall the Schoking and recent Murder of the School Master and children he never could have compromised the Honor of the Nation by such disgraceful Conditions."[23]

Bouquet had seen as much of the terrible consequences of war as any man in North America at the time. He had fought in the mountains and valleys of Europe and the dark, dense forests of the Ohio Country. While Johnson's and Bradstreet's toils had been completed, by the time Bouquet and his eleven hundred men were able to mobilize it was already October. Bouquet was a disciplinarian and a professional. He personally inspected his army's weapons on a daily basis, and he kept in regular communication with his commanding officer. Had he been born in England and not Switzerland he could very well have held Thomas Gage's commission as commander-in-chief of North America's armed forces. Alas for Bouquet he was not, yet he remained steadfast to his duties nevertheless.

He and his army began their march into the Ohio Country with the deepest of resolve. They began their journey on October 3 and pressed on for ninety-two miles toward their destination. They camped, they rested, but they never broke stride unnecessarily; with winter approaching they could not afford to. As they marched they passed the ruins of Logstown, burned down long ago after the death of Tanacharison in 1754. It was a stark reminder of the fragile political world that was Indian America. They marched in a column more than double that of the force that Bouquet led at Bushy Run and encountered no resistance. The march took them a total of eleven days, and on October 14 they marched triumphantly to the Muskingum River. The heart of the Ohioan Rebellion would soon become its final resting place.[24]

When Bouquet and his men arrived they were hurriedly met by two ragged couriers from Colonel Bradstreet's force. The men explained that they had been captured by the Delaware, and when the tribal sachems heard of Bouquet's approach they promptly released the prisoners with hopes of discussing terms of peace. The former captives carried with them a document affirming this marked with the signs and symbols of over ten different Delaware chiefs; most prominent among them was the celebrated prophet Neolin himself.

Using Bradstreet's men as messengers, Bouquet agreed that he would like to discuss terms with the sachems and established a meeting for three days later. Bouquet was aware that he would hold most of the cards at the council because of the weakened state of the Indian rebellion. The Great Lakes peoples had shown that they were not interested in prolonged combat, and Johnson had made peace with the remaining Iroquois defectors.

Pontiac was still trying to rally support deep in the Illinois Country, but aside from them the Ohioans were effectively alone. The battle that they had fought for over a year was winding down, and Bouquet correctly believed that he was in a position to end it completely.

The scene at the council fire on October 17, 1764, remains one of the most compelling of its era, and stands as a benchmark in Indian American history. Henry Bouquet sat surrounded by some of the most influential sachems in all of the Ohio Country; men like Custaloga and Tamaqua were present, but neither was the primary orator. That honor

"The Indians delivering up the English captives to Colonel Bouquet near his camp at the forks of the Muskingum . . . in Novr. 1764" (*Library of Congress*)

would fall only to Guyasuta, the new Half-King of the Ohio Country. For Bouquet and Guyasuta it would have been a moment of great circumstances. These two men had battled each other ferociously only one year earlier at Bushy Run, and now they stood face to face in an entirely new capacity to discuss a subject with which neither had much experience: peace.[25]

Guyasuta delivered the following speech, both poetic and calculated, honest and regretful:

> Brother, Yesterday you desired us to be strong in doing Good and we have done our Utmost to be ready to let you hear us today as you desired. It's owing to the Western Nations & our foolish Young Men, that this War happened between us. It is neither your fault nor ours we Now throes away every thing that is bad so that non of it shall remain, & we leave you the direction of our thoughts for the future.

Now we have thrown away every thing bad, nothing remains in our hearts but good. We take fast hold of this chain of friendship, and we, the Chiefs of the Delawares, Shawanese and Senecas, living upon the Ohio, who are related to the Six Nations, request you will do the same, as we cannot hold it fast without your help, and we must both look up to God, who now sees every thing that passes between us, for his assistance. Do not think that what we say comes from our lips only, it proceeds from the bottom of all our hearts; therefore we again request that you will join both hands with ours to this belt of friendship. We have respectfully told you that we have thrown away every bad thing from our hearts: that you should hear nothing but good from us. Colonel Bradstreet has desired us to deliver up your flesh and blood; we now assure you it shall be done, as you have long desired to see them. Our reasons for not complying with this request sooner, was that Colonel Bradstreet held us by open hand and you by the other; so that we did not know which way to carry them. But we now desire that you will inform us at what place you choose to receive them; whether at Fort Pitt, or the lakes. We have been very diligent in collecting ourselves together, with the few prisoners you see, to meet you. Brethren, you have now heard all we have to say at present, and we think we have done every thing required of us by Col. Bradstreet, who sent me to their nations with these articles of peace.[26]

Guyasuta's speech had resonated with Bouquet; in reality it had only served to affirm his general opinion that the Ohioans were exhausted. The British and Indians who treated that day had come a long way, and there were still miles to go. For the colonel his top priority had to be prisoner exchange. Since the Indian rebellion had gotten under way, hundreds of white settlers had be taken from their homes and brought to the desolation of the western Ohio Country. Bouquet stipulated that all must be returned, even if at a later date, and the logistical nightmare of locating and receiving all of those prisoners was one that proved too large for one man, even one as sturdy as Bouquet, to tackle.

The agreement that Bouquet and Guyasuta came to was that all prisoners in the immediate vicinity would be returned in the next series of days, and all others in different parts of the Ohio Country as soon as possible. In a show of great seriousness, Guyasuta offered to personally arrange the release of white settlers posted around the Muskingum and Scioto valleys. To achieve this he would need to travel to and negotiate with the Delaware, Shawnee, and Wyandot; his eventual success in these endeavors is evidence of the respect he commanded.[27]

When Bouquet and his men located the white prisoners in and around their immediate whereabouts, the colonel wrestled with one startling development: the prisoners were not prisoners at all. One of the great misconceptions of Indian "kidnapping" is that even though it is often a traumatic affair at the onset, once captives are brought back to the Indian camps they are often adopted. As a general rule in Indian warfare, any male of fighting age would be killed, but women and children were almost always taken. The children would be adopted into the clan as equals, and the women would be married to the warriors of the village. The tradition was centuries old, and from the native perspective hostage taking was a regular practice following a battle. Because the tribal communities tended to be small, the death of a dozen or more warriors could shatter an individual village. To honor those dead, and more pragmatically to replace them, the captives would be adopted to strengthen the overall size and strength of the group. Words like "captives" and "hostages" have specific and painful connotations from the Western perspective, but the Indians' viewpoint was entirely different.

Bouquet was able to collect a number of white captives during his 1764 mission, but not all wanted to be "rescued." Some of the captives told him that they had been living in Indian hands since the time of Braddock's defeat nine years earlier. For those that would not go willingly he made sure that they returned to the British east. It was a heartbreaking scene for all parties involved. Children kidnapped in their infancy but now in adolescence were taken from their mothers; though they were Indian, these mothers were the only ones the children had ever known.[28]

With Bouquet's exit that summer the saga that was the rebellion of 1763 came to an end. While Pontiac still toiled in the Illinois region, violence around the Great Lakes and the Ohio Country gradually diminished. At the center of this finale were the two men who perhaps most embodied the struggle. Henry Bouquet proudly wore the British redcoat, even though the Swiss-born colonel had not a drop of English blood to speak of. Standing across from him was Guyasuta, the man who began the insurrection and perhaps did more than any other native sachem to achieve a peaceful conclusion.

By the spring of 1765, Guyasuta had secured his position as a peace chief in the Ohio Country. Since Britain had suppressed the Indian rebellion and the Iroquois had been reestablished as the supreme native power of the region, Guyasuta had rediscovered his traditional Seneca roots and used his newfound power to its fullest advantage. As a condition of Bouquet's treaty seven months earlier, Guyasuta and the Ohio sachems met with their British counterparts at Fort Pitt to engage in a full prisoner exchange. With the Irishman George Croghan in attendance, Guyasuta delivered a cautious speech, resigned to his fate:

> When you first came to drive the French from this place, the Governor of Pennsylvania sent us a message that we should withdraw from the French, & that when the English was settled here, we should want for nothing. It's true, you did supply us very well, but it was only while the War was doubtful, & as soon as you conquer'd the French you did not care how you treated us, as you did not then think us worth your Notice; we request you may not treat us again in this manner, but now open the Trade and do not put us off with telling us you must first hear from your great man before it can be done. If you have but little goods, let us have them for our skins, and let us have a part of your rum, or we cannot put dependence on what you tell us for the future.[29]

For Guyasuta it was something of a homecoming. For much of the previous two years the sachem had dwelled in the

Muskingum River valley as a rebel leader and a fugitive, but with the assurance of peace he was more than willing to return home. The Forks of the Ohio, however, was not the place that he had known in his youth. In 1765 it was dominated by the imposing presence of Fort Pitt, whose tall, broad, earthen walls made a strong statement that the British Empire was firmly in possession of the Three Rivers. The fight that he had led for twenty-four months was a lost cause, and Guyasuta was firmly convinced that the British could prove a strong ally in his future endeavors.[30]

Although Guyasuta had been one of the most feared and wanted men of the frontier for almost two years, the British were more than willing to form a partnership with him. With a domain that extended to five continents, even the novice imperialist knew that success in an aboriginal world was about collaboration more than conquest. In Guyasuta they believed they had a powerful ally who would aid in the implementation of British policy throughout the Ohio Country. Where the British were mistaken was in their assumption that Guyasuta was vested in their success. Should the policy in question benefit his own people, the sachem certainly would have been on board; if it only served to advance British interests, however, he would prove to be quite obstinate.

Because of Guyasuta's new role as Britain's premier advocate in the Ohio Country, Sir William Johnson never kept him too far out of reach. In July 1765, Guyasuta joined the secretary of Indian affairs in treaty with other Ohio sachems to negotiate a complete and final peace. Though the violence had largely been quelled already, the nine days of deliberations were largely designed to finalize and review the conditions and terms of the agreement. By this point, Johnson had become one of the single most important administrators in British North America, and in his own honor he had constructed a new base of operation in upstate New York called Johnson Hall. Built in the Georgian style and made of wood fashioned to look like stone, Johnson Hall mimicked the grace and style of an English country house; its unmistakable two stone blockhouses to its front though revealed that he built it in a very dangerous world. In some ways it was colonial America in a microcosm. Although it tried its best to imitate its English homeland, it could never shake the unmistakable roughness that exposed its provincial roots.[31]

By the time the deliberations ended on July 13, Guyasuta had affixed his mark to the treaty, a European custom that appeared unavoidable, and confirmed the peace that all parties anticipated. He had been able to accept the fate of his rebellion since Bouquet's treaty a year earlier. At forty years old, Guyasuta was prepared to believe that the wars of his youth were a natural progression in this new colonial world. The French and British had violently worked out their differences, and the concession made was by New France. It was a difficult venture to be sure, but necessary; in this regard Guyasuta viewed cooperation with the British as his own people's concession. The notion that North America could be preserved as an Indian world alone was a belief of his father's generation, and as one of the elders of his community it was his responsibility to recognize that dream as an old one.

To believe that reclamation of his ancestral lands was possible was to deceive the young Seneca warriors at his service. The best decision for him, and therefore the best decision for them, was to join with their new British brethren. Their two worlds, originally an ocean apart, were now closer together than ever before; Guyasuta was determined to be the bridge between them.

SIX

Unwavering Commitment

DUAL ALLIANCES IN AN AGE OF UNREST

G uyasuta was one of many sachems inside the foreboding walls of Fort Pitt, and he had found himself in a familiar situation. Though the British Crown had announced that no Anglo-Americans would be allowed to settle and survey Indian lands, since the rebellion had ended they had done just that.

Guyasuta was in an unenviable position. Since he first visited Johnson Hall two years earlier, he had become a valuable ambassador to the Indians of the Ohio Country. He was a trusted ally of Sir William Johnson, and the two of them often toiled in pursuit of plans to maintain a fair and equitable policy of British North America toward its Indian peoples. Guyasuta therefore had to wear two hats; to the British he had to present Indian complaints, and to his own people he was a sounding board. His loyalty was always to his native brethren, but he often was placed in the middle of a continual struggle that pulled him in all directions. For peace to truly prevail, Guyasuta knew that the Indians had to remain a present issue in the larger scope of imperial policy makers, but the Ohioans themselves also had to be willing to make some concessions. He was joined at council by the Ohio Country's foremost leaders, including Tamaqua and Custaloga.

With a copy of John Bradstreet's disgraced treaty of 1764, Guyasuta rose and spoke: "By this treaty we agreed that you had a right to build forts and trading-houses where you pleased, and to travel the road of peace from the sun rising to the sun setting. At that treaty the Shawanese and Delawares were with me, and know all this well . . . be strong . . . and wipe away the reproach of their former breach of faith, and convince their brothers the English that they could speak the truth."[1]

Since late April, Guyasuta had been acting as the primary orator to his British counterparts at Fort Pitt, and though he had a good working relationship with George Croghan, the key diplomat stationed at the fort, the two men were finding very little common ground. As Guyasuta spoke over the two-week session, he straddled his duties of representing the angry Ohioan chiefs and appearing as reasonable to the British. The result was great discontent among all parties, and the fact that there was not an official document on which either side could base its argument meant that the council was essentially meaningless. The British had outlawed settlements, but the 1763 motion was never meant to be permanent. The Crown had no way of genuinely controlling Anglo immigration into Indian territory. Aware of this, hundreds of settlers flooded the Ohio River valley to carve out their own homesteads, paying no mind to its standing Indian occupants.[2]

Sir William Johnson spent much of 1768 attempting to explain this to his superiors. Because no document existed to protect Indian rights, or at least define their land in some way, the problems of the Indian rebellion that began five years earlier were certain to surface yet again. While he struggled with the politics of his own people, he found in Guyasuta a willing associate in spreading peace through his own means. Johnson and Guyasuta had developed an interesting partnership over the previous three years; both were former warriors now fighting the battle for peace. Of their many strategies developed at Johnson Hall, one in particular centered almost entirely around Guyasuta's effectiveness in the Ohio Country. Since the Mingo communities had once been a part of the Iroquois world and given Guyasuta's status in the region, Johnson believed that he could employ Guyasuta to persuade the Delaware and Shawnee to return to the fold of their Iroquois overlords. At any rate, good relations would never be possible until a proven and official boundary between Indian land and British territory was defined.

The council at Fort Pitt was like many others after the Indian rebellion had ended. They were often emotional, but rarely productive. Pontiac was all but silenced by that point, yet his undying inclination toward war was still a thorn in the side of Sir William Johnson. The men had met two years earlier at Oswego in 1766 and officially ended the rebellion, but Pontiac's unknown whereabouts never ceased to haunt the British. The treaty, Johnson hoped, would settle the dispute once and for all. Johnson received his wish in the summer of 1768 when the Board of Trade in London finally agreed to negotiate a settlement with the Indian peoples of the frontier. In August 1768 approximately three thousand native peoples met with the secretary of Indian affairs at Fort Stanwix on the New York frontier to determine where the new border would fall.[3]

The demographics of the Indian delegation present were revealing. Since the end of the rebellion Johnson had pressed to reestablish Iroquois, and therefore British, supremacy over the Ohio Country. As it turned out, the vast majority of peoples at Fort Stanwix were from the Six Nations itself. For Johnson the proceedings were of the utmost importance, and to accommodate the many sachems and warriors he had local contractors fashion a great council house, as well as a number of sleeping quarters and auxiliary buildings. The meeting was a who's who of power brokers from across the North American colonies, and its attendees included the royal governor of New Jersey Sir William Franklin, Dr. Thomas Walker of Virginia, and the chief justice of New Jersey Frederick Smyth.

Although the agreement would directly impact the Ohioans as it was their lands that were up for grabs, Johnson believed that the treaty would serve to remind those subjects that the Iroquois were their traditional overseers, who had full right to represent the Ohioans' interests in council. From August to November, Johnson and the delegates of the Iroquois Confederacy traced out a new "official" border of the imperial frontier, and while the Ohioans had no idea, their imperial masters had sold their traditional hunting lands out from underneath them for a meager £10,460.[4]

The agreed division ran from Fort Stanwix in New York and proceeded southwest to the confluence of the Ohio and Kanawha rivers; it then continued down the Ohio River to its confluence with the Tennessee River. Called the Treaty of Fort Stanwix, it served as the crowning achievement in the diplomatic career of Sir William Johnson. Shortly after the treaty was signed, settlers poured into the freshly minted British territory; the Shawnee and Delaware already present put up heavy resistance.

Not even the administration of British North America was in full accord with the decision. John Stuart, the superintendent of Indian affairs for the Southern Department, had finalized negotiations with the Cherokee in October at the Treaty of Hard Labour, and Johnson's proposed boundary directly contradicted the one that he had defined almost a month earlier. While the Shawnee and Delaware were forced to deal with the realities that their homes were taken away from them, an act that epitomized the notion of virtual representation, the delegates present at Fort Stanwix still had questions that needed to be answered. It was discussed that the line would begin at Fort Stanwix, but depending on which side of the fortification would greatly determine the control of a strategic piece of land called the Oneida Carrying Place. If the line began on the eastern side of the fort, the Carrying Place was controlled by the Iroquois; if it began to the west it was held by the colony of New York. As momentous as the Treaty of Fort Stanwix was, its realities and unintended consequences soon undermined the euphoria felt by its creators.

The measure of the treaty was one of great uproar in the Ohio River valley. The Shawnees and Delawares were pressed from their lands, and because they were represented by the Iroquois they had no choice but to abide by the decision. For the Ohioans, it was an ultimate act of betrayal, particularly to the Shawnees. While the Delaware maintained some of their tradi-

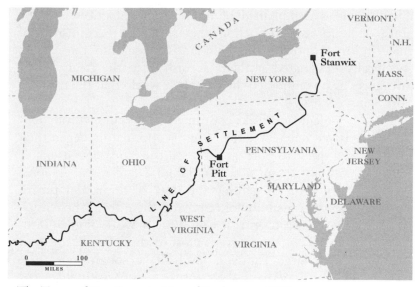

The Treaty of Fort Stanwix Line of Settlement, 1768.

tional land holdings, the Shawnees were forced to vacate every-thing and relocate farther south down the Ohio River as refugees. This was nothing new for the Shawnees; they are often referred to as "wanderers," with a long history of forcible removal courtesy of decisions made out of their sphere of influence. Over the next three years when white families began to move onto Indian land to claim it as their own, the Shawnees grew belligerent; small pockets of violence, generally with both parties lashing out, began to unsettle the Ohio Country.

During this time it fell to Guyasuta to preserve whatever tenuous peace could be salvaged during the great period of upheaval. Using Johnson Hall as his base of operations, the sachem would venture back and forth to the Ohio Country to try and placate the Shawnees. Johnson wrote that Guyasuta was a "Chief of much Capacity and vast Influence," and that he was "very useful on such Occasions." At one particular meeting at Fort Pitt in 1773, Guyasuta's dual obligations required him to deliver a wampum string of peace to the Shawnees from Johnson, and then return to Johnson Hall with a list of complaints from the same constituency that he was sent to appease.

The Shawnees complained of unfair trade practices and the abuse of liquor as a distraction; they spoke of the injustices of the Virginians moving on their lands, even into those areas specifically designated as theirs according to the treaty. Their grievances again embodied the turbulent world that the treaty of Fort Stanwix created.[5]

Even as violent outbreaks continued to manifest throughout the Ohio River valley, wealthy Virginia speculators began their profit-driven quest to purchase and sell the lands now available to them. Among them were Dr. Hugh Mercer and Colonel George Washington. Regarding the state of the settler turned squatter, and the possibility of removing them from their situation, Washington writes that it would be "a Work of great difficulty; perhaps of equal cruelty, as most of these People are poor swarming with large Families, [and] have sought out these retreats on which perhaps their future prospects in like way wholey depend."[6]

The situation was quickly becoming a zero-sum game. From as early as the fifteenth century, when a white settlement entrenched itself on Indians lands there was almost no way of eradicating it without open warfare; even then, most often the settlement would remain. Therefore, when a new squatter encroached on Indian territory, native resistance was generally fierce and deadly. Washington noted in a letter to a fellow speculator: "Any person . . . who neglects the present opportunity of hunting good lands, and in some measure marking and distinguishing them for his own, in order to keep others from settling them, will never regain it."[7]

When Guyasuta and Washington had their chance encounter in 1770 along the shores of the Ohio River, it was in this world and under these circumstances that they met. Washington was seeking fortune, and Guyasuta was in the midst of a peace-making expedition into the depths of the Ohio River valley to treat with the Shawnees. It was a world quite distant from that of the Indian rebellion seven years earlier, but still much closer than either party was comfortable with. The violence had ended on a large scale, but the inherent racially motivated prejudices of both Indian and white alike made the Ohio Country one of the most unstable regions in all of North America.[8]

While most in the east believed the Indian war was a thing of the past, the confusion created by the Treaty of Fort Stanwix would serve as a stark reminder to those detached parties in the east that the problems of land and possession were far from settled. In October 1773, the Shawnee resistance movement of the Ohio River valley would claim its first victims.

Daniel Boone was no stranger to the American frontier. Born in Pennsylvania, Boone was raised on the far reaches of English society, and he took to the wild and uncharted expanses of North America as only a provincial could. In 1755, Boone served as a driver at Braddock's defeat, and since 1769 he had developed a reputation as a pioneer as one of the first men to explore and survey the vaunted Kentucky region. Sitting past the farthest reaches of the Virginia colony, Boone had always heard rumors of the rich and fertile possibilities that the relatively uncharted area had to offer. Once he had seen them for himself, however, it was decided that he would lead the first group of true, permanent settlers into the region in 1773.

While Boone marched with his family and fifty other settler families, he unknowingly (or perhaps uncaringly) led his party directly through the heart of the emerging Shawnee rebellion. Though Boone was a relatively unknown commodity at the time, joining him on his trek into the unknown was a Virginian named William Russell. As the well-respected brother-in-law of Patrick Henry, Russell was easily the most notable member of the enterprising group. On October 9, as Boone and his followers negotiated the treacherous Appalachian Mountains of today's West Virginia, he sent many of the young men, including his son James and Russell's son Henry, on a relatively routine adventure to gather supplies. As the youngsters set out they were soon attacked by a party of Shawnee, Delaware, and Cherokee warriors. While many were killed outright, both Boone and Russell's sons were tortured to death brutally. Many speculated that the killings were perpetrated in such an egregious fashion as a means of sending a distinct message regarding the Shawnee opinion of the 1768 treaty.

The deaths of the children of Boone's parties became an explosive news story in the American colonies. Not since the

Boston Massacre three years earlier had British North America been so riveted by an isolated series of events, and in the Ohio Country itself the killings signaled a new, ominous chapter in Indian-white relations.[9]

Almost overnight the Ohio River became a great tangible boundary between old and new, Indian and American. To settle on its shores was to flirt with danger, and to cross the river was to court death. Those who settled on its southern banks were generally the most rugged of frontiersmen with a natural disdain for government and an evident distaste for their Indian neighbors. Of all the settlers below the safety of the waterway, three distinctly stood out as especially daring. At the most extreme south was a party at the mouth of the Little Kanawha River, among them one George Rogers Clark who would make his mark in the approaching American Revolution. Farther north was the encampment of Ebeneezer Zane at the mouth of Sandy Creek. Zane was a noted guide in the dense and dark region and most believed he was fully capable of handling himself in the politically unstable region.[10]

In the year that had passed since the Boone murders, sporadic yet intense violence had made the entire Ohio River valley a tense and unnerving place. At the heart of the region stood Fort Pitt, the mighty bastion of imperial power, and much of the white population tended to flock around it in times of uncertainty. At Pittsburgh, word had developed that some kind of punitive measure should be taken against the unruly Shawnees, yet no official word from any colonial legislature indicated that such a venture was coming. Even though the ownership of the profitable Ohio Country was in dispute between Pennsylvania and Virginia, neither had determined how to best deal with the terrible calamity that was developing under their noses. When a matter of profitability was at stake, say the deed to a particularly valuable piece of land, both colonies had jumped to claim it as their own; yet in the face of a potential war they were both conspicuously quiet.

It appeared that if the Shawnee were to be punished, it would have to come from the frontiersmen themselves.

To lead such a venture though the Ohio Valley settlers believed that they would need an experienced and battle-hardened veteran; unfortunately, none of them fit that mold. The obvious choice was one Michael Cresap, a Seven Years' War veteran who owned a small trading post at Redstone Fort less than twenty miles upriver. Cresap was granted a large tract of land from the colony of Virginia itself, and he had been stationed in the valley for some time as a result. When the settler militia approached him regarding a potential attack, Cresap was quick to quell the discussion of inevitability around him. He explained to the settlers that the Shawnees were to blame for the violence that had befallen the region, but war was far from a foregone conclusion. In his experience, Cresap explained, the colonial legislatures of Virginia and Pennsylvania were reluctant to declare war because it was a costly venture that in many cases was nothing more than an easy way out. Sound diplomacy, he argued, could still win the day, and he took his newfound followers north to the village at Wheeling to simmer.

Once Cresap and his men arrived at Wheeling they found nearly every settler family in the immediate area desperately sheltered there. The situation was much worse than he anticipated, and after some confused correspondence with the commandant of Fort Pitt, Cresap rallied the population to volunteer for a strategic strike against the Shawnees. He believed that the tribal sachems intended war at all costs, and a preemptive strike by his rabble could deliver a deciding blow before the entire valley was engulfed in battle.[11]

On April 27 Cresap and his armed militants spotted a small party of Shawnee canoes floating down the Ohio River; sensing their opportunity, the Virginians proceeded to chase their foes for almost fifteen miles. It was a confusing scene for both sides, and the lack of organization turned the pursuit into a chaotic free-for-all. When the settlers finally caught up with their Shawnee foes, a modest firefight ensued at a place known as Pipe Creek. Although the engagement was brief, with neither side inflicting enough damage to consider it a victory, Cresap's expedition would serve as a seminal event in the emerging Ohio Valley conflict of 1774.

The response to the Pipe Creek skirmish was immediate and fierce. For the native peoples of the Ohio River valley that had been relocated by the Fort Stanwix Treaty, life had become increasingly difficult. The Shawnees were the primary belligerents in this new war, yet the remaining Delawares and Mingos of the Ohio Country were being drawn in it more and more each day. In every instance that a Shawnee party attacked and killed a white settler family, the first response was also to avenge their deaths by killing an Indian in retaliation, often regardless of tribal affiliation. One such people, Guyasuta's former Mingos, had been saddled with a particularly troublesome burden.

Without Guyasuta, who reattached himself to his Iroquois heritage and now served as the Half-King for the entire region, the few Mingo leaders left became quite powerful. Among them was Logan, son of a Cayuga mother, who served as the de facto sachem for the remaining Mingo peoples of the valley. By the time word of Cresap's battle had reached Fort Pitt, it was major news throughout the region, and Logan would have been aware that such an incendiary action would have consequences far beyond his control. Logan had preached peace to the settlers, and had been insistent that the actions of the Shawnees were not the fault of his people. Three days after the skirmish at Pipe Creek, though, that argument disappeared forever.

On April 30 Logan and a party of thirty other Mingos had encamped for the night on the shores of the Ohio River at the mouth of Yellow Creek. They had been on a long hunting expedition, and as they remained on their side of the river in accordance with the 1768 treaty Logan had little fear of any territorial repercussions. The events of three days earlier had already taken hold, and a general panic had swept across the region. While Logan was away from camp, likely making preparations for the next days' hunt, several members of his party were persuaded to cross the river and invited into the cabin of a local rum trader named Joshua Baker. After sufficiently inebriating themselves with the alcoholic beverages provided by the settlers present, a party of men led by an unruly frontiersman named Daniel Greathouse moved into the cabin and proceeded to gun down the entire party. Among the dead were several members of Logan's family, including his brother. The lone survivor of the attack was an infant; its mother had begged for its life and convinced the settlers that its father was white. She was murdered and scalped, and in all a dozen were killed.[12]

The event that had become known as the Yellow Creek Massacre illustrates in devastating fashion the two sides of frontier savagery. While the circumstances of the killings at Yellow Creek place blame differently, none disputes the result. One account indicates that the massacre was no massacre at all, simply an act of preemptive self-defense: "Mrs. Baker told Dan'l Greathouse that a squaw told her (in a drunken fit) that the Indian intended to murder Baker's family before leaving. Greathouse went & raised a party of abt 30 men . . . twelve Indians were killed in all."[13]

Still others redirect blame back to Greathouse and his men: "Could any person of common rationality, believe for a moment, that the Indians came to Yellow creek with hostile intention, or that they had any suspicion of the whites, having any hostile Intentions against them, would five men have cross the river, three of them in a Short time dead drunk, the other two discharging their Guns, putting themselves entirely at the mercy of the whites, or would they have brought over a Squaw, with an infant paupoos, if they had not reposed the utmost Confidence in the friendships of the whites, every person who is acquainted with the Indians Knows better."[14]

The terrible consequences of a prejudiced heart and a woefully ignorant eye had turned the Ohio Country on its head. After the murders at Yellow Creek hundreds fled the region out of fear of a general Indian reprisal. Like they had done a decade earlier in 1763, families abandoned their homes and livestock and flooded across the Allegheny Mountains. Logan was devastated, as his family was murdered; the singular assurance from the British that such atrocities would never happen again, the Treaty of Fort Stanwix, seemed null and void.

The Yellow Creek Massacre was merely a catalyst; while the conflict had originally been a Shawnee venture alone, the indiscriminate killing of Logan's family drew the Mingo into the fray as well. To avenge the deaths of his fallen kin, the Mingo transformed the late spring of 1774 into a widespread and terrible bloodletting; the white settlers of the Ohio Country paid for the sins of Daniel Greathouse by the hundreds. For Guyasuta, a former leader of the renegade Mingo, the events proved to be terribly frustrating. According to his agreement with Johnson, it was his duty to control the Mingo and repatriate them into the Iroquois world, and with every death his failings became more and more evident.

On May 5, the Shawnee clarified their intentions to their British counterparts, and challenged the colony of Virginia to stop them:

> We have received your Speeches . . . we look upon it all to be lies. . . . It is you who are frequently passing up and down the Ohio, and making settlements upon it, and as you have informed as that your wise people have met together to consult upon this matter, we desire you to be strong and consider it well. . . .We see you speak to us at the head of your warriors, who you have collected together at sundry places upon this river, where we understand they are building forts, and as you have requested us to listen to you, we will do it, but in the same manner that you appear to speak to us. Our people at the Lower Towns have no Chiefs among them, but are all warriors, and are also preparing themselves to be in readiness, that they may be better able to hear what you have to say. . . . You tell us not to take any notice of what your people have done to us; we desire you likewise not to take any notice of what our young men may now be doing, and as no doubt you can command your warriors when you desire them to listen to you, we have reason to expect that ours will take the same advice when we require it, that is, when we have heard from the Governour of Virginia.[15]

Virginia had heeded the Shawnee warning, and the man who was one of the most controversial figures in British North America was in his second year of service as the royal governor of the colony of Virginia. Born in Tymouth, Scotland, in 1732, John Murray, the Earl of Dunmore, had become one of the fastest rising political figures in the American colonies.

Dunmore was an experienced politician, having held the same position to New York three years earlier; he hoped to have an impact now. He was a member of the old aristocracy of Great Britain, and his family estate had existed since 1686. He lived in a time of opulence, in an age and class where he could take comfort in the fact that he was born into untold wealth and prosperity, and his children and grandchildren would be as well. The peerage system of the British Empire allowed for an upper class to exist in untold luxury, supported by twin pillars of land ownership and heredity, while the vast majority of British citizens saw nothing but squalor throughout their lives. This mechanism allowed men like King George III to remain in power, and it was precisely what many in the lower classes believed was the fundamental fault line responsible for separating the American colonies from the rest of the empire. As Lord Chesterfield, a contemporary of Dunmore, famously penned: "We, my Lords, may thank Heaven that we have something better than our brains to depend on."[16]

Dunmore was in a class of his own when compared to other royal governors of the eighteenth century. The position of governor was explicitly reserved for the upper echelon of British society, and most in the position never left the confines of the British Isles to visit their namesakes. In their place often served a lieutenant governor to manage the daily affairs of the colony, and they did so with limited interruption. Lord Dunmore administered his title in a more direct fashion, which is certainly why he was transferred from the governorship of New York to Virginia, the richest and most politically powerful colony, in 1771.

Governor Dunmore was no stranger to the Ohio River valley, and four years earlier he had toured Fort Pitt to gain a better sense of his colonial holdings. Although Pennsylvania had also claimed the Ohio Country, its governor was not likely to show his face in the heart of the frontier. In preparation for his tour, Dunmore had relied heavily on the advice of a Virginia Provincial of growing influence: George Washington. By all accounts Washington greatly admired Dunmore, whose picturesque stature weighed heavily on the aspiring gentryman. One letter from Washington to the governor just before the Shawnee conflict humbly begged that the provincial militia of Virginia be given the same respect as the British Regulars: "The officers have an entire confidence in your Lordship's disposition to promote their just rights. They have no other dependence, and they hope to be put on an equal footing with those other officers, whose pretensions are not better founded than their own. . . . The part

I take in bringing this matter to a hearing will, I hope, meet with your Lordship's excuse, as I am, with the greatest respect, my Lord, your Lordship's most obedient and most humble servant."[17]

For Dunmore, though, Washington's inquiries fell on deaf ears. Dunmore was a notorious imperialist, and he did not hide his disdain for men like Washington. A man of wealth and refinement, Dunmore was born into a specialized caste system unique in the modern world. Some Americans were wealthy, but they were at best men of commercial fortunes. After traversing the frontier three years earlier, Dunmore developed a distinct distaste for the likes of the Ohio River valley. He would describe the people that he encountered critically, with special emphasis on their opinions of his dominion over them. "The Authority of any government . . . [is] insufficient to restrain the Americans; and that they do and will remove as their avidity and restlessness incite them . . . they do not conceive that Government has any right to forbid their taking possession of a Vast tract of Country."[18]

When news of the unrest caused by the Ohioan Rebellion reached the colonial capital of Virginia, many speculated as to what, if any, outcome would emerge. As a colony Virginia was torn between protecting its own interests and acquiring new ones. Since the end of the Seven Years' War Pennsylvania and the Old Dominion had battled over who precisely controlled the Ohio Country. From Dunmore's perspective, Fort Pitt and the Ohio River valley were his for the taking; Virginia had spent more than any other colony in defense of the region, and it was an investment that he expected a return on. In contrast, if the colonial legislature sat idly by and did nothing, their Quaker competitors to the north could sweep in, end the Shawnee and Mingo uprising, and reestablish order in their own favor.

Many other royal governors may have handled the decision with more tact, but Dunmore was never known for policies that split hairs. He believed that the best way to settle the dispute between the colonies *and* dispel the Indian violence was by asserting his own authority in the valley through brute force. When the nineteenth-century Prussian political philosopher Carl von Clausewitz famously stated that warfare was merely politics by other means, Lord Dunmore provided a perfect example in practice. From his seat of power, the governor saw the unrest in the Ohio Valley as a great opportunity that, with the right maneuvering, could become quite profitable.

Like his acquaintance George Washington, Dunmore had invested a substantial sum of his own personal wealth in land speculation throughout the Ohio Country and beyond. If he was to suppress the Ohioans, a task he believed that his Virginia militia could do handily, the land would be his for the taking. Using the right political spin, the governor could transfer his own personal gains into a larger victory for the entire colony of Virginia and many of his fellow legislators would profit. Virginia would be the uncontested ruler of the region, and he would establish himself as the premier administrator in all of British North America.

If an invasion of the Ohio River valley was to come to fruition, it could also have a larger, more clandestine benefits that the British upper echelon would quietly hope for as well. Since the end of the Seven Years' War, the political atmosphere in British North America had become tense, slowly building to talk of open rebellion against the Crown. After the French were defeated, royal accountants estimated that it would cost £220,000 annually to defend America and the Caribbean; Parliament enacted unpopular levies and duties on the colonies to help foot the bill. Controversial measures such as the Sugar Act of 1764 and Stamp Act of 1765 drove thousands of colonists to boycott British goods and take to the streets in protest. Furthermore, the Townshend Duties of 1767 aggravated the divisive situation to a level unseen in the British Empire. Finally, in March 1770, British Regulars fired on a group of unarmed civilians in Boston and five people died.[19]

If Dunmore could lead Virginia's large and powerful militia against the Ohioans, it could serve as a much needed distraction for the colony; talk of rebellion and "taxation without representation" would hopefully fade away quickly and quietly. The thirteen colonies could rally around such a victory and be reminded how mighty the benefits of empire could be. Furthermore, and perhaps on a more devious and practical level, if the showdown with the Ohioans was a difficult one, the army of American-born Provincials would be too weakened to even consider participating in a revolution. It was a convenient little conflict for Lord Dunmore, and a once-in-a-lifetime political opportunity.[20]

The march to war was far too enticing to pass up, and from his pulpit of power the governor mobilized over two thousand men for a full-scale invasion of the Ohio River valley. They would all be Americans, and they would all be Virginians. If victory came, one colony would be able to reap the benefits of the conquest. The expedition would be a concentrated delivery of brute strength from two different forces that would converge in a pincer maneuver against the Shawnee villages throughout the region.

The first column would march in a westward trek through the mountainous gorges of today's West Virginia under the command of Colonel Andrew Lewis. A veteran officer of Virginia, Lewis took on the mission willingly. He was present at Fort Necessity with Washington in 1754 and was captured as part of Grant's failed attack on Fort Duquesne in 1758. A much more capable soldier twenty years later in 1774, Lewis stood as one of the most daring leaders North America had to offer.

The second column that would march southward would leave with another thousand men from Fort Pitt, led by none other than Lord Dunmore himself. The two parties agreed to join forces at the mouth of the Great Kanawha River, and from there move forward to sweep the resistance out of the Ohio River valley altogether. While Lewis led his men in stern fashion to the meeting point and arrived on October 9, Dunmore's forces were delayed at Fort Fincastle in Wheeling, West Virginia. When Lewis wrote to Dunmore regarding the delay, the governor responded by ordering him to continue to a new location at the Shawnee towns along the Scioto River. It was an unusual deviation from their intended plan, but Lewis heeded his orders and marched his men down the Ohio River unaware of what dangers lay ahead of him.

On the morning of October 10, as Lewis and his army continued southward, they received word from their scouts that a large number of Indian warriors were drawing near; by the time the Virginians could address the threat, they found themselves in the middle of an ambush. Under the general leadership of the Shawnee chief Cornstalk, over six hundred Ohioan warriors rushed Lewis's men. Aware that the Virginians were in the area, the Mingo and Shawnee positioned themselves in such a way that they could trap their opponents against the Ohio River in a hammer-and-anvil engagement. With nowhere to run, the Virginians were forced to do battle with the native warriors.[21]

While Lord Dunmore's party remained several miles away and largely unaware of the struggle, Lewis and his one thousand men took to the trees to find cover. Lewis knew from his previous experience that traditional rules did not apply in frontier combat, and he had learned how disastrous attempting to follow them in the face of an enemy like the Ohioans could be. The site of the engagement was well-known among the Indian communities nearby, and their knowledge of the terrain gave them a distinct advantage over the Virginians. Known as Tu-Endie-Wei, or "point between the waters," the site had become known as Point Pleasant among the land speculators that passed by in the years earlier.

As the battle raged, Lewis and his men did their best to survive. Though they had greater numbers than their enemies, the close-quarter combat largely negated their musket. During an exchange, Lewis's brother Charles was struck down in a hail of bullets. To their credit, the Virginians maintained their composure and discipline during the exchanges. From the Ohioan viewpoint, the ambush was designed to crush the Americans quickly; because the Virginians had almost twice as many men, a drawn-out battle would eventually turn in their favor. As the morning drifted to afternoon, the Virginians threw down their muskets and resorted to hand-to-hand combat.[22]

Lewis and his men, veterans of numerous frontier campaigns, had no difficulty using this very heated and personal style of combat. Had it been a party of British Regulars, like at Braddock's defeat, Cornstalk and his warriors would have likely overrun their opponents. As it turned out, the very complaint that Braddock most vocally chastised the Provincials for was what ultimately kept them in the fight on this day almost twenty years later. While the Regulars were organized and structured, the American Provincials had learned the value of fighting in a

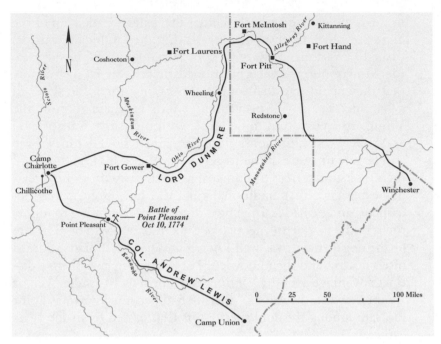

Lord Dunmore's War, 1774.

uniquely Indian style. Redcoats would never drop their firearms and take to trees; for those reasons the Indians often had an easy time defeating them.

At Point Pleasant, however, Lewis and his men were able to adapt, and though Cornstalk was heard shouting orders to his warriors to "be strong!" and continue the fight, it was apparent that his flash ambush had failed to produce the quick result he had hoped for. By midday the Indians began their retreat. The greatest British victory over an Indian force in colonial history was achieved by Provincials—and almost no Britons at all.

At the end of the battle, Lewis registered seventy-five Virginians killed and another one hundred and fifty wounded; most estimate that almost forty Indian warriors had died. The Battle of Point Pleasant would prove to be a breaking point in the Ohioan uprising, and a turning point in American history. After Lewis and his men left the field, they proceeded to their destination as instructed by Lord Dunmore.

Situated eight miles from the Scioto River, Dunmore and Lewis established a makeshift fortification that they called Camp Charlotte. It was there, in the heart of the lands granted to the Indians, that the governor was able to negotiate a peaceful settlement with the battered Shawnee Cornstalk. As a punishment for their actions, Dunmore insisted that all lands granted to them by the Treaty of Fort Stanwix south of the Ohio River be turned over to the Colony of Virginia. It was a resounding success for the royal governor. He had initiated an expensive and risky venture to subdue the Indian rebellion, and at Camp Charlotte he collected his winnings. Thousands of acres of land in today's West Virginia and Kentucky now belonged to him, making his colony the most powerful in British North America.[23]

Although the agreement was signed and Dunmore was satisfied with his gains, the Mingo sachem Logan whose family was killed at Yellow Creek refused to accept the defeat. Why should the Mingo surrender simply because the Shawnees had? He made his resistance known, and shortly after the signing at Camp Charlotte Dunmore took a final action to ensure his cooperation. In a display of sheer force, Major William Crawford marched southward and decimated the Ohioan village of Sawkunk. It did not break the spirit of Logan, but it did convince most of the warriors present that furthering this rebellion would only lead to their downfall. At this moment Chief Logan delivered what still stands as one of the most emotionally charged speeches in American history:

> I appeal to any white man to say, if ever he entered Logan's cabin hungry, and he gave him not meat; if ever he came cold and naked, and he clothed him not. During the course of the last long and bloody war, Logan remained idle in his cabin, an advocate for peace. Such was my love for the whites that my countrymen pointed as they passed, and said, Logan is the friend of the white men. I have even thought to live with you but for the injuries of one man. Col. Cresap, the last spring, in cold blood, and unprovoked, murdered all the relations of Logan, not sparing even my women and children. There runs not a drop of my blood in the veins of any living

creature. This has called on me for revenge. I have sought it: I have killed many: I have fully glutted my vengeance. For my country, I rejoice at the beams of peace. But do not harbour a thought that mine is the joy of fear. Logan never felt fear. He will not turn on his heel to save his life. Who is there to mourn for Logan? Not one.[24]

With the treaty at Camp Charlotte came to close one of the single most confusing and challenging events in American history. Known as Lord Dunmore's War for the calculated and highly political nature of its implementation, the events of 1774 in the Ohio Country offer a wonderful opportunity to explore the immense interconnectivity of the colonial American experience. In the 1950s historians began trying to understand the larger meaning of the conflict; while experts toiled though, politicians acted. To make the site of the Battle of Point Pleasant a more marketable tourist destination, West Virginia officials labeled it as the site of the "first battle of the American Revolution." It was a terribly misleading designation and not based on the historical record. Therefore, for sixty years that title has skewed the true meaning of the conflict in the minds of thousands of visitors.[25]

While Lord Dunmore's War is certainly connected to the American Revolution, it is by no means a *beginning* of anything. The events of 1763 set into motion a turbulent new world in which revolution was almost unavoidable. The Battle of Point Pleasant stands as a vital connection to the end of the Seven Years' War, and a direct line to the American Revolution. It is an intermediary event in a larger Revolutionary era, a period that truly begins with the fall of New France and ends with the Treaty of Paris in 1783.

If a label for the start of the American Revolution must be produced however (and it *should,* if only to upend the "first battle" campaign of yesteryear), it would be the Treaty of Camp Charlotte. While Dunmore had largely concerned himself with gobbling up large tracts of land, he also made sure to address the emerging colonial discontent. As part of the negotiations, he requested that should the American colonies rebel, the Ohioans would remain neutral. He knew that the British had a strong ally in the Iroquois Confederacy, but the unruly history of the Mingo, Shawnees, and Delawares prompted him to believe that an American-Ohioan alliance could develop if revolution truly took hold. To ensure that they did not join on the side of the American rebels, Dunmore believed that total Ohioan neutrality would be the best course of action.

When the American revolutionaries hit their stride in the west three years later, they were able to do so because their only potential enemies, the Ohioans, still abided by the neutrality agreement made that night at Camp Charlotte. Although the Provincials who murmured for separation from Great Britain did not know it at the time, Dunmore's treaty with the Ohioans had ensured that their fledgling revolution would survive its tenuous first years.

In the fall of 1775, Guyasuta was living in a world rendered unrecognizable by change. A year earlier Sir William Johnson, his closest confidant in the British world, had died. During a conference in July 1774, just before the Ohioan Rebellion broke out into open combat, Johnson rose to speak and suddenly collapsed to the floor. While his death was listed as a seizure caused by suffocation, modern medical specialists are nearly certain that a stroke ended his life. Whether it was the result of years of tense negotiations, or the worrisome state of the Ohio River valley, Johnson's passing would leave a void that few could fill as the thirteen colonies teetered on the brink of revolution.[26]

More than two thousand people from around the continent attended Johnson's funeral, including governor of New Jersey William Franklin. In the days that followed delegates of the Iroquois Confederacy performed a ritualized celebration of his life and recognition of his death; he was their greatest advocate in a cold, imperial world. After the ceremony the sachems were also charged with performing another, this time to officially recognize the man that would succeed him.

Born in Ireland in 1740, Guy Johnson was the son of Sir William's younger brother. When he traveled to North America in 1756, in the midst of the Seven Years' War, he settled in the Mohawk Valley and was soon deputized by his uncle. By 1763, that year of such great measure, Guy Johnson married his cousin Molly, the daughter of Sir William. By the time the superintendent of Indian affairs suddenly died in 1774, Guy was the most likely candidate to replace him.[27]

Although Sir William was gone, his legacy lived on through what was expected of his replacement by the natives that he had represented. Guyasuta developed a good working relationship with Guy Johnson, who made it his charge to clean up the messy situation in the Ohio River valley. Throughout the early part of 1775 Guyasuta was still exercising his influence over the Ohio peoples by negotiating the release of prisoners taken during Lord Dunmore's War. While Guyasuta worked on his behalf, the new superintendent Johnson was already feeling the strains of a continent hurtling toward revolution.

A year earlier in 1774 several American colonies began the process of establishing localized private legislatures called Committees of Correspondence that operated outside of the scope of British authority. The existence of such impromptu legislators had always been on the tongues of those Provincials seeking greater freedom, but they never materialized. The fact that there were now thirteen of them indicated that this new movement was much more volatile than any before it. Finally, in that same year, Johnson and other colonial administrators were enraged when several delegates of all but one of the thirteen colonies met in Philadelphia at what would become known as the First Continental Congress.

Developments in North America had gotten much worse than the creation of a joint legislature, however. In April 1775 a group of British Regulars were intercepted when marching on a weapons cache in Massachusetts. Their progress was impeded by a party of armed rebels, and the result was almost unthinkable: open combat. The battles of Lexington and Concord had finally given teeth to the Provincials' new clamor for revolution, and it would fall to Johnson to ensure that the Indians of the frontier were prepared to do their part to stop it. A month later, Guy

Johnson received orders from General Gage to collect as many Iroquois warriors as possible and march to Canada. From there, he was to await orders for an attack on New England, the heart of the rebellion. Leaving Sir William's great symbolic homestead of Johnson Hall far behind, Guy arrived at Montreal on July 17 with over one hundred Loyalists, and only ninety Mohawk Iroquois warriors.

The reason that Johnson had found so little success in rallying willing Iroquois to join him was because the Haudenosaunee were generally as divided as the white American populace when it came to revolution. For the previous two decades the British had been under the impression that the Iroquois were fully committed to the British cause, not recognizing that their alliance was only based on mutual success. The Six Nations still reserved the right to act autonomously, and when the British realized that their support was not certain, they began to turn up the heat to draw the Iroquois to their side.

On Johnson's march to Canada, he first stopped at Oswego to try and gain a vote of support from the Iroquois; when he failed he moved on, knowing full well that negotiations had only just begun. What resulted was a race to gather as many Indian allies as possible. If the British were convinced that the cooperation of the Indians would be essential, then the American rebels would need to win their favor as well. Therefore in October 1775, six months after the first shots at Lexington Green, commissioners of the Continental Congress ventured to the steady walls of Fort Pitt to find their own Indian allies.[28]

The Americans were not seeking an open alliance on October 27; they were merely hoping to sustain neutrality among the Ohioans. In their speeches they clarified this point, and they continuously flattered the sachems present. As the Iroquois Half-King, Guyasuta was chief orator at this conference, and he pledged that that Ohioans would respect their oath of neutrality taken a year earlier, and that he would do his best to convince his Iroquois brethren in New York to do the same. While the Americans were pleased with the result of the conference, others were not. Following Guyasuta's promise, a Delaware sachem called White Eyes rose in anger. He believed that Guyasuta had no right to exercise that kind of authority to speak for his people, and he angrily declared that the Iroquois yoke would be thrown down. The Delaware, he decided, were free.[29]

For the next twelve months, the British and Americans would empty their diplomatic coffers in preparation for war by seeking out Indian support in an endless string of councils. Though Guy Johnson was still a novice and had yet to convince many that he was as capable a negotiator as his late uncle, he did recognize the importance of a unified partnership with the Iroquois Confederacy. In November 1775 Johnson traveled to London with a prominent loyal Mohawk named Joseph Brant. For weeks Brant and Johnson met a host of celebrities including King George himself. While it was a life-changing experience for Brant, Johnson knew that by parading him around the Old City he would gain popular support for addressing Mohawk grievances, and therefore earn enough political capital to create a royal push for achieving full alliance with the Iroquois as a whole.

In December 1775, the Continental Congress agreed that they may need to call on an Indian ally "in case of real necessity." The next spring they would begin their strong, sustained push to counteract what their British opponents were mustering. Appointed in April 1776 by Congress, George Morgan was given the title of Commissioner for Indian Affairs, Middle District, at Fort Pitt. The heart of the American movement to gain Indian support was to be in the Ohio Country.[30]

The British, however, focused their attentions more northward, in New York. Believing that their long-standing covenant would be upheld, the royal effort was more focused in the Iroquois Confederacy's central powerbase. In June 1776 Fort Niagara, the mighty post on the shores of Lake Ontario, was a busy and momentous place. Its commandant was Colonel John Butler, who was determined to sway the Six Nations to his own viewpoint. He would rely on the arguments provided to him, most notably that the Americans would swindle away Indian lands and dishonor their treaties:

Your Father the Great King has taken pity on you and is determined not to let the American deceive you any longer—tho' you have been so foolish as to listen to them last year and believe all their wicked stories—they mean to cheat you and should you be so silly as to take their advice and they should conquer the King's Army, their intention is to take all your Lands from you and destroy your people, for they are all mad . . . and full of deceit. They told you last Fall at Pittsburgh that they took the Tom Hawk out of your hands and buried it deep and transplanted the Tree of Peace over it. I therefore now pluck up that Tree, dig up that Tom Hawk, and replace it in your hands with the edge toward them—that you may treat them as enemies.[31]

As the most numerous group in attendance, the Seneca nation had the duty to respond. One sachem, Flying Crow, responded to Butler's advances: "It is true [the Americans] have encroach'd on our Lands, but of this we shall speak to them. If you are strong Brother, and they but as a weak Boy, why was our assistance [needed] . . . ? You say they are all mad, foolish . . . and deceitful—I say you are so and they are wise for you want us to destroy ourselves in your War and they advise us to live in Peace."[32]

In this moment the experienced Colonel Butler lost his patience with the Seneca and took to insults; he reiterated their foolishness and silliness and openly disrespected the Seneca as cowards. At that point Guyasuta ended the tirade with a response of his own, stating, "We must be Fools indeed to imagine that they [the British] regard us or our Interest who want to bring us into an unnecessary war."[33]

For Guyasuta, the neutrality that he maintained was not one of obstinacy to resist an imperial power, but a hard-earned position developed after a lifetime of war. In his own youth he had been swayed by the empty promises of a foreign power, and his alliance with the French twenty years earlier had left him alone and abandoned. What the British had begun doing, in his mind, was simply a repeat of that same persuasive diplomacy, and its effect on the young Iroquois warriors was no different. Guyasuta watched as the elder sachems of the Iroquois Confederacy resisted choosing a side in the coming struggle, but the young warriors migrated by the dozens to travel to Canada and commit to the British cause. To them the imperial glories of the Iroquois Confederacy were never a part of their own world; the power and domain of Iroquoia was a distant memory of generations past. The British promised them a return to an age of uncontested Iroquois rule, and the warriors in their twenties and thirties created an image of what their past must have looked like decades earlier. As in all societies, the image that a later generation creates of its distant past is never accurate, and always skewed with values and traditions that had never truly existed. In the rashness of their youth the young Iroquois were far more anxious for war than their elders, and the fifty-year-old Guyasuta only hoped to impart the wisdom of his youth to them.

Although the aging sachem placed great faith in his decisions, because they were born of his own experience, even he was finding it increasingly difficult to convince anyone that the coming American Revolution was a mere repeat of some European conflict twenty years earlier. A month after the conference at Fort Niagara, Guyasuta found himself exercising his position as Half-King yet again in the Ohio Country. It was now mid-July, and only a few days earlier the Continental Congress signed and published its Declaration of Independence from Great Britain. Although there had been spurts of violence already, Guyasuta knew that all-out rebellion and open warfare was coming to North America. Around the council fire at the Forks of the Ohio, Guyasuta was presented with a peace belt designed and decorated with thirteen diamonds, the wampum string of the united American colonies. Although he maintained his position as Half-King to speak on behalf of the Ohioan peoples present, Guyasuta delivered a message to the Americans that was more of a personal warning than a prepared statement. He said, "We will not suffer either the English or the Americans to march an army through our country."[34]

In this pronouncement Guyasuta spoke not just for the Iroquois and their subjects, but for all native peoples of the frontier. He had spent much of his adult life leading Indian forces with no single tribal allegiance, and speaking of all Indian nations as one had become a habit. It also made him a visionary, ahead of his time.

It had been well-known that the Continental Congress in Philadelphia hosted some of the most furious debates in American history. Individual colonies had expectations and demands that did not often match those of their provincial allies. At the Fort Pitt council Guyasuta included a recommendation of his own. He explained to the congressional delegates that they would be best served to act as one and put their differences aside. If they failed to do so, their entire revolution could collapse as a result. Guyasuta ended the treaty with an assurance that the Ohio Indians would remain neutral in the war, and the Iroquois retained their impartial stance as well. It was a moment of celebration for the American commissioners, for they knew that an uninvolved Indian populace would save them a great challenge; they were already facing insurmountable odds against the Royalists (those loyal to the Crown and in British service).

At the conclusion of the council, the commissioners presented Guyasuta with a sealed package. For much of the previous year, the fifty-year-old sachem trekked back and forth from the Patriot base of Fort Pitt to the Royalist base at Fort Niagara to maintain peace and neutrality among the groups. His efforts allowed for the Continental Congress to plot against the British without fear of Indian reprisal, and six months earlier on January 27, 1776, they had passed the following measure: "Resolved, That a commission issue to Cayashota, giving him the rank of a colonel, and that a silver gorget be presented to him."[35]

That night in July at the Forks of the Ohio, Guyasuta opened a package to reveal a silver, inscribed gorget to be worn around his neck, a gift from the Continental Congress in Philadelphia. The gorget, a small piece of ceremonial armor that protected the neck, was viewed as the last vestige of the medieval knight, and it symbolized the traditional values of an aristocratic gentleman soldier. With the gorget though also came something even greater; he had been awarded the commission of colonel in the American Continental Army. The aging Guyasuta draped the gorget around his neck and said farewell to his American associates.

Though the Americans may have been confident of their achievements at Fort Pitt, Guyasuta was far from aligned with their cause. In a matter of weeks the hawkish wing of his people would begin to gain ground, and Indian America would change forever. Guyasuta may have been celebrated in Philadelphia in early 1776, but he would soon become one of the Americans' fiercest enemies in their revolution.

SEVEN

The Cause of the Crown

The Siege of Fort Stanwix and the Battle of Oriskany, August 1777

At fifty-two years old, Guyasuta sat motionless in the forest. He was hundreds of miles from the Ohio Country, but he was fully prepared to fulfill his obligation to his Seneca heritage. Around him sat over four hundred Iroquois warriors, and on the tree line above him were several dozen American Provincials who remained loyal to the British Empire. They had recently received word that a belligerent force of almost eight hundred American rebels was marching toward their position, and the Indians poised themselves for an ambush.

In front of them flowed a bubbling creek that softly cut its way through New York's Mohawk River valley. It was around this creek that the Iroquois and Loyalists maintained a clandestine position in anticipation of their enemies' clumsy approach; by the end of the day it would be called Bloody Creek. Guyasuta looked into the eyes of the young warriors who surrounded him and saw the tense anticipation that he himself had felt many years earlier. They sat patiently, having quickly applied makeshift war paint, each taking slow, measured breaths.

This attack would not be routine for any of them. For the previous six months Guyasuta had led raids across the New York frontier and Ohio Country, reclaiming the territory for the Iroquois Confederacy in the unique style of terror that had made him famous for the last two decades. He knew that his life and the balance of power that defined Indian America would change forever after that day. Making their way toward him were seven hundred New York farmers, and joining them were over one hundred Oneida warriors. As critical members of the Six Nations, the Oneida had been part of his tribal brotherhood all his life.

If he was to be victorious, he would have to attack his own Iroquois brethren. It was a scenario that many thought impossible, but the Oneidas' decision to join the Patriot war effort and deviate from the remainder of the Iroquois Confederacy left him with no choice. The Americans had essentially declared war on Guyasuta in an ultimate betrayal, and they would suffer the consequences—even at the expense of civil war. As he surveyed the landscape, awaiting the sounds of animal hoofs descending toward his position, Guyasuta looked proudly to his nephew Gyantwachia, who had organized the Seneca in preparation for the attack. Gyantwachia, like his uncle, was born in the Genesee River valley, and the English speakers had translated his name as Cornplanter. Although he was younger than Guyasuta, Cornplanter was firmly attached to his Seneca roots and considered himself fully Iroquois. Guyasuta's experiences as a Mingo leader in the Ohio Country were long behind him, and it only took the sight of his powerful nephew to bring him back to the Iroquoian worldview and all that was at stake.

They had agreed that the ambush would begin only when the bulk of the enemy forces crossed the rocky stream ahead of them. As the front of the Patriot column first splashed into the trickling waters, though, some of the warriors in the distance let loose a terrifying yell. Aware of what they had just walked into, the New Yorkers raised their rifles. The Battle of Oriskany was on.

In 1776, as both the Americans and the British prepared for war, both sides felt strongly that the native peoples of North America would play a determining role in the conflict. For the British, the best possible outcome would be for the Iroquois Confederacy to honor their long-standing covenant with the Crown and join to crush the rebellion; for the Americans it was that the fragile neutrality displayed to that point would continue.

The role of the Indians is often one of the most confusing and difficult questions faced by historians who specialize in the Revolutionary period. Until the 1970s, scholars and researchers often ignored or diminished the Indians' effects on the outcome of the war, while overemphasizing the actions of George Washington or the bravery of his subordinates. As a result, the actions of men like Guyasuta, Cornplanter, Joseph Brant, and the other sachems who helped redirect the conflict were overlooked. Early on, much of this disregard may have been racially tinged. That changed, however, when a new generation of historians abandoned the "top-down" view of history that defined their predecessors and began looking at all classes of people. The sources had always been there, but their value had not been recognized. New perspectives on old stories emerged, and much like accounts from the perspectives of slaves, workers, and women, the Indians too began to have their voices heard more clearly.

Perhaps the single most challenging hurdle to understanding the Indians' role in the American Revolution is that they were never a monolithic group. This unique collection of North American peoples was as different from one another, if not more, than the Europeans themselves. Their respective nations rarely cooperated with one another on a large scale, and they were never totally united. When the Indians abandoned neutrality and ultimately chose sides, the process amounted to not one, but many different decisions.[1]

To begin, remaining neutral is a luxury reserved for powerful, singular, and most important independent people. The Iroquois Confederacy in 1776 had gained back some of its control, but some factions had become more powerful among the Six Nations than others. The council fire did still technically burn, and all nations were represented, yet they retained their individual powers and exercised them more than ever before. Although it would eventually break down, historians cannot make determinations based on what is known now, only judgments on what was known then. The largest single reason the Iroquois could not remain neutral was their lack of the final, and most precious, feature needed for neutrality: independence.[2]

The Indian of the eighteenth century was, like the settler of the same time, the creation of a multicultural, multi-ethnic patchwork of peoples that was British North America. Trade had first tied the Haudenosaunee to the English, and it was trade that lured their subjects toward the French. Therefore, if the Iroquois wished to remain impartial, the resulting trade stoppage would prove catastrophic. North America's Indian populations were able to split their loyalties between the French and English thirty years earlier because both sides could provide plentiful amounts of goods to satisfy them, but their decision was not so difficult at the onset of the American Revolution.

The American rebels relied almost completely on British goods, and though the war itself caused something of a cottage industry to develop, those supplies could barely sustain the colonists. The Iroquois realized that the only way to keep a safe and steady supply of European goods coming into their lands, and thereby keep their fragile economy afloat, was to side with the British. The Iroquois were sturdy, headstrong, and committed to their own values, but their dependence on European goods in many ways made their decision for them.

To illustrate this point, the abundance at the Loyalist base of Fort Niagara made a convincing argument. Following one council at the fort, a Seneca sachem was overheard saying: "When our white Brethern call us to meet them at their Towns, we all flock like Bees—not that we want to take strong hold of their Friendship but to share the Goods they bring with them."[3]

While the subjects of the Iroquois maintained their neutrality well into the conflict, longer than any other eastern nation, they too shed light on the notion of trade being the single most crucial factor in choosing sides. Captain Pipe, an influential Delaware sachem, explained this to the Americans at Fort Pitt in 1777. "Great Stress is laid on your inability to supply our wants

& we are ridiculed by your Enemies for being attached to you who cannot even furnish us with a pair of Stockings or a Blanket—this obliges us to be dependent in a great measure on them."[4]

Joseph Brant painted by George Romney in London, ca. 1776. (*Library of Congress*)

If there was a singular figure instrumental in persuading the Iroquois to join the British it was the Mohawk Joseph Brant. Since his travels with Guy Johnson the year before, Brant had become the most recognizable American Indian to the average Londoner. He had met with the king himself, had his portrait painted by some of the finest artists in the city, and was even draped with the ceremonial apron of the Masonic Order. For Brant, the glitz and glamour of the British Empire was no longer ephemeral, but a real, tangible feature of his life. When he returned to North America in the summer of 1776 he was fully convinced that the American rebels, if victorious, would pilfer Indian lands out of sheer necessity. The strength, comfort, and prestige of the British worldview ensnared Brant, and his sole mission became to rally Iroquoia to his side.

Upon his return to the continent, Brant wasted no time joining in the war effort. By August 1776 the Mohawk aligned himself with the forces of General William Howe as he prepared his assault on New York in an attempt to destroy General George Washington's Continental army. Though Washington escaped and the revolution limped on, Brant had been continually impressed by the calculated severity of the royal officers at the Battle of Long Island and was reassured that an alliance with them was his best course of action.

After hostilities had ceased at New York City, Brant returned to his ancestral homeland to visit with his family; he had been gone for over a year. Shortly thereafter he continued his trek northwest to the gates of Fort Niagara. Although Iroquois neutrality remained in place, the movement was quickly losing steam. Activity at Fort Niagara proved a testament to that. Its counterpart Fort Pitt had almost no Iroquoian presence, yet the Loyalist base on Lake Ontario was almost continuously inhabited. For Brant, his arrival at Fort Niagara was a great homecoming; the response that he received, however, was unexpected. He held council with the sachems, explaining what he had seen and how he believed the Americans would behave if they managed to win the war. It was a passionate oration, but that winter the chiefs of the Six Nations present were not convinced. Brant left the post, angered by their reluctance, but he rejoined the British war effort nevertheless.[5]

By July 1777, however, those present at the council fire began to change their opinion. The economic strains of neutrality were now being felt, and with the war fully under way there was little chance of relief. The traditional channels that brought the firearms, glassware, metalwork, liquor, and supplies that had bolstered the native economy for the last several decades had again run dry; action needed to be taken. Therefore, with an approaching fiscal disaster at their backs, the Iroquois abandoned neutrality. The dispute, however, was just beginning.

As a confederation, the Iroquois were a collection of six nations seeking mutual benefit. Although they were firmly entrenched as members of the coalition, the individual nations retained their rights to act in the best interests of their people. When the vote to end neutrality came, there was little argument, but the vote regarding which side to join proved contentious. The Mohawk, Onondaga, Cayuga, and Seneca all favored a British alignment; while Joseph Brant was not present, his arguments from seven months earlier certainly weighed on the council's minds. The remainder of the confederacy, the Oneida and Tuscarora, believed that only an alliance with the Americans would benefit them.

As complex as the process was, the Haudenosaunee divisions were largely due to the efforts of one man. Samuel Kirkland, a Presbyterian minister, had lived among the Iroquois for almost eight years by the time the revolution began. Born and raised in Connecticut and a graduate of the College of New Jersey (now Princeton University), Kirkland was a staunch advocate of the Patriot cause. As he preached the gospel to the natives in the

Mohawk River valley, he grew very close to the Oneida and Tuscarora and became something of an unofficial ambassador. The two nations placed their faith in him, and when he promised that the Americans would recognize their sovereignty after earning their own independence, his word was enough for them to throw their support to the rebellious colonists.[6]

The resulting dissension among the Oneida and Tuscarora was a turning point in the history of Indian America. For the first time in almost two hundred years the mighty Iroquois Confederacy was split; the issue was great enough that both sides regarded civil war as a possibility.

With the decision made, the formerly united Six Nations began to act largely as six separate entities battling on two different sides. The Seneca, with Guyasuta in attendance, prepared for war by selecting the two sachems who would lead their people as war chiefs. The first was Sayenqueraghta. At seventy years old, the man called Old Smoke was one of the most experienced candidates for the position. He had fought in the Seven Years' War and was selected initially in 1751 as a war chief. He was instrumental in the Devil's Hole Massacre and fought against the Cherokee and Choctaw in 1765. The second man whom they chose to rally behind was much younger than Sayenqueraghta, but every bit the leader. Gyantwachia, or Cornplanter, had also walked the line of neutrality. While the Seneca still wavered with indifference, he famously stated, "war is war, death is death; a fight is hard business." Many looked to him now to bear the torch that his uncle Guyasuta had held during Pontiac's Rebellion.[7]

The Mohawk had already selected Joseph Brant as their war chief months earlier, and he was fully engaged in the royal war effort in the colony of New York. In the spring of 1777, the commander in chief of His Majesty's forces in North America, General John Burgoyne, was preparing the largest single invasion of American territory in the short history of the war. Taking as his launching point the province of Quebec, which effectively was all of Canada and the Great Lakes region, Burgoyne planned on sending a dual-pronged military juggernaut into the New York frontier to dismantle the rebel cause. While it was a venture that would require patience and timing, Burgoyne

believed that by capturing Albany and all of its precious surrounding water routes he could sever New England from the rest
of the continent. Also discussed, though it would never come to
fruition, was the possibility of a third corresponding force marching on Philadelphia itself to deliver a final killing blow.

The strategy for America reflected the immensity of the
British Empire. While the plan was formulated in London
between Burgoyne and Secretary of State George Germain, its
impact would be felt a world away on a continent of uncertain
future. The entire venture on paper was bold, but even more
impressive was Burgoyne's direct involvement in its implementation. Upon his arrival back in the North American colonies,
Burgoyne himself would lead approximately eight thousand
troops from Canada southward along Lake Champlain and proceed to Albany. He would at the same time send a smaller force
of two thousand men under the command of Barry St. Leger to
sail through Lake Ontario, land at Oswego, and march into the
Mohawk River valley. Though St. Leger's movements would
serve as a diversion more than a tactical necessity, the two forces
would converge at Albany, giving the Crown total domination of
Lake Champlain, Lake George, and the highly prized Hudson
River. Such an accomplishment would allow Burgoyne to control
the entire waterway from Quebec to New York City. In 1777, the
British still considered the American Revolution to be a brief
bump in their larger imperial strategy, and to snuff it out early
was the best that the administration in London could hope for.[8]

The entire Saratoga campaign would require precise execution, however, in challenging terrain. The New York frontier
possessed all the hardships that any single piece of territory
could offer. The expedition would need to cross mountains,
wind through desolate valleys, and live with the constant threat
of marching through enemy territory. Burgoyne would need to
select an officer who could handle the burden, and his new
Indian allies were central to its success.

The target of Great Britain's wilderness march would be a
strike at one of the most hallowed and critical pieces of territory in all of North America. Though dangerous and vast, New
York's Mohawk River valley and its surrounding area were well
known for its complex series of waterways that allowed near

direct access from the Atlantic Ocean to the heart of the frontier. For the last century before the war, traders from France and Britain had found that by sailing down the St. Lawrence River and linking with Lake Ontario, goods could be easily moved inland with the assistance of willing native guides.

The plan called for the expedition to begin at Oswego, which had been fortified initially by the British in 1727. Though the small post was destroyed in the Seven Years' War, the location still held strategic importance. After sailing out of Lake Ontario, smaller vessels would traverse eastward on the Oswego River, linking next with Oneida Lake. From there, vessels would navigate the much tighter Wood Creek. Natives would play a vital role at this point, as it was here that the only portage of the entire journey was required. Small bateaus would be docked, and goods would be carried almost two miles across the Mohawk River valley on foot; it was the only time that a shipment from Europe would ever need to cross dry ground after leaving its European port of call. After the trek, the goods would be reloaded aboard a waiting bateau, sailed down the Mohawk River briefly before connecting with the Hudson. It was a taxing journey, and one that required some trial and error, but explorers on the North American frontier found that their risks were rewarded in profitable ways.[9]

Hundreds of commercial parties gained safe passage through a remote region thanks to this series of waterways, leading the British Empire to decide in 1758 that it should fortify its most vital point. The portage, called Deo-Wain-Sta, or "the Great Carrying Place" by the Indians, had become a vital component of native life as it was the place where all traders had to pass, and therefore a crucial point of economic exchange in the New World. Near the site of today's Rome, New York, a fort was commissioned and in four years it was completed. It nearly mirrored the design of Fort Pitt (though on a much smaller scale) and it was named after the officer who oversaw the construction of both fortifications, General John Stanwix. As a tiny beacon of British power in a vast frontier, Fort Stanwix would go on to become a site of great importance for Indian diplomacy; the immensely unsettling Treaty of Fort Stanwix that led to so much bloodshed was completed there in 1768.

As peace reigned though in North America following the end
of the Seven Years' War, it became less of a priority to maintain
a garrison at the site, and as the British found themselves
unchallenged in North America they abandoned the post. Even
though it was dilapidated and left to the elements, its position
retained its great importance. At the outset of the American
Revolution the outgunned rebels of the area found a new home
in its crumbling walls. They rebuilt much of the site, and
though it had been deemed useless by the British, it became a
small symbol of hope for the fledgling Patriot cause.

Though the post at the Carrying Place was renamed Fort
Schuyler after Major General Phillip Schuyler of the
Continental army, most of the men stationed in its walls still
called it by its original name. By May 1777 it was back as a
viable fortification. Under the command of Colonel Peter
Gansevoort, the 3rd New York Regiment worked tirelessly to
make old Fort Stanwix as strong as possible to once again take
command of the entire Mohawk River valley.[10]

At that same time, however, plans were already in motion far
away in Canada to capture the site. While Gansevoort's men
sawed and hammered away their time, a friendly scout of the
Oneida nation approached the colonel. As he was still Iroquois,
the man claimed to have privileged information. An Oneida, he
had thrown his support to the Patriot side, and it was his duty
to pass on any intelligence he had acquired. He explained that a
joint Anglo-Iroquois force was rallying in Canada, and they
would be at his location within the next few weeks. Already the
Iroquois internal divisions were playing a critical role in the outcome of the American Revolution, and Fort Stanwix was just the
beginning.

The Oneida scout provided advanced warning of Barry St.
Leger's wing of the invasion as laid out in London eight months
earlier. By June 13 General Burgoyne had begun his march
toward Albany, and ten days later the invasion of the Mohawk
Valley was under way. On June 23, St. Leger left Lachine, near
Montreal, leading an impressive force of manpower. The column that he created was as diverse as the British Empire itself,
consisting of Redcoats from the 8th and 34th Regiments of
Foot, accompanied by eighty Hessian mercenaries, and nearly

three hundred and fifty Loyalist Americans from the command of John Butler of Fort Niagara. The entire group was accompanied by a host of animals, goods, and one hundred Canadians to manage its supply train.

From their starting point in Canada the British had fully welcomed the Iroquois' recent shift away from neutrality. While encamped on the St. Lawrence River, a group of rebel prisoners had been presented to the general and upon interrogation they revealed that the Patriots had occupied the remnants of Fort Stanwix. St. Leger gave careful consideration to this news, and the prisoners of war also revealed that Colonel Gansevoort was fully aware of their approach. They continued by claiming that the post held six hundred rebel troops, and that any advancements that the British made would be well scouted ahead of time. With this new intelligence in hand, St. Leger was convinced by one of his Indian agents that perhaps it was time to approach the Iroquois about joining him on the expedition. They would have been a major addition as they knew the land better than any of St. Leger's men, and from what he had gathered they were anxious to fight.[11]

Like a storm surge St. Leger's force landed at Oswego on the shores of Lake Ontario by July 14. Once there, the general held a conference with the Mohawk and Seneca sachems and warriors present. Among the chiefs in attendance were Joseph Brant, Cornplanter, and Guyasuta. The parties agreed that a joint action would be required, and overnight St. Leger added almost eight hundred Iroquois warriors to his army.

St. Leger's march was a strong one. They maintained a brisk pace and were kept well informed by their newly acquired native scouts. While speed was always essential on missions such as his, intelligence and adaptability were just as critical. En route, St. Leger received word that Colonel Gansevoort had had extra supplies delivered to Fort Stanwix in preparation for the oncoming attack, and the general jumped to action immediately. He requested the presence of the Mohawk Brant, and promptly dispatched two hundred warriors and thirty British Regulars to intercept the convoy. Although they were unsure where exactly the supply vessels were, their familiarity with the water systems limited their scope to a small search area.[12]

Brant and his Iroquois rushed toward Fort Stanwix, hoping to catch their prey before the vital provisions could be delivered, but by the time they were within sight of the post it was too late; two hundred Massachusetts militiamen had already unloaded the supplies, and all were safely within the walls of the fort. It was a deflating development for the Anglo-Indian allies, and Brant settled for the capture of the delivery ship's captain. He quickly sent word back to St. Leger that he had achieved only a small victory, but the damage was done. Before the supplies arrived, Fort Stanwix would have been an easy target. The British and Indians could have surrounded the post and waited until the starving men inside surrendered. Now, with a fresh resupply and plentiful stores, the siege could last for weeks; those were weeks that St. Leger did not have. He presumed that General Burgoyne would be waiting for him at Albany, and when timing was the essence, an extended engagement against a small fort was not a luxury that he could afford.[13]

The following day the bulk of St. Leger's thirteen hundred men emerged from the forests outside Fort Stanwix. Just as he had anticipated, the Patriots had put themselves in the best possible position to withstand a lengthy siege. To avoid such a measure, St. Leger decided that he would engage in some of the great traditions of his native allies to perhaps circumvent a battle altogether. At midday, St. Leger aligned his soldiers in formation and marched them around the walls of Fort Stanwix. He hoped to intimidate his foes, and when the Iroquois followed behind in full war paint, what he created was an impressive and overwhelming display of sheer imperial power. After several minutes of parading, the general offered the flag of truce and read aloud a message from General Burgoyne allowing for safe quarter upon surrender; the Americans inside declined to respond. Although St. Leger's column was over twice as large as Gansevoort's, St. Leger proceeded with operations and gave orders to begin a prolonged siege. St. Leger acted in a professional manner, and directed his men very efficiently, but he was likely disturbed by the Patriots' refusal to capitulate.[14]

The positions that his men took were ideal for a siege, and the personnel assignments reflected St. Leger's inherent distrust of Provincial militia. He positioned his artillery and Redcoats from the 8th and 34th Regiments, his best men, at the top of a

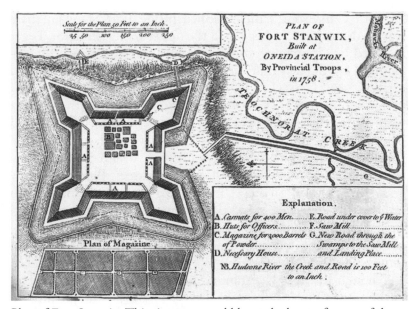

Plan of Fort Stanwix. This tiny post would be at the heart of many of the critical actions in New York's Mohawk River valley. (*Narrative and Critical History of America*)

small bluff overlooking the fort, the most advantageous location available. He next assigned the American Loyalists to the south of the fort, and the Iroquois agreed to set up their camps between the British and the Mohawk River. This was not an oversight by St. Leger; by placing the Iroquois along the banks of the waterway they would provide effective interference in the case of an American force attempting to break the siege. If the Patriots did try to advance on his position from the south, they would first encounter the warriors' wrath. St. Leger used Brant's, Cornplanter's, and Guyasuta's men as a first line of defense, but more appropriately as a tripwire.

The Indian chiefs, expecting the siege to be long and drawn out, established their camps as instructed. Despite the fact that the bulk of St. Leger's force was Indian, the two allied groups would rarely interact. The Indians would sleep and reside in their own camps, just as the British, Hessians, and Americans would. Although they moved as one force, they generally separated into their own unique enclaves when off-duty.[15]

With Gansevoort's men trapped inside Fort Stanwix, there was no doubt that St. Leger had the upper hand, but as St. Leger assumed his dominant positions around the fort, he was deeply troubled by the fact that the majority of his artillery had yet to arrive.

His scouts quickly discovered the problem. After the Oneida warned the Patriots of St. Leger's advance, Gansevoort ordered his men to cut down trees across the Carrying Place. When the British horses lugged their heavy cannon toward the fort, they were stopped by an abbatis of heavy fallen trees. Before the siege could truly begin, St. Leger had to use precious manpower to remove those obstacles, and the Indians had no interest in participating. For much of the next two days the British lost valuable time, with the Iroquois serving as the bulk of the force that remained around the fort.[16]

Though it was only a minor delay in the grand scheme of an entire campaign, it offered St. Leger's enemies enough time to mount a response. Underscoring the regional nature of the Patriot war effort, the counterattack to the British invasion was conducted entirely by local forces. St. Leger's orders were part of a larger invasion plan that had been formulated and ordered by London itself, but Gansevoort, who hoped to defend Fort Stanwix, did so not from General Washington's orders, or even from Philadelphia, but entirely on his own. On July 30, two days before the British had reached the Mohawk River valley, a party of American-aligned Oneida warriors alerted Nicholas Herkimer to the movements of St. Leger and his Iroquois allies. As the head of the Committee of Safety of Tryon County, Herkimer had become a de facto local adjunct of the larger revolutionary movement around the colonies. He had no contact with any larger units of the Continental army, and to that point the only military background he had acquired was twenty years earlier in the French and Indian War. As the rebellion launched into full swing two years earlier, the modest bit of combat experience he possessed made him the only man eligible to serve as colonel of the district militia.[17]

When word reached him that St. Leger's forces, Brant's Mohawk, and Guyasuta and Cornplanter's Seneca were marching toward the valley, Herkimer jumped to action. He set out an immediate bulletin to all available men of fighting age to arm themselves, and by August 4 he had assembled eight hundred able-bodied militiamen at his disposal. Though they were willing, Herkimer's forces were largely inexperienced first- and second-generation immigrant farmers, and the following day many dropped out of the expedition prematurely due to fatigue. Encamped at the Oneida village of Oriska, the Mohawk Valley's lone Patriot response effort appeared to be unraveling before it began.

As unprepared as he was, Herkimer was nothing if not resilient. In an impromptu council the Provincial colonel formed an agreement with the war chief Han Yerry, a noted Patriot sympathizer among the Oneida. Impressed at the gravity of the emerging situation and anxious to deliver a blow to his British enemies, Han Yerry agreed to lead nearly one hundred Oneida warriors alongside Herkimer's now depleted seven hundred Provincials. Though unknown at the time, Herkimer's American-Iroquois force was put on course to collide head on with St. Leger's British-Iroquois.

Nicholas Herkimer's lack of combat expertise was evident by his hesitancy to attack St. Leger directly. Shortly after forming with the Oneida, the colonel sent forward a messenger to alert Gansevoort of his impending arrival at the besieged Fort Stanwix. Included in the correspondence was a proposed plan for the commandant to order a sortie toward the approaching Patriot army. It was a bold plan that would require the men inside the fort to suddenly charge the British positions around them, and it would only be successful when Herkimer and his men were close by. When Gansevoort received the communication, he was to fire three booming cannon shots as a secret indicator that only Herkimer would understand. Only ten miles away, the Provincial colonel waited for the signal; it never came.

The runner that Herkimer had sent was not able to penetrate the picket of St. Leger's position, and the message was delayed. That same night, the Mohawk Joseph Brant received word of the Americans' approach thanks to the efforts of his sister Molly. Still a person of national significance in Canada, Molly Brant rendered service that was only illustrated in a small measure the night of August 5. She had been the common-law wife of the late Sir William Johnson, and bore him nine children. Even after the great negotiator's death she remained firmly committed to the British worldview and was active throughout the period.

In the early morning hours of August 6, both parties planned for the very real possibility of a military engagement at sunrise. Despite the fact that they were planning at the same time, the two commanders could not have been more distant. In the British camp St. Leger, Brant, and Cornplanter had devised an effective strategy to turn the tables on their approaching American foes by setting an ambush approximately halfway between Fort Stanwix and their enemy's reported position. While the Indians would carry most of the burden of combat, St. Leger was confident that they would rout their foes. Ten miles to their west, though, Herkimer was struggling just to keep his own men under his control.

The Patriot council had lasted all morning, and Herkimer still waited anxiously for Colonel Gansevoort to signal the receipt of his message. As his men grew increasingly uneasy, the officers beneath him began demanding that Herkimer take Fort Stanwix by force, regardless of his previous plans. It was a hard lesson in leadership for the fifty-one-year-old colonel, and it was only when his militiamen began calling him a traitor and turncoat that Herkimer finally gave in to their wishes. In an interesting twist, their charge of treachery was fueled by the fact that Herkimer's brother was only miles ahead serving under the command of St. Leger himself.[18]

The place that the Indians chose to set their trap was at a particularly challenging interval along the banks of Oriskany Creek. Decided on largely by the Seneca, the spot in which they posted their ambush was at a point where the ground sloped almost fifty feet; the hope was that while the Americans struggled to negotiate the hill the Indians would collapse in on them and find victory quickly. The Loyalists that joined Cornplanter that day arranged themselves on a modest bluff overlooking the planned point of attack. They were members of the Kings Royal Regiment of New York, one of the first regiments raised from Provincials who wished to remain loyal to King George. As the morning sun continued to rise on August 6 and Herkimer led his men toward Fort Stanwix, neither party knew how drastically their fates were about to change.

The morning of August 6 would be the greatest test that the brief military career of Nicholas Herkimer would ever face. By 10 A.M. he had abandoned his own principles, along with his disciplined first instincts, and given way to the masses that now fell in behind him. He did not wait for the signal of three cannon shots as intended, and the result was a line of six hundred provincial militiamen stepping in a lively two-by-two stretching almost a mile behind him. The road that they walked was relatively well-traveled in its day, but quite simple. On one side was a marshy and unstable plot; on the other was more solid, elevated ground. While Herkimer led his men, he made sure to hug the edge that was more stable for his column to travel across.

As the American force continued its march, the ground before them began to slope. It was a drop-off that they were all aware of, but no reports indicate that Herkimer was hesitant at all about leading his men into it—he was after all doing so from the front. As the colonel moved down the hill on horseback, he saw before him a small ford across Oriskany Creek. The creek was a minor tributary of the Mohawk River, and here it was only one meter across. It was a paltry crossing and a minor bump in the rhythm that he and his men had developed over the last hour of trekking. The stream was narrow but rocky, not unlike dozens of others than filled the Mohawk River valley.

Colonel Herkimer continued across the waterway and began to briskly ascend the hill on the other side. He may have looked behind him to keep watch over his line's progress, as it now looked like a great snake with almost one-third of its body divided by the sudden ravine, but there was no indication that he ever sensed danger.

As his line continued to cross the creek, the colonel himself was nearly on flat land and the heavy, cumbersome supply train was now beginning its journey downhill. Though the Americans and their Oneida scouts did not know it, all the while they were struggling with the ravine they were surrounded by almost five hundred Seneca and Mohawk warriors waiting in the dense cover. Painted in all varieties of ceremonial reds and blacks, Brant, Cornplanter, and their associates including Guyasuta all sat poised to strike only feet from the unsuspecting Patriots.

In an ambush like this one, timing was essential. The purpose of lying in wait was to catch one's opponent at their weakest point, and therefore at their most vulnerable. If the ambush was executed properly the outcome would look something like at Devil's Hole. It would be remembered as an event in which the victimized force was off-balance and unaware; the end result would be recalled not as a battle, but a massacre. If the trap was blundered and the enemy was given the opportunity to take heed of their surroundings, then an action like Bushy Run might ensue. In 1777 though, Bushy Run stood out as an anomaly; it was the only time that a British force had ever run a warrior band from the field of battle.

The plan devised by Brant and Cornplanter, and relayed to their Mohawk and Seneca warriors, respectively, was to have the Royal New Yorkers on the bluff ahead freeze the American column, and then in the confusion the Iroquois would spring their trap from either side of the jammed Patriot force.

By the time that Herkimer had crossed the stream though, some of the warriors were already beginning to stir, and when the wagon wheels of the cattle carts were heard the less experienced fighters broke the silence and revealed their position by shouting war cries. It had startled the Americans, but the timing was off. The layout of Herkimer's line was designed in such a way that the confused warriors attacked believing that their timing was accurate. At the front of the line was the colonel, and behind him approximately four hundred militiamen. Behind them was the supply line, including the wagons that the warriors perceived as the end of the line, but there were still two hundred men following after. When the Indians initiated their attack, it was no longer a surprise and they had to move swiftly, because a quarter of Herkimer's total strength still had yet to enter the ravine.

By the time that Colonel Nicholas Herkimer heard the snapping and popping of musket fire, he was already up and away from Oriskany Creek; when he heard the war whoops, though, he knew that he had to return as quickly as possible. Turning his horse around, Herkimer rushed back into the ravine that he had just left, but did so at a pace that was unsustainable. Already as he headed back he had seen that his line was fully engaged and surrounded by an Iroquois force almost equal to his own; it would have been hard to digest in the midst of the forested chaos, but his own dead and wounded men were a testament to the enemy's ferocity.

In the first volley fired by the Iroquois they had already managed to greatly weaken the Patriot force; Colonel Ebeneezer Cox was one of the first men killed. It was no shock and certainly no coincidence that Cox died so quickly. Since the Seven Years' War it had been regular practice among North America's Indian warriors to locate and kill officers first. Although they had no tradition of a hierarchy of power on the field of battle, the Indians knew that the white army relied entirely on its chain of command for control. Although the loss of an officer greatly weakened any army, in Europe it was considered poor form to target an officer; this, however, was not Europe and the frontier often created its own set of rules.

While Herkimer was descending back into the bloody madness of the ravine, his identity as a commanding officer was recognized instantly and he became a primary target. Before he could reach the bottom of the slope he was struck by so many musket balls that he was thrown forward. He had been wounded in the leg, and his horse had died. His men saw his injury and in the midst of the violence around them they scooped him up. They attempted to take him away from the killing, fully aware of what fate awaited the wounded against an Indian enemy, but the colonel insisted he remain. They quickly unlaced his saddle from the back of his lifeless animal, sat it against a tree, and placed Herkimer on it. Badly injured, the colonel boldly barked orders from his seat and, while still smoking his pipe, repeatedly filled the hollow with shouts of "I will face the enemy!"[19]

The fighting had lasted for thirty minutes with no sign of stopping, yet because of the premature nature of the attack almost half of Herkimer's men had yet to engage the Indians. None of the Patriots had any real combat experience to speak of, and many of those who had not entered the now smoke-filled ravine turned away from the cries deep inside, and ran. While the New York farmers fled the scene of the battle, Joseph Brant and his Mohawks gave chase. The Seneca remained vigilant along the creek, and Brant's men had little trouble running down the scattered American force. Scalped bodies of the slain were said to be found as far as a mile away from the ravine itself, and this was no doubt from the efforts of the Mohawk warriors in hot pursuit.

In the midst of the fighting, Herkimer's entrapped men had managed to claw their way out of the ravine. Although their ability to escape their precarious position was a victory in its own right, it was only then that the battle could be fought on any terms other than those of the Iroquois. To work their way away from the gurgling creek, the Patriots and Oneida resorted to hand-to-hand combat, as the Seneca and Mohawk had found great success throwing aside their muskets and swinging away with the tomahawk. When the Oneida battled their fellow Iroquois on opposite sides of the struggle, it was done without remorse; in the midst of the smoky carnage it appeared that the Iroquois civil war would be a bloody and exhausting affair.

With the new development that the Americans had survived the initial offering of the Indians, members of the Loyalists looking on ran back toward the bulk of St. Leger's camp in an attempt to draw reinforcements. Suddenly, though, with the prospect of a long and costly battle ahead of them, both sides were surprised when rain began to fall across the valley. What began as a brief sprinkle soon turned into a torrential downpour; it served to momentarily cool the hostilities and both sides used the natural diversion to regroup.

The wounded Herkimer took advantage of the thunderstorm to position his men on some high ground close by. Although it was not ideal, it was much better than being assaulted from all sides of a deep ravine. At the same time on the British side the Loyalist John Butler used the break to interrogate prisoners that his Iroquois allies had taken. Through his inquisition he had discovered the exact origin and size of Herkimer's army as well as the blundering attempt to communicate the message of sortie to Gansevoort a day earlier. Had Butler heard three cannon shots, which he never did, he now knew exactly what that meant.

The storm began to break, and the Loyalist reinforcements arrived soon after. Knowing full well how disorganized and untrained the Patriots really were, the oncoming Loyalists took to deception to gain an upper hand. They astutely turned their

A mid-nineteenth century engraving of the Battle of Oriskany. Gen. Nicholas Herkimer is at the far left, continuing to give orders after his horse was shot from beneath him. (*Library of Congress*)

jackets inside out so that only the dull interior was showing, and from a distance they gave the appearance of American militiamen, not Loyalist enforcers. Coincidentally the term "turncoat" actually held some literal meaning in this regard. When the disguised British auxiliaries arrived, their overall effectiveness was stifled when one of Herkimer's Patriots recognized the face of his Loyalist neighbor and the ruse fell to pieces. The fighting that followed was intense and largely hand-to-hand as well.

Though the Battle at Oriskany was still under way, it was at eleven o'clock that same morning when Herkimer's original messenger was finally able to reach Fort Stanwix. Though the British had caught wind of the scheme, they erroneously believed that it had been unsuccessful. In reality it had not failed, it had only been delayed. By the time that Colonel Gansevoort received word that Herkimer was approaching, certainly too late, he decided the general plot of sortie was still a valid option. Using the Oriskany engagement as a distraction, Gansevoort issued a general order that sent two hundred fifty of his remaining men into action. The order of sortie was an old military axiom in which a besieged force suddenly rushes the positions of their attackers; the strength of the maneuver is that it disregards the normal stages of a siege and succeeds through unconventional methods.

In the case of Fort Stanwix the sortie initiated by the Patriots did just that and much, much more. Knowing that the bulk of the forces that had surrounded the fort had been Iroquois, and that those warriors were now engaged four miles away at Oriskany, the colonel instructed his men to raid the large Indian encampments along the Mohawk River. Rather than attacking St. Leger's Regulars and Hessians, an assault on the empty native camp would allow his men to replenish their supplies through pillaging the Iroquois stores. In a flash, the garrison of Fort Stanwix poured into the Iroquois camp and stripped and spoiled their entire stock of food, ammunition, and supplies.

After pilfering the possessions of the distant Seneca and Mohawk, the Patriots then turned their attention to the Loyalist camp. Like the Iroquois, the Loyalists too were fighting with Herkimer's men at Oriskany Creek, and Gansevoort's men were able to gather not just supplies but also vital intelligence from the Tory position.

The brilliance of Colonel Gansevoort's sortie against the empty camp was perhaps most felt in the distance at Oriskany. As the Patriots and Loyalists, as well as Oneida and Seneca/Mohawk forces, continued the fight, an Indian scout ran quickly from Fort Stanwix with news that the camp site had been raided. Upon hearing of this unexpected development, Cornplanter, Guyasuta, and Brant suddenly issued an order to retreat back to the Mohawk River. Those supplies that Americans stole from the Indians were meant to sustain them not just during the siege, but for the rest of the season. If they had been totally depleted, and they had, the Iroquois war effort would be neutralized almost instantly.

As the vast majority of the British force at Oriskany were not British at all, but Iroquois, when the warriors fled the scene the remaining Loyalist forces had no choice but to retreat as well. Herkimer's force may have been a collection of untrained farmers, but with no Indian support the Loyalists were outnumbered almost five to one. When the Loyalists retreated back to St. Leger's general position, however, the battered Patriots could not give chase. Because of the violent and surprising nature of the engagement, the Indians inflicted much more damage than they sustained. At best estimates the natives only endured a 15 percent loss from their total force, and had Gansevoort's sortie not drawn them away from the creek, the number of deaths they inflicted could have been dramatically higher. At the end of the Battle of Oriskany Herkimer's force suffered an almost 50 percent casualty rate.[20]

Badly wounded and in need of medical attention, Nicholas Herkimer withdrew his forces away from Fort Stanwix to safety. The siege did not end, and the Battle of Oriskany was viewed as a British victory despite the fact that the Indians devised the overwhelming amount of strategy and inflicted the majority of the damage. Over a decade later, one Seneca veteran of the affair recalled:

> We met the enemy at the place near a small creek. They had 3 cannons and we none. We had tomahawks and a few guns, but agreed to fight with tomahawks and scalping knives. During the fight, we waited for them to fire their guns and then we attacked them. It felt like no more than killing a Beast. We killed most of the men in the American's army. Only a few escaped from us. We fought so close against one another that we could kill one another with a musket bayonet. . . . It was here that I saw the most dead bodies that I have ever seen. The blood shed made a stream running down on the sloping ground.[21]

While St. Leger took account of the forces lost in his apparent victory at Oriskany, Brant and the old Seneca Sayenqueraghta approached the British general with a new plan of their own. Hoping to destroy the wounded Herkimer and his ragged militia, the sachems expressed a strong interest in pursuing the Patriots and finishing what they started earlier in the day—but St. Leger refused.

The British general was not on a seek-and-destroy mission against rebel militia; he was still expected to meet General Burgoyne at Albany. Such an expedition against a weak and minor regional force would only be a distraction from achieving his overall goal. That night Joseph Brant, Cornplanter,

Sayenqueraghta, Guyasuta, and their many warriors all met in council to determine the best course of action given the day's events. It was on that night that they collectively decided to send the symbolic bloody hatchet to their former Oneida brethren. The gesture was an official diplomatic declaration of an inter-Iroquois war.[22]

Shortly thereafter, many of the camps went their separate ways based on the outcome of the Battle of Oriskany. When Brant and the Mohawk and Cornplanter, Guyasuta, and the Seneca agreed to join St. Leger, they did so under the impression that they would only serve as an auxiliary force to the larger Loyalist army. When the battle began, though, they had certainly done the bulk of the fighting, and after Gansevoort's men raided their camps they had suffered the most overall damage. It appeared to the Iroquois that the general had taken advantage of their support, and most of the warriors abruptly abandoned the siege of Fort Stanwix.

After setting off on their own, Joseph Brant led his Mohawks on a punitive raid against the nearby Oneida village of Oriska. Once there, his warriors raided the site and took whatever prisoners they could. In traditional fashion the Mohawk tortured the Oneida and prompted a brutal retaliation. The Oneida later attacked the Mohawk sites of Canajoharie and Tiononderoge, leaving terrible scenes of massacred bodies in their wake.

Following his rout at Oriskany Creek, Colonel Herkimer and his men took shelter at the small post of Fort Dayton. Despite the fact that Fort Stanwix was still under attack, his men elected to stay away in hopes that another recovery force would come to relieve it. While the men sat idle, field physicians speculated whether or not the colonel's leg could be saved and ultimately elected to perform surgery. To repair the injury suffered at the start of the battle, an impromptu procedure was performed but terribly botched; though he showed great bravery in the face of the enemy only days earlier, Nicholas Herkimer would die as a result of a careless amputation.

On August 21, fifteen days after the terrible battle, a Patriot army under the command of General Benedict Arnold came to the rescue of the besieged Fort Stanwix and forced St. Leger's men away from the post.

While Cornplanter remained in New York with his Seneca, Guyasuta left the colony to begin he long trek back to his obligations in the Ohio Country. It is not known what his precise movements were, but there is sufficient evidence to suggest that he played a prominent role in the raid of a small settlement outside of Fort Ligonier in December 1777 that claimed the lives of four frontier settlers. Despite the fact that there was a heated rivalry now among the Six Nations in New York and Canada, Guyasuta was still the Half-King of the Ohio Country, and the Ohioans were beginning to slide away from neutrality to the cause of the Crown. If the trend was to continue, and there was no sign that it would stop, his presence would be more vital than ever before.

By 1778, the Ohio Country was quickly proving to be a thorn in the side of the Patriot strategy. In February, the American general Edward Hand led approximately five hundred militiamen westward from Fort Pitt to capture a stock of supplies delivered to the belligerent Indians by their British rivals. His mission would be to locate and remove the contraband and deliver a potentially crushing blow to his native foes. The Shawnee, Wyandot, and Ojibwa had aligned with Great Britain, and only the Delaware attached themselves precariously to the Americans.

Though ambitious, Hand's expedition would be doomed from the beginning as the column was undersupplied and, when an early thaw developed, Hand was forced to turn his men around near Mahoning and return to Pittsburgh through the slush and mud. With no enemy to fight, and a rambunctious throng of untrained soldiers at his disposal, Hand oversaw one of the costliest events of the early war when a small Indian camp was unexpectedly discovered. Approximately forty miles from the mouth of the Beaver River, Hand writes: "I detachd a party . . . to Secure them, they turn'd out to be 4 Women & a Boy, of these one Woman only was Saved."[23]

What Hand had discovered was a friendly Delaware encampment. While most of the natives had fled, in their bloodlust Hand's forces murdered every remaining member of the group except a lone young woman. Because this was the only action of the expedition, it pejoratively became known as the "Squaw Campaign."

In Philadelphia, the situation was growing grim. Many of the Ohioan nations had aligned themselves with the British by 1778, and their affections were won because of a steady supply of goods coming into the Ohio Country from Fort Detroit and Fort Niagara. If the American cause hoped to gain any ground in the region in which they were greatly outnumbered, they would need to stop that precious flow of goods. A venture such as that would require a staunch Indian ally, and as almost all of the land-owning tribesmen of the region had joined the British cause, the Delaware were the only option that the Americans had.

Despite the terrible nature of the "Squaw Campaign," the Delaware agreed to a council at Fort Pitt. On September 19, prominent sachems including White Eyes, John Kill Buck, and Captain Pipe (whose family was killed by Hand's Expedition) met with Andrew and Thomas Lewis of the Continental Congress to discuss terms of union. Also looking on were Indian agent George Morgan and Colonel Daniel Brodhead. While the particulars of the treaty were being discussed, Morgan would write, "There never was a Conference with the Indians so improperly or villainously conducted."[24]

The topics of discussion centered basically around two points. The first granted Americans the right to pass freely through Delaware territory en route to Fort Detroit; the second gave the Americans the opportunity to build a series of forts in Delaware territory. In exchange for their cooperation, the Indians would receive a vast supply of arms and supplies to suit their needs. After centuries of rule under the Imperial Iroquois Confederacy, the Delaware were not accustomed to receiving such beneficial offers directly and appeared anxious to sign.

All of these stipulations appeared to solidify a bond between the two nations, but the misleading explanations and intentionally poor translations on the part of the Americans later exposed their attempted deceptions. Most noticeable to those in attendance, many with a great deal of experience with the Delaware Nation, was that the interpreters on the American side were intentionally offering confusing, and sometimes even incorrect, translations to the sachems. Regarding the forts, the Americans explained to the Delaware that the measure would simply allow the Americans to better protect the women, children, and elders of the territory. It was under these pretenses that the sachems agreed, while the Americans fully expected the Delaware to offer their own warriors to garrison the fort and lead attacks on enemy positions. Other natives later claimed that the Americans promised postwar land grants to the Delaware with insinuations of potentially becoming a fourteenth state after independence was won. Whatever the terms of agreement, the result was monumental. Unlike previous councils, the 1778 meeting actually produced a signed document; it was the only convention to do so. Therefore the Treaty of Pittsburgh, as it came to be known, marked the first time that the United States signed a formal treaty with any Indian nation.[25]

It was a major triumph for the Americans in a year of major triumphs. Earlier in February 1778 the Continental Congress signed a formal treaty of alliance with France, and in June, George Washington's army finally left its winter quarters at Valley Forge to continue the struggle for freedom.

In the eyes of Guyasuta, during the most chaotic period in Iroquois history, the idea of a Delaware alliance with the Patriots was a direct conflict with the larger mission of the British-allied Indians of North America. The war would rage on, and in the midst of the American Rebellion the Indian peoples of the New World continued the fight for their own version of liberty and independence.

EIGHT

The Cause of His People

THE SULLIVAN–CLINTON AND BRODHEAD EXPEDITIONS AND THE BURNING OF HANNA'S TOWN, FALL 1779

The siege of Fort Stanwix was a failure. The British plan to take command of New York's frontier ended in disaster as well. When the Seneca and Mohawk left the Mohawk River valley after the Battle of Oriskany, Great Britain's fortunes suffered; while it was not an immediate result of the Iroquois' absence, they were sorely missed. General John Burgoyne's great plan to capture the colony of New York came to a screeching halt when he was defeated at the Battle of Saratoga and surrendered his army on October 17, 1777. The larger consequences of the loss played havoc on the outcome of the war.

Because of the unexpected failure of the Saratoga campaign, of which the siege of Fort Stanwix was a part, the American rebellion received a much needed shot in the arm in the form of new, profitable alliances. France had ached to avenge its loss in the Seven Years' War, and after the Americans defeated Burgoyne's men success actually seemed possible. It was only when the British were halted at Saratoga that France became fully invested in the Patriot cause. Money, weapons, and support poured into North America to aid the weak and disorganized army of George Washington, and suddenly the war turned in a new direction. The steady pace of British victories subsided and the Continental army had a chance to regain some ground. Just as the native peoples had found success by subsisting off French goods decades earlier, the Americans would now benefit from France in a similar way.

The collapse of the Saratoga campaign did not end Britain's efforts on the New York frontier, but it did alter their appearance in a drastic way. The days of marching large, drum-beating regular armies out of Canada into the region were gone; what replaced it was a uniquely American resistance set on preserving the Crown. After vacating the Mohawk River valley following the rout at Oriskany Creek, Joseph Brant and his Mohawks, along with Cornplanter and his Senecas, initiated a hard and fast series of raids across the frontier. They located Patriot villages and settlements and fell on them with harsh disregard. They initiated a war that would grant no quarter to the enemy, and from the Iroquois vantage point the more fearsome their actions, the more effective they would be.[1]

No village was safe. Whether it was a settlement of English New Yorkers, a German homestead, or even a Patriot-allied Oneida community the warriors of Brant and Cornplanter would locate and uproot it in violent fashion. It was not dissimilar to the frontier assaults of 1764–65, but unlike before when these types of raids were considered uniquely Indian ventures, they now had a contingent of prominent allies at their side. In many cases fighting alongside the Iroquois were the Loyalists of the North American continent. It was a marriage formed at the Battle of Oriskany when both the Indians and loyal Americans drew the sword against their own brothers for the first time; the fact that victory resulted only served to validate their bloody covenant. The mixing of worlds that occurred in colonial America resulted in a common community between the frontiersman and Indian, and while we usually ascribe Indian irregular warfare to the rebellious patriots, the Loyalists were a very real product of that same regional amalgam. Therefore, when the Provincials took to the trees at Braddock's defeat, and when the Virginians broke from tradition at Point Pleasant, those were tactics learned from the natives in a cultural exchange, and the

Loyalists now employed them just as effectively in 1778 as the Patriot militia.[2]

The campaigns of General Burgoyne had fallen off, but the New York frontier now belonged to the new Iroquois-Loyalist alliance. In their singular efforts the British were still successful despite the fact that their officers and Regulars operated hundreds of miles away; the campaigns of terror registered in the vast expanses of the continent were effective, and thus not unnoticed for long. In Philadelphia that summer the Continental Congress received numerous reports of how deadly the frontier raids had been, and the delegates collectively agreed that a serious discussion of Indian affairs was in order. It was out of this meeting that the need for a treaty like the one at Fort Pitt was born, and the discussions of potential military intervention in New York and the Ohio Country were first deliberated. Their actions were slow, however, and the reality that they were fighting and financing a bloody war handcuffed the congressional delegates in their ability to effectively defend the frontier. As 1778 continued, the worst was yet to come for the Patriots.

In June, three large parties of warriors came together at the Indian village of Tioga in northern Pennsylvania. They met under the auspices of the Iroquois in friendly territory to discuss plans for taking their so-far productive war effort to new heights. These representatives of three worlds would become bound together as one in a way never before thought possible. They were the Mohawks led by Brant, the Senecas under Cornplanter, and a group of Loyalists under the command of Colonel John Butler, affectionately called "Butler's Rangers." These three men were not strangers, and their collective efforts had proven deadly at Oriskany Creek. Their efforts had transformed the New York frontier into a great war zone, and Fort Niagara to the west operated as something of a home base for their raids. As they met in council, they elected to extend their reach beyond Iroquois territory and unexpectedly take the fight into the backyards of their Patriot enemies. To that point in 1778 the three parties had been largely operating independent of one another, sometimes in pairs, but never as one unified force.

John Butler was born in Connecticut and fought with great bravery on the side of the British in the Seven Years' War. He was in the fullest sense of the word a Loyalist; he believed deeply in the British Empire, which had allowed him to become one of the richest men in the colonies. Like all Loyalists he understood that Great Britain was the home of his father and grandfathers, and it was under the domain of the king that his way of life had come to dominate five continents. After giving his best years to the Seven Years' War, Butler was simply not prepared to turn his back on the love of king and country that defined him most. To this day Butler is revered for his service to the empire, and his bust is in the Valiants Memorial in Ottawa, Canada.[3]

When the three war chiefs met in council that night, they decided that the most effective way to deliver a killing blow to the Patriot war effort was to strike at the site most central to its success. As Napoleon would later affirm, an army truly did march on its stomach, and if Butler, Cornplanter, and Brant could eliminate a major supply source, they could potentially stop Washington's army in its tracks. Their target would be the breadbasket of the Continental army just south of Tioga—the nutrient rich farmlands of the Wyoming Valley.[4]

Situated in central Pennsylvania in the Susquehanna River watershed, the Wyoming Valley and its surroundings extended in all directions like a great fertile crescent of the American colonies. The lands had been settled decades earlier by English and German farmers and by 1778 its communities were well established and prosperous. With the great Allegheny Mountains to its far west as the unofficial boundary between the colony of Pennsylvania and the open frontier, the Wyoming Valley owed its fertility to the Susquehanna River and became one of the most successful agricultural centers in the New World. Its plentiful stores of wheat, grain, and livestock fed much of the American East Coast, and it supplied Washington's armies with as much foodstuff as any other region.[5]

An attack on the Wyoming Valley would send a strong message to the Americans, no doubt, but the area was not without its pitfalls. The Patriots had established a number of posts throughout the valley, many directly within reach of the Iroquois-Loyalists. To make a maneuver on such a high-value target as the Wyoming Valley would require stealth and surprise, but it was certainly possible. The likely immediate damage was enticing, but the eventual chaos forced the decision to strike.

By June 30 Butler's Loyalists had descended southward into the Wyoming Valley and caught the entire region off guard. His first order of business was to establish a base in the area, and after locating a small fortification called Wintermute he promptly settled himself there. The post was a local militia stronghold, and Butler and the Iroquois took control rather easily after allowing its occupants to go freely as long as they vowed to never pick up a rifle in anger again. The militia soon surrendered their stores and supplies, and Butler began the implementation of his new campaign.[6]

With this forceful action the Iroquois-Loyalists announced their presence in the Wyoming Valley, and only days later a local Patriot militia force had begun to congregate for retaliation at the small post called Forty Fort just a short distance away. Sensing that the operation was under his control, Butler offered no resistance when Joseph Brant and his Mohawk began raiding settlements far north of their position, and he was confident that Cornplanter and the Seneca were sufficient to see the job through. As the invaders collected intelligence on the enemy force that had collected in response to their arrival, the British began to formulate a strategy to deal with this latest threat.

The purpose of their invasion was not to keep or even hold any territory, it was merely to seek and destroy. All that Butler and Cornplanter sought to do was to ruin the Wyoming Valley, but they saw no tactical value in retaining it. If they were to have a showdown with the local Patriot force that amassed at Forty Fort, it would be a lose-lose situation for the Iroquois-Loyalists, as the only prize of such a battle was the land itself, which held no value for them. Instead of marching on the much weaker, impromptu Patriot column, Butler and Cornplanter elected to fall back on the same strategy that they used a year earlier at Oriskany: ambush.[7]

The Seneca located a position that was just outside the Loyalist base at Fort Wintermute and between it and the Patriot Forty Fort. Once there, they promptly disguised themselves from view and awaited the approach of their unsuspecting enemies. To draw the militia toward them, Butler had ordered that his Rangers burn Fort Wintermute to feign retreat; to do so was no major loss because the fort would be abandoned soon after anyway. With the smoke rising in the distance on July 3, the unsuspicious Yankees ran toward the blaze under the pretense that their enemy had miraculously begun to flee. As the Patriots ran, excited by this sudden turn of events, they were within one hundred yards of Butler's Loyalists when they unknowingly fell into the arms of Cornplanter's Iroquois.

The fighting was intense, but it was never competitive. For over forty-five minutes the untrained Patriot militia tried to adapt to the irregular strikes of the Iroquois, but they could never manage a tenable battle line. The Iroquois soon fell on their enemies with tomahawks swinging, and the Patriots fled in a chaotic and messy retreat. Though it was a triumph for Butler's Rangers, the Iroquois had not yet achieved what they considered a satisfactory victory; of the original three hundred Patriots that engaged the Indians, sixty managed to escape the encounter. Only five men were taken prisoner, and Butler estimated himself that there were nearly two hundred and thirty scalps taken that day.

The following morning, with the only defensive force of the Wyoming Valley vanquished, Butler and his Rangers moved southward to accept the surrender of the exposed Forty Fort and all the men inside. Despite the brutality of the campaign, Butler took great pride in the fact that all of the men that capitulated were spared: "what gives me the sincerest satisfaction is that I can, with great truth, assure you that in the destruction of the settlement not a single person was hurt except such as were in arms, to these, in truth, the Indians gave no quarter."[8]

The Wyoming Valley campaign had pleased British administrators in Canada and it was viewed as a surprising adjunct to their overall strategy, but across the thirteen colonies it was seen very differently. News spread quickly of how devastated the American militiamen had been, and by 1778 the prejudiced opinion of Indian attacks had deeply permeated the American consciousness. Even in the face of the irrefutable evidence that the Iroquois had spared the forces captured at Forty Fort, the campaign was still labeled the Wyoming Valley Massacre.[9]

This misleading title led to brutal and intense retaliations in central Pennsylvania by angry settlers seeking revenge. Two months after the initial Iroquois-Loyalist invasion, a militant force led by Thomas Hartley of York raided and burned a dozen Indian villages, citing the Wyoming Valley Massacre as their primary motive. Despite the fact that the Seneca and Cayuga had been the primary combatants in the Wyoming attack, Hartley's men targeted settlements of Delaware and Mingo that had had nothing to do with the assault. It was combat fueled by intolerance on both sides, and as usual, justice was the first casualty.

After the smoke had settled along the Susquehanna River, John Butler and his Loyalist Rangers continued their crusade against Patriot homesteads in the Mohawk Valley. In accord, American militia leaders William Butler and John Cantine reacted by destroying the Loyalist villages of Onaquaga and Unadilla in southern New York. What had begun as a tactical raid spiraled out of control into a regional conflict, and the outcome was a frontier divided and ready to explode. While the actions of the parties provided the tinder, it was the steady campaign of misinformation and sensationalism that ignited the blaze. One of the figures caught in the middle of the erroneous yarns woven that fall was Joseph Brant. Although Brant was not present at the Wyoming Valley invasion, most white settlers in the east and west claimed that he had been at the center of the entire venture. It was untrue, and, even worse, the Indians were accused of savagely murdering their prisoners at Forty Fort, where no captives had been taken, much less harmed in any way.

Angry and enraged by the perceived ignorance of the Patriot rumors, Brant convinced himself that no action could clear his name, and his only recourse was to exceed his now infamous reputation of brutality himself. Brant soon joined Walter Butler, the son of John, along with three hundred Seneca under Cornplanter for yet another offensive against the New York countryside. Joining them this time was a party of fifty soldiers from the British 8th Regiment of Foot, and their target was a Patriot position in a vast countryside called Cherry Valley.

On the cold morning of November 10, Brant and Butler led their army in a clandestine approach toward the Cherry Valley post and the thirty homes that surrounded it. When the joint Anglo-Iroquois force fell on the targeted fortification, its commandant was killed while running from a nearby house. After the Seneca gained access to the tiny outpost, they killed the men inside without hesitation. With the strong house firmly in their hands, the young Butler and his troops stood guard while Cornplanter's warriors turned their attention to the households nearby.

The Seneca tore through the town, and as they had done many times before, the Loyalists stood by as their allies burned down homes. What they had not anticipated, however, was what the Iroquois did with the noncombatants that they captured in the process. In one of the most brutal events of the entire American Revolution, Butler and the Loyalists stood frozen as the Seneca murdered the women and children of the Cherry Valley. By the time that they realized the full intention of the Seneca, the Loyalists were powerless to stop the slaughter. In all, fourteen American militiamen and as many as thirty women and children were killed. For the entire summer of 1778 the Patriot frontier filled its taverns with overdone stories of senseless murder and carnage, and in November at Cherry Valley the Iroquois gave them their massacre.[10]

By the spring of 1779, the news of the Wyoming and Cherry Valley massacres had shaken the Patriot world, and proven to policy makers in Philadelphia and General George Washington that action needed to be taken. The maneuvers of the Iroquois and Loyalists in New York and Pennsylvania had convinced Washington that victory would not be possible without the elimination of their ever-present threat, and a strategy was soon devised to neutralize them. At the heart of his native opponents' success, Washington believed, was their penchant for war and need for goods, and his past experiences gave him more than enough evidence to justify a directed assault against them. While he gave the Iroquois much of the credit for the raids that they and Butler had instigated, he never doubted that they would fade away without British support. While Brant and Cornplanter were sturdy and daring leaders, Washington concluded that Fort Niagara was their great lifeline; if the post on Lake Ontario could be captured, the allied-Iroquois would have no choice but to capitulate.[11]

The expedition that he devised would never take its collective eye off Fort Niagara, but its overall effect would be measured by how much damage could be done to the Seneca, Cayuga, Onondaga, and Mohawk. The march would be two-pronged, designed to leave from two points simultaneously—Easton, along the Susquehanna, and Pittsburgh, along the Allegheny— and each force would demolish all the Iroquois settlements that they could find. If possible, when both teams accomplished their initial goal, they could combine in New York to make one great charge at Fort Niagara. After some deliberation and much correspondence, General Washington found the men that would lead such a dangerous expedition in the form of the thick-skinned officers John Sullivan and Daniel Brodhead. Washington wrote the following letter to Sullivan before his campaign:

> The Expedition you are appointed to command is to be directed against the hostile tribes of the Six Nations of Indians, with their associates and adherents. The immediate objects are the total destruction and devastation of their settlements, and the capture of as many prisoners of every age and sex as possible. It will be essential to ruin their crops now in the ground and prevent their planting more.
>
> I would recommend, that some post in the center of the Indian Country, should be occupied with all expedition, with a sufficient quantity of provisions whence parties should be detached to lay waste all the settlements around, with instructions to do it in the most effectual manner, that the country may not be merely overrun, but destroyed.
>
> But you will not by any means listen to any overture of peace before the total ruinment of their settlements is effected. Our future security will be in their inability to injure us and in the terror with which the severity of the chastisement they receive will inspire them.[12]

On June 18, General John Sullivan and a force of four thousand men began their march northward along the Susquehanna River. With his orders in tow, and total war on the docket, Sullivan wrote to General James Clinton in Schenectady, New York, that he should lead a brigade of men from his current posi-

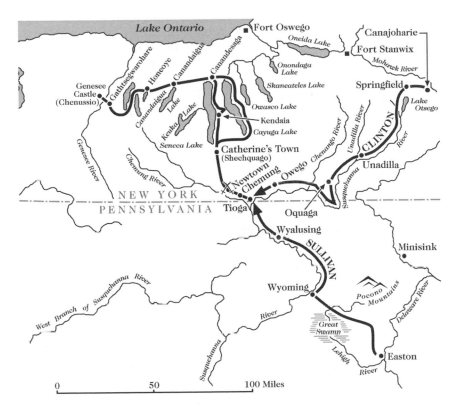

The Sullivan–Clinton Expedition, 1779.

tion through the Mohawk Valley. When Sullivan worked his way closer, Clinton was to turn suddenly south and meet him at Otsego Lake. Along the way Sullivan suggested that Clinton burn and destroy any Iroquois villages that he could find. Sullivan's march was long and slow from the beginning and by June 23 they had only moved fifty miles. Sullivan set up a post in the Wyoming Valley to await supplies and was delayed there until July 31.

For another fourteen days they marched, and after arriving in New York they established a forward base of operations dubbed "Fort Sullivan." Their initial target was the Indian village of Chemung, and after gathering some intelligence they were surprised to find it completely abandoned. Regardless of the news, Sullivan sent his troops to the site to raze the village and its supplies; his mission was to destroy the Iroquois settlements, not the Iroquois themselves. En route his party was ambushed but the attack was only a minor impediment. Later that day Sullivan's men left Chemung in ruins and its supporting grain fields ablaze. Victory came at the point of a sword for Sullivan, and unfortunately for the natives his reign of terror had just begun in Iroquoia.[13]

General John Sullivan took his army of four thousand across the Finger Lakes of New York, and penetrated the Genesee River valley, leaving scorched earth in his wake. As the ancestral home of Guyasuta and Cornplanter, the Genesee was a staggering loss for the Iroquois. In a great strategic blow, the Americans could now subsist on the foodstuffs left behind by the warriors. When Sullivan's expedition had consumed their fill, they simply burned whatever precious grains and crops remained in their wake. By the arrival of winter, as Sullivan turned his forces back toward New Jersey, more than forty Iroquois towns had been reduced to rubble.

Across the Allegheny Mountains, while Sullivan cut a path of destruction across New York, the second component of Washington's great annihilation of the Iroquois began to take hold. Led by Colonel Daniel Brodhead, the commandant of Fort Pitt, the other half of the expedition was anxious to engage their native foes. Unlike Sullivan's men in the east, Brodhead's soldiers had been posted in the heart of the hostile frontier for months. While those on the other side of the mountains knew of Indian attacks only in spurts, dubbed "massacres," Brodhead and his Pittsburghers lived with it on a daily basis. The colonel wrote regularly to General Washington regarding his feelings toward the Iroquois, and he was not one to mince words. Brodhead wrote: "It would give me great pleasure to make one grand push against the Mingos . . . who will not and ought not be treated with but at the point of the Bayonet."[14]

Brodhead, a surly man, was a product of the Pennsylvania frontier. He had grown up on a homestead that was regularly attacked by Indians, and his service in the military was already stellar. He fought at the Battle of Long Island, and wintered with Washington at Valley Forge. The general trusted him, and for Brodhead, to deliver a devastating blow to the natives around Fort Pitt seemed like a genuine pleasure.

Before embarking in Aug-
ust 1779 Brodhead wrote of
the Mingo-Seneca that he
would "revenge the past, to
carry the war into their own
country, and strike a decisive
blow at their towns." This was
a particularly bold plan considering the importance that
his intended targets had
among the Ohio Indians.
Among their great sachems
was Guyasuta, and although
he had long rescinded his
Mingo identity for his Seneca
roots, he still held a great
affection for his former people. This mission would not
be for the faint of heart;
Brodhead's expedition would

The Brodhead Expedition, 1779.

need to completely eliminate the Mingo-Seneca to be successful,
otherwise the subsequent retaliation would be hellish for frontier settlers.[15]

Brodhead's expedition left Pittsburgh with over six hundred
men, whose first true engagement came days later at the mouth
of French Creek. The lopsided battle saw the Americans surprise
a Seneca hunting party and kill several of them; no Americans
died. Continuing northward up the valley, Brodhead encountered surprisingly little resistance as most of the communities'
warriors were at war in other parts of the colony. The uncontested damage wrought by the mission was catastrophic for the
Mingo-Seneca people. At the village of Yoghroonwago alone the
Americans destroyed over one hundred and thirty houses and
almost five hundred acres of crops. The villages of Conewago,
Buckaloon, and Mahusquechikoken were subsequently left in a
similar state . . . burned to the ground.

For Guyasuta this expedition was an unexpected and terrible
turn of events. He knew that the people in those villages were
noncombatants, and the most helpless among them. Women

and children charged only with collecting grain were suddenly thrust into the heat of battle with no recourse. Brodhead's men forced them to flee into the forests, and their homes were razed before their eyes. The fields that they had planted and nurtured for months were set on fire, and the vital sustenance that they supplied would be left as smoldering embers.

Between the cumulative efforts of Sullivan, Clinton, and Brodhead, Iroquoia had been left a wasteland. From the beginning of the Seven Years' War to 1779, the homeland of the Iroquois had been unmolested, and now retribution for decades of frontier raids came in the form of utter destruction. The Iroquois were devastated by the raids not just in their ability to wage war but in their ability to survive. The food that they had grown in their villages was supposed to last them for the entire winter, and stood as the one bit of sustenance that they had not relied on trade with the Europeans to acquire. With those precious grain stores wiped out, the destruction wrought by the Patriot raids would be felt for months. Hundreds stood to die of starvation alone, and an entire population teetered on the brink of annihilation.

It was everything that General Washington could have hoped for regarding the British-allied Iroquois. They would no longer be able to wage war against the Americans, and even the Loyalists who lived and fought among them began to flee to the safety of Canada. The campaign of terror that had defined the frontier for the previous two years seemed to have ended, and a Patriot victory in the war was beginning to look possible. This sudden turn in his favor came at the expense of hundreds of Iroquois families, but war required difficult decisions. In 1753 as a young man Washington trekked the corridor of the Allegheny River himself with Guyasuta at his side. He knew those villages and saw their inhabitants; twenty-five years later the fact that they were now gone signaled a major victory in a war that the twenty-one-year-old Washington could have never imagined. A boastful Brodhead wrote to Washington after his return to Fort Pitt: "I have happy presage that the counties of Westmoreland, Bedford, & Northumberland, if not the whole western Frontiers will experience the good effect of it."[16]

Even with the unfortunate reality that Fort Niagara was never attacked and remained a Loyalist stronghold, Brodhead and

Sullivan still managed to besiege the critical post on Lake Ontario. The winter of 1779 had quickly descended on the American frontier, one of the coldest on record in North America. The combined lack of foodstuffs caused by the Patriot scorched-earth campaign and the harshness of the wintery conditions caused a massive refugee crisis among the Iroquois, and hundreds of men and women funneled toward Superintendent of Indian Affairs Guy Johnson.

Making his winter quarters at Fort Niagara, Johnson estimated that nearly one-third of all Iroquois on the continent had lost their entire livelihood as a result of the Sullivan/Brodhead campaign. He was in as good a position to make such an assertion as anyone because with the snowfall came the bulk of the starving families seeking aid. The winter of 1779 saw the fort filled with hungry and desperate people, all of them believing that Johnson would be the solution to their problems. While the terrible scene was viewed as a regrettable side effect of the Patriot victory, the image of Fort Niagara depleting its own supplies to feed the huddled masses was well worth the damage.[17]

There was, however, a great casualty of the 1779 campaign, owing to it being such a general and violent measure, that many Patriots did not care to notice. As Sullivan made his way across New York, he paid little attention to which Iroquois villages he burned. He measured his success in destruction, and along the way he inflicted irreversible losses indiscriminately across Iroquoia. While the British-allied Seneca, Cayuga, Onondaga, and Mohawk all suffered for their actions, the American allied Iroquois, like the Oneida and Tuscarora, also felt the brunt of the attacks. For this reason, the majority of the warriors that had attached themselves to the Americans switched their alliance to the British. Although some ventured to the unwelcoming Patriot post at Fort Stanwix, most humbly filed into Fort Niagara with the rest of their Iroquois brethren.

Along with the scores of refugees at Fort Niagara that winter were the chiefs that had led the Iroquois into battle with the Loyalists, most notably Joseph Brant, Cornplanter, and Guyasuta. Their people had sought sanctuary there, and the war chiefs themselves joined them in their plight, although sources indicate that the leaders were much more comfortable at Fort

Niagara than most of their lesser tribesmen. Brant was given a royal stipend every week that he largely kept for himself and his family, though technically it was meant to be distributed among the Mohawk that he represented.[18]

During this great period of desperation along Lake Ontario, Guyasuta passionately pleaded for assistance in avenging the attacks on his people. Johnson was aware of how much havoc had been caused, but he remained steadfast in his position that no militia or Regulars could be spared to avenge the loss of Guyasuta's Mingo-Seneca villages. Johnson's position had toed the royal line, and the idea that a quick British victory would be the best way to end the Iroquois' hardships was not one that Guyasuta ascribed to easily. He wanted retribution immediately for the American campaign against his people, but it would never come in the way he sought. The reality was that after the 1779 campaigns the Iroquois would never regain their prowess and never implement meaningful war on the frontier again. Johnson may have recognized this in part, but the the ramifications are only visible to historians in hindsight. The Loyalist-Iroquois story of the American Revolution effectively ended that winter at Fort Niagara, and any subsequent success that Guyasuta, Cornplanter, or Brant would have would be regional at best.

Guyasuta had spent his life listening to the promises of equality in partnership from European powers, and in his younger years he had allowed them to dictate his own actions. But now as a fifty-five-year-old sachem he scoffed at the naiveté of his youth. His body bore the scars of allegiance to France, and his once-great people were now reduced to begging as a result of their allegiance to Britain. Now in the twilight of his life, Guyasuta would have recognized that the fight was reserved for younger men, but his efforts could still be effective in a diplomatic capacity. When the winter ended in 1780 he left Fort Niagara and sought to influence change in his own ways in the Ohio Country.[19]

For the remainder of 1780, Guyasuta visited the villages of the Ohio Country on what could best be described as a morale boosting tour. Before leaving Fort Niagara, Guy Johnson had indicated that Guyasuta would be best served holding council with the various nations of the region to express Johnson's commitment to their cause, and to reassure them that the British Empire was still concerned about their interests. Considering the circumstances on the continent, that story was becoming increasingly difficult to sustain. To their south, George Rogers Clark had captured the British stronghold of Vincennes in the Illinois Country for the second time, and the French had thrown their full support behind the American cause. Shortly after, Spain had declared war on Great Britain, and "Mad" Anthony Wayne routed the forces of King George at Stony Point, New York.

Despite the bad news accumulating for the British, and the dwindling hope that the American rebellion could be stifled early, Guyasuta continued to take his message of staying the course through the Indian villages of the Ohio. As Half-King, he was still respected and his services in the defense of the Ohio Indians from decades past still kept him in high regard. At Fort Niagara Johnson had hoped that the old sachem would be able to rally the Indians together at Fort Detroit, but as Guyasuta soon discovered, that would be nearly impossible.

For much of 1780, the major war chiefs of the Ohio Country who would have had to sign off on a conference as big as Johnson planned were far from their homelands. While the Wyandot still maintained a stout presence, most of the warriors from the region were in Kentucky doing battle with Patriot forces in the mountainous forests. Although he was ambitious, Guyasuta's campaign in the Ohio River valley largely fell on deaf ears. Among the native peoples there was a developing sense that victory was still in sight, but they would need to act more independently of their British allies to find it.

Under these pretenses Guyasuta led approximately thirty anxious Wyandot warriors against the forward operating base of Fort McIntosh, some thirty miles north of Fort Pitt along the Ohio River. Fort McIntosh had become an experimental post that was part of a larger design to fortify a route toward Fort Detroit. While it was only a starting point, and few additional forts would actually be constructed, Fort McIntosh had proven to be a valuable asset to the Continental army and could hold a garrison of a thousand men. By the summer, the news coming from the east was not promising. In May, the British had captured Charleston, South Carolina, and defeated the Patriots handily at Ramsour's Mill, North Carolina. When Guyasuta took his recently acquired warrior party to Fort McIntosh, their raid was a brief one; the damage may have been minor, but it reminded the Americans that the Ohioans were still a significant threat.

Following a winter break, Guyasuta took to the diplomatic trail again in 1781, but soon found that the willingness of his spirit was simply not enough to overcome the weakness of his own body. Falling ill, Guyasuta was sidelined for much of the year at Cattaraugus in western New York. Though he was not out on the trail, the revolutionary world continued to turn; in his absence the delicately balanced Ohio Country was beginning to feel the strains of American victory. The largest portion of the fighting in the East was now focused in the South, and already the Patriots had tallied stirring victories at the Battles of Cowpens and Cowan's Ford. In the American South the possibility of the tide turning in their favor had emboldened Washington's men, but in the Ohio Country that same sense of joy could not have seemed farther away.

Only months earlier, in the fall of 1780, Colonel Daniel Brodhead had received correspondence at Fort Pitt alerting him to an impending crisis with the Delaware of the region. Since signing the Treaty of Fort Pitt two years earlier, the Delaware had grasped onto an unstable alliance with the Americans despite the fact that their fellow Ohioans had joined the Loyalist cause. In the face of increasing pressure from the Indian nations around them, the Delaware were primed to break their vow of cooperation and wage war against the Patriots. Brodhead received a letter that winter from the village of Coshocton stating: "I am so much mocked at by the Enemy Ind's for speaking so long to them for You. Now they laugh at me, and ask me where that great Army of my Brothers, that was to come out against them so long ago, and so often, stays so long. . . . They further desire me to tell You now to make haste and come soon, the sooner, and the greater Your Number the better."[20]

For the length of the war Coshocton had been the most prominent Delaware village in the Ohio Country, and the fact that it was now preparing its warriors to align with the British was a defeat that Brodhead could not endure. Therefore, after waiting out the worst of the winter, Brodhead prepared his men for a strategic preventive strike against the unruly Delaware village.[21] In April 1781, the colonel organized an expedition to travel to Coshocton along the Tuscarawas River and punish the Delaware himself. Because he was acting alone, without the aid of the Continental Congress or Pennsylvania, Brodhead ordered the march out of Pittsburgh of his own volition. Knowing that his men had so few provisions, he was certain that the Delaware had even less.

Brodhead's militiamen utterly devastated the village of Coshocton, taking prisoners and burning acres of crops in a replay of the scorched earth campaign he had led against the Iroquois two years earlier. Despite the fact that the colonel wanted to execute all the Delaware warriors of the region, his men persuaded him otherwise and they began their return trip to Pittsburgh. Only weeks later, Daniel Brodhead was officially relieved of duty. It was a shocking blow that reverberated throughout the Ohio Country, and it was soon followed by an act so heinous that the region would be damaged beyond repair.

For most the revolutionary era, the Delaware of the Ohio Country were deeply divided regarding which side they would support. As the war progressed, many of the warriors went their separate ways; while the British allies made the long trek to Fort Detroit, the American supporters remained at the village of Coshocton. This seemed to have kept the Delaware balanced between the two worlds, but it was not sustainable or practical. As the Delaware leaned more toward total collusion with the British, many of the noncombatants among them found a welcome home in the Moravian missionary towns spread throughout the Ohio Country. These villages were open, welcoming places established by Europeans for the purposes of spreading the tenets of the Moravian Church, and though they were still in a hostile environment, it was as close to neutrality as many of the Delaware could find.

In 1781, a month before Cornwallis's surrender and five months after Brodhead's destruction of Coshocton, the peaceful Christianized Delaware who resided in the religious havens of the Ohio Country were forced to follow their tribal leaders to British territory to the North. By that point, the Delaware had thrown their full support behind the Crown and in the opinion of the Indian partisans there was no place for neutral villages. That September Delaware and Wyandot warriors marched on the religious outposts and forcefully relocated their Indian inhabitants to their new homes along the Sandusky River on Lake Erie. It was a flagrant use of power against the weakest members, but it was done largely in the interest of their own safety.

Meanwhile, on October 19, 1781, on the Yorktown Peninsula in the colony of Virginia, Charles O'Hara, an officer serving with General Charles Cornwallis, surrendered his commander's sword to Benjamin Lincoln, a general on George Washington's staff. This event marks a convenient endpoint to the American Revolution; Washington gets his victory, and America waves its flag proudly over a defeated imperial army. While it is true that celebrations were under way in Boston, New York, Philadelphia, and Virginia's Chesapeake coast, the frontier found little solace in those distant events.

During the blustery winter of 1781–82, the Christianized Delaware were feeling the effects of their forced removal six months earlier. Although they remained with their families, the crops that they had grown to sustain themselves through the season were left in their original villages to the south. The people were starving, and there were almost no authorities to keep them in this place far from home. With nothing to feed their children, many decided to return to the old villages to harvest their crops and promptly return with their stores resupplied. In all one hundred men, women, and children began the long hike back to their old residences in the sanctuary of their vacant settlements.

It did not take long, however, for the realities of the war-torn Ohio Country to catch up with them. Before they could reach their unharvested fields, a party of one hundred and sixty Pennsylvania militiamen crossed their path on March 8, 1782, under the command of Lieutenant Colonel David Williamson. Williamson's men had been assembled in hasty fashion after a series of Indian raids farther east, and they sought only revenge in the swiftest form possible. The Pennsylvanians had been on the hunt for the Indians that killed their neighbors and burned their homes for several days, and with no warriors in sight it became clear that *any* Indians would suffice. The Christian Delaware were quickly surrounded and gave themselves willingly to the heavily armed militia; there were no weapons among them.

The Pennsylvanians detained the Delaware crudely and voted unanimously to kill their captives. After the meeting ended, some of the troops joyfully informed the prisoners of their fate, and the witnesses say that the Delaware prayed and sobbed for the remainder of the night. While the Pennsylvanians attempted to sleep in their camp, they were kept awake by the Delaware singing hymns in the cold darkness of the forest; many of the hymns were the same ones that the militia themselves sang in their own churches back east.[22]

The next morning Williamson's men awoke to find that some members of their party had left the camp to protest killing the Delaware, but that development was not enough to stop those that remained. As planned, the Pennsylvanians bound the Delaware by their hands and feet, and clubbed them repeatedly on the head with a heavy mallet. With their prisoners stunned, the soldiers completed the execution by scalping them in brutal fashion with enough force to kill them. Two victims survived, and their account stands as the best description of the event known as the Gnadenhutten Massacre.[23]

In total, the Pennsylvanians murdered twenty-eight men, twenty-nine women, and thirty-nine children that day. Their mutilated bodies were piled up, burned, and buried in a mass grave; their village was plundered and set on fire as well. The spoils of the victory were so great the Pennsylvanians needed eight horses to carry it home.

By July 1782 Guyasuta had found himself at a crossroads. For the previous five years he had operated in accord with the larger alliance that the Seneca had maintained with the British Empire, but despite his efforts he had yet to be convinced that the cause of his people had truly benefited from that difficult and uneven relationship. The Iroquois had spilled blood in the name of suppressing the American rebellion in order to reap the rewards promised to them in the event of peace, but the British had been unwilling to do the same in the name of their native allies. Sullivan's and Brodhead's campaigns presented the British with an opportunity to stand mutually with the Iroquois to defend Indian rights, and they declined in a cold and passive manner; the Gnadenhutten Massacre therefore was the last straw.

Guyasuta had argued passionately for British assistance after the destructive raids of 1779 and he received no help; following the events at Gnadenhutten, however, he was determined to have his voice heard. After enlisting the aid of approximately sixty soldiers from the King's 8th Regiment of Foot out of Fort Niagara, the fifty-eight-year-old sachem prepared for a devastating assault on the second largest town in all of the Ohio Country. Joining him were one hundred Mingo and Seneca warriors, and his target was the Patriot foothold called Hannastown.

Guyasuta had vowed to himself following the winter of 1779 that he would continue the struggle for Indian sovereignty with or without British assistance, and as the Crown had begun preliminary peace discussions with the Americans following the defeat at Yorktown, it now appeared that an independent operation was his only choice.

In July 13, 1782, the Indian warriors and their modest band of Redcoat allies moved stealthily southward down the Allegheny River from Lake Chautauqua, New York. The chief directed the men to Kittanning, where they abandoned their canoes so as not to draw attention. Guyasuta was well aware that their target was best attacked on foot. The soldiers, who were mostly Loyalists, were making their own statement with this attack; having sworn an allegiance to the Crown they had lost everything with American independence.

The impending attack on Hannastown was a last stand for both sides, and even the Loyalists were defiantly painted in the colors of their Iroquois allies. Their target was chosen deliberately for its Patriot roots. Founded in 1773 along the Forbes Road, Hannastown was built by Pennsylvanians in response to the Virginia-based monopoly over the town of Pittsburgh. It had been home to many of the pre-revolutionary stirrings that led to the rebellion, and the meetings that took place there even produced their own document of defiance toward the Crown a full year before the Declaration of Independence was ever penned. The town stood as a great symbol of the new America in the Ohio Country, and to Guyasuta it was representative of the style of expansion that had forced his people off their own lands.[24]

Marching approximately forty miles through the night, Guyasuta's joint Anglo-Indian force came within striking distance of the site. But the party was spotted a mile north of Hannastown and—as the party was in full war paint, an unmistakable warning to the people of the frontier—the alarm was sounded. Sheriff Matthew Jack frantically ushered the citizens into the meager fort that protected the town, and by the time the full extent of the attack had come almost sixty people were huddled within its walls.[25]

The fighting lasted the entire day, and though only one citizen was killed, the destruction wrought was the worst ever on an American settlement on the frontier. In total over thirty homes, several dozen acres of crops, and the county jail were left as smoking piles of ashen rubble. The warriors slaughtered more than one hundred head of cattle and plundered all available ammunition and horses. With revenge in his heart over the villages of his people burned by Brodhead's campaign three years earlier, Guyasuta had orchestrated the most complete Indian victory of the American Revolution; the city of Hannastown would never be rebuilt, and its ruins would be lost to history. This absolute eradication of the Ohio County's second most important settlement would be one of the last major battles of the Revolutionary War.[26]

In this final act, Guyasuta had made his great statement on behalf of the Iroquois and Ohioans whom he had spent his life defending. For all intents and purposes the British-Patriot war was over, and the Americans were already celebrating their prospective independence. If viewed in that manner, the burning of Hannastown was entirely unnecessary; the war was long behind men like George Washington and Thomas Jefferson. But Guyasuta was not trying to further the Loyalist cause or weaken the rebellion, he was making a profound statement in the heart of the frontier that the Indian war extended far beyond that. As the young men around him celebrated their victory, both Iroquois and Loyalist alike, Guyasuta grew tired; in camp he rested, and sleep had finally come, but peace for Indians remained a distant dream.[27]

In 1783, an ocean away from the Ohio Country, delegates of the new United States of America, and those from France and Spain, met with representatives of King George III, sovereign of Great Britain, to decide the terms of peace that would create the first modern republic in over two thousand years. According to the agreement, the United States of America was given a parcel of land more than twice the size of the American colonies that extended as far west as the Mississippi River, as far south as Florida, and as far north as the Great Lakes. France would be rewarded with profitable fishing rights off the Canadian coast, and with acquisitions in the form of the Caribbean island of Tobago and the African territory of Senegal. Spain, for its meager efforts, was given the territories of East and West Florida.

The Treaty of Paris was a rousing success for the enemies of the Crown, and with the signing of that agreement the world that Britain created after the Seven Years' War unceremoniously disintegrated into the ashes of history. Despite the joy felt in those victorious empires after the American Revolution, few stopped to consider the nations left out of the treaty. On the frontier of North America the continent's Indian peoples had never participated in any treaty, and they never agreed to peace. To them, whether they were Iroquois, Ohioan, or Cherokee, the war that they waged for the last twenty years was far from over. They battled expansion and for their own territorial rights; the betrayal of the Treaty of Paris was only magnified when the British signed over to the Americans what little land the Indians had left east of the Mississippi.

With the agreement, the Revolutionary Era that began at the end of the Seven Years' War came to a close. If the Indians were to continue their struggle, they would be left to their own devices, as never again would a rival empire trample through the wilderness of North America to enlist their services in the manner that defined the period. For two centuries if one European empire proved distasteful to the Indians, there was always an alternative, but now that system had ended. Competition was gone from the frontier, and so too were all its shared benefits. If the Indian nations were to resist expansion and seek a return to a world long since lost, they would have to do so as a unified force, and disregard their tribal differences. There was now only one obstacle to achieving this dream: the United States of America.

NINE

He Wonders at His Own Shadow

THE UNITED STATES OF AMERICA AND THE NORTHWEST INDIAN WAR, 1793

In April 1793, as the waters of the Ohio River flowed by briskly, Guyasuta wondered at the sight before him. As a young man he had marveled at the river's capacity to take him to distant places, and he rode its tides as far south as Kentucky decades earlier. But now the river was different; its colors shone less brightly, and its destination had changed dramatically. For most of his life the Ohio River was a haven, a great passageway away from the troubles of the politically turbulent east to the peaceful solitude of the west. It had always been on his side, and it seemed sometimes that its currents rushed by on his behalf.

It was remarkable how forty years could change even the Ohio River. Before him, on that same waterway that he idolized in his youth now floated the most impressively destructive military force ever conceived in the history of North America. An American army over two thousand men strong was solely committed to exterminating the Ohioan way of life. He knew that it would accomplish its goal, there was no doubt of that, but what surprised him most at the age of seventy was how little he cared. It was not a sense of helplessness; he had felt that before. This was a sense of apathy that only came with old age.

Guyasuta had given up fighting his battles with musket and tomahawk years earlier, and he was resigned to the fact that the only war he fought now was against his own body. Yet, as the American force sailed beyond his vision, he could not help but consider the totality of his own life's battles. Had they been reduced to this? The Ohioans that were rebelling against the American states were winning battles, but the war that they waged was destined to fail. They could have pursued another route; his nephew was waging his own diplomatic struggle in New York, and Guyasuta fully supported him. Was violence, though, the only means to achieve their ends?

He did not have the answer. His life had become one of stability and relative comfort on his small camp outside Pittsburgh. He remembered the Forks of the Ohio when only the forest claimed it as its own, when the French brought their war to his home, and also the moment when he realized that his world changed forever with the completion of Fort Pitt. Out of that great struggle emerged a city, and a nation, and regardless of his feelings toward them, Pittsburgh was now his home. As he turned back toward his camp, his mind slipped away from the aches and pains that came with each step and remembered a time when he walked tall. The years had taken their toll, and Guyasuta could not help but feel that the new war being waged was merely a continuation of his own.

In October 1784, a year after the signing of the Treaty of Paris, delegates of the newly confederated United States of America met in treaty with the Iroquois Confederacy at Fort Stanwix in central New York. While they had come to terms with their European enemies, the Americans had never formally ratified peace among the Six Nations. Present were the men that so feverishly battled against the Patriots during the revolution and it was those same war chiefs that spoke on behalf of their people. Joseph Brant began the proceedings by reaffirming that "we must observe to you, that we are sent in order to make peace, and that we are not authorized, to stipulate any particular cession of lands."[1]

In this regard Brant was correct. As much as the Americans pressed the Iroquois to give up strategic parcels of their ancestral territory, the Six Nations remained far too divided to ever give any one sachem enough power to make such a concession. The Mohawk chief soon left the days-long council, and much of the diplomatic process was taken over by the Seneca Cornplanter. The only charge that any of the natives were given by their fellow chieftains was to negotiate peace with the new United States, and at the (second) Treaty of Fort Stanwix that mission was accomplished. Although the result was promising for the American delegates at Fort Stanwix, the long spell of combat that preceded it had left the traditional power of the Iroquois in shambles, and whatever terms they agreed to other than a cessation of hostilities were not likely to hold much weight in their former territories.

Three months later in the Ohio Country, the Americans continued their expedition to gain territory through peace negotiations with delegations of the Ohio Indians at Fort McIntosh along the Ohio River. This council, held in January 1785, sought territorial concessions and negotiated peace with members of the Wyandot, Delaware, Chippewa, and Ottawa. The parties agreed that the Indians would give up their claims east of the Cuyahoga River, and it too was viewed as a resounding success.[2]

The issue that the Americans failed to recognize while signing such simple and superficial agreements was that the landscape of Indian America had changed. Since the end of the American Revolution treaties like the ones signed at Fort Stanwix and Fort McIntosh were simply not viable due to the fact that the traditional channels of power used to create social and political hierarchies among the Indians had vanished. The Iroquois no longer held sway over the Ohioans, and in the absence of a regular British presence the Great Lakes peoples had greatly intermingled in the affairs of the nations to their east. As new lands in Kentucky and Illinois opened for settlement, their sachems had established a regular presence in the Ohio Country; just as the definition of "American" changed after the Treaty of Paris, so had the identity of "Indian."

Suddenly one's tribal affiliation paled in comparison to one's political persuasion among the native peoples of North America.

While during the Revolutionary Era it would be relatively rare for a warrior to break free from the traditional treaties signed by his tribal elders, the singular threat posed by the United States had allowed that to change. If an individual was deeply attached to honoring the agreements of his people he was able to do so, but if a warrior party felt strongly against it they would be welcomed readily in another group that was more in line with their own sentiments. In this new North America one's actions relied on a village or social affiliation more than tribal heritage.

In the face of these recent developments, the treaties signed by the Americans became deeply divisive issues in council fires across the Ohio Country, and a new movement had begun to stir that would alter the region and the nation forever. While the men that signed the accords in New York and Pennsylvania stood firm in favor of their original decisions, farther west the treaties were viewed as nothing short of cowardice. If those two documents were honored, then the United States would gain full command of the Ohio Country and its lands would be open for settlement just as before, and this time because expansion had already pushed so far westward there would be nothing left for the Indians who sought refuge in its forests and valleys. While the Iroquois were seemingly willing to give up their hold on the Ohio Country, the warriors who actually resided there were not so anxious; there was still a palpable level of anger on the frontier, intense enough to create a political movement of cooperation not yet seen among American Indians.

To complicate matters further for the Americans' cause, even though the Treaty of Paris had given them title to all lands west to the Mississippi and north to the Great Lakes, the forts constructed by the British largely were still garrisoned by British-Canadian militia. Throughout the Ohio Country and Great Lakes region small posts of British Provincials remained based on the simple fact that the Americans had no way to enforce their removal. Because all of Canada remained in British hands, there was no sense of urgency to surrender any of their vital forts. Since the Revolution had ended, there was a very real concern among most administrators in Canada that a safe zone was necessary along its border with the United States, for as weak as the Americans were, the Canadians were even more vulnerable.[3]

It was in the diverse make-up of North America that Britain found its great buffer. Operating from Canada, the new superintendent of Indian affairs Sir John Johnson began an ambitious campaign to unify the frontier's Indian nations into one monolithic pan-Indian alliance. In 1782 John Johnson, the son of Sir William Johnson, had assumed his father's old position when his cousin Guy Johnson was sent to London in disgrace for falsifying war reports. He was as capable as either of his predecessors and equally savvy.

Despite the fact that such a movement was already under way, his promise of weapons and supplies made joining such a confederation appealing for most young warriors of the continent. Although he was outwardly willing to assist such a revolutionary new idea, Johnson was operating solely for his own benefit; in truth he cared little for the fate of the Indian cause. From the British perspective, the more difficulties the Americans faced the less likely they were to invade Canada, so in that regard an angry native rebellion would provide a timely and expensive diversion.[4]

Johnson's plans were fully supported by the old cadre that surrounded his predecessor, and most active among them was Joseph Brant, who remained one of the single most powerful men among the Six Nations. Brant was never a hereditary chief, but his immense political capital accrued during the American Revolution made him as effective as any single man in all of Iroquoia. After a meeting at Niagara the Mohawk leader agreed to venture deep into the Ohio Country and hold council with the many peoples that resided within it, fully bent on pitching the beneficial nature of a unified tribal alliance. Johnson promised to likewise send a schooner called *Faith* through the Great Lakes to support him with weapons, ammunition, and supplies. At the village of Lower Sandusky on Lake Erie, before warriors from as far away as Florida, he began his oration with staggering effect.

> It is certain that before Christian Nations Visited this Continent we were the Sole Lords of the Soil! . . . the Great Spirit placed us there! and what is the reason why we are not Still in possession of our forefathers birth Rights? You may

Safely Say because they wanted unanimity which we now So Strongly and Repeatedly recommend to you. . . . Therefore let us . . . be unanimous, let us have a Just sense of our own Value and if after that the Great Spirit wills that other Colours Should Subdue us, let it be so, we then Cannot reproach our Selves for Misconduct. . . . The Interests of Any One Nation Should be the Interests of us all, the Welfare of the one Should be the Welfare of all the others.[5]

Although he would only play a modest role in the larger alliance that became known as the Western Confederacy, Brant's early efforts were critical in the formation of the shared identity that defined it. He had been to London twice, and had as much credibility on the field of battle as any war chief in North America. He proposed a radical shift in native policy away from tribal alliance and redirected the anger and frustration of recent abuses toward unified cooperation. He served as the greatest firebrand of a renewed Indian uprising against these new United States, and by August 1786, Brant had rallied over fifteen hundred different warriors from across the Indian world, including Hurons, Wyandots, Shawnees, Delawares, Ottawas, Chippewas, Miamis, Mingos, and even the Creeks and Cherokees. But while he was a pronounced voice, he was not indicative of the entire Iroquois people.

Opposing him was the equally regarded Cornplanter of the Seneca. Since the signing of the Treaty of Paris, Cornplanter had rapidly become the face of American-Indian cooperation among the old power base of the Iroquois Confederacy. He and his Seneca were generally in agreement in maintaining the terms of the Treaty of Fort Stanwix signed with the Americans two years earlier; while he still held sway in Iroquoia, Brant's more hostile form of politics seemed to be much more popular elsewhere. The contrast between the Mohawk Brant and the Seneca Cornplanter reflected blurring loyalties in Indian country following the American Revolution. Both were Iroquois, and both ultimately sought peace; their means however were radically different despite the similarity of their desired ends. Just as Brant had pressed for unity and resistance, Cornplanter struggled equally for a diplomatic reconciliation with the new United

States: "The United States will take care that none of their Citizens shall intrude upon the Indians within the bounds which in the late treaties were allotted for them to hunt and live upon."[6]

The rift between these two men represented the rift between the larger nations of Indian America as a whole. Many Iroquois, including Guyasuta, rallied behind the peaceful negotiations that Cornplanter sought; many more, however, trekked to the Ohio Country in pursuit of war. For the young warriors who were anxious to fight, 1786 was merely the continuation of a decades-long struggle for Indian sovereignty. Although the Europeans divided the years of combat into the Seven Years' War, Pontiac's Rebellion, Dunmore's War, and the War of American Independence, for the Indians it was simply one long series of hostilities against different foes for the same reasons. This was a strong belief among the new generation of Indian war chiefs, and in clashing with the United States they were merely fighting the wars of their fathers. The men who had actually participated in those wars found the entire premise erroneous: there could be no Indian autonomy. Guyasuta, now in his sixties, had actually been in those battles, and he joined in the quest for peace because he recognized that what Brant and the other war hawks were creating was simply propaganda to incite rebellion.

Brant was hardly operating with the full interests of all Indian peoples for the sheer purpose of solely advancing the Indian agenda. Native resistance following the American Revolution was highly complex, and rarely fit into the Western understanding of traditional hierarchal values. Brant's primary objective in rallying the Ohio Indians together was peace with a separate land for the Indians, the same could be said for Cornplanter, but both of their efforts were also centered on restoring the traditional power of the Iroquois. Since the end of the revolution the Six Nations had largely disintegrated and had been reorganized into three primary factions: Brant led a community in Upper Canada, Cornplanter in western Pennsylvania, and Red Jacket, nephew of Cornplanter, along Buffalo Creek in western New York. They all agreed that peace had to be the final aspiration, but Cornplanter and Red Jacket shied from war while Brant did not. Brant, however, would lead a confederacy only if the war was on *his* terms, and only if it guaranteed a fortuitous result for *his* Iroquois people. If the individual members of the Confederacy decided to battle the Americans on their own, Brant would have no part of any such venture.

In a show of their support of peace-making efforts, the United States charged Cornplanter and Guyasuta with venturing into the rumbling Ohio Country to make the argument for harmony with the Americans. Although the old sachem Guyasuta's words generally fell on deaf ears among the Shawnees, Cornplanter had proven quite disruptive to Brant's unique brand of fiery politics. Regardless of their optimism, realities dictated to the Americans that the outdated policy of treaty-signing they had been using to gain territory and quiet the Indians of the frontier was failing. In the event of a general uprising, which was becoming more likely every day, Congress was convinced that it would need battle-ready troops for the new nation to truly take control of the Ohio Country.

The Western Confederacy of Indian peoples had become a worrisome development for the United States Congress, but the native groups were still forming a cohesive identity and lacked an overall strategy. As their discussions of engaging the Americans continued, many involved became restless and increasingly belligerent. Among the most anxious to initiate open warfare were the Shawnees, and while many of the sachems at Lower Sandusky still were hesitant to begin fighting right away, the people called the "wanderers" did so without reservation. Using calculated strikes at particularly vulnerable posts in the great wilderness of Kentucky, the Shawnees immediately shocked the frontier using the same effective tactics that had proven so deadly for the last four decades. With every murder, raid, and skirmish the American settlers in the region became more hesitant, and soon they fled in a mass exodus.[7]

Knowing full well the ultimate outcome of such raids, the American general George Rogers Clark ordered the prominent Kentuckian Benjamin Logan to retaliate with deadly force. Logan had been a major leader in the defense of Kentucky during the American Revolution, and worked his way to second in command of all Patriot forces in the territory. When the fighting receded in 1781 he was a particularly vocal advocate that the region should be entered into the new Union as a state separate from its overseer of Virginia. He knew the area well, and he had fought the Ohioans enough to know their weaknesses.

After being ordered into action by Clark, Logan led a combined force of American Regulars and buckskinned Kentucky militia on a raid into the well-known Shawnee settlements along the relatively small Mad River in modern Ohio. A mere sixty-six miles long, the river was marked by numerous Shawnee cabins along its banks. Knowing that the warriors of the villages were off instigating their raids to the south, Logan and his men tore through the exposed communities and destroyed all the residences and farmlands that they encountered. It was yet again an example of the type of campaign that Sullivan and Brodhead initiated eight years prior, and though it was draconian, it worked.

Among the captives taken during Logan's raid was the influential sachem Moluntha. Moluntha was a familiar face to the Americans as he had been very active against them during the revolution; in their haste the militiamen executed him in a maneuver driven largely by a desire for revenge. Although the raid greatly weakened the Shawnees in Kentucky and was celebrated by settlers in the territory, Logan's success would ultimately serve only to strengthen the resolve of the other confederated native groups against the United States. Over the next three years the frontier would erupt in brutal Indian war, and they would inflict casualties on nearly fifteen hundred American settlers.

Much of the violence stemmed from the utterly undefined territory that the Indians held, and the claims that the Americans believed they held title to. While many of the confederated Ohioans scoffed at the treaties of Fort Stanwix and Fort McIntosh, the Americans believed that the resulting exchange had given the land to them unconditionally. This miscommunication resulted in hundreds of deaths on both sides, and it was only further complicated by misguided legislation drafted by the United States Congress. In 1787 the Americans passed the Northwest Land Ordinance under the guidance of the Articles of Confederation. Although the act is best known for the official creation of America's first "Northwest Territory," it also stated that if an Indian population resided on a given piece of land then the land was rightfully theirs. The provision was designed to circumvent the brewing Indian rebellion in the territory, yet it also sent the larger message that those lands were now open for settlement to hungry and ambitious American pioneers.[8]

To remedy this new problem to reassert the United States' claims over the Ohio Country as assigned already, a new treaty was ordered by Congress in January 1789. It was to be signed at the then four-year-old Fort Harmar built along a critical bend in the Ohio River, near present-day Marietta, Ohio. The original purpose of the pentagonal fort (named for Josiah Harmar, a trusted associate of Washington's in the American Revolution and a leader in his new country's quest to control the Ohio Country) was to prevent settlers and Indians from attacking each other. To ensure that this new treaty would be conducted appropriately the governor of the Northwest Territory himself would be present. Arthur St. Clair was a veteran of the American Revolution and a trusted military officer, and when he arrived at Fort Harmar he thought very little of the native sachems around him. The Treaty of Fort Harmar was sealed January 9, and in the midst of a cold winter almost thirty Indian chiefs from eight Ohioan and Great Lakes peoples affixed their marks along with St. Clair himself. Nothing new came out of the treaty, which to the Americans was merely a resigning of the Fort Stanwix and Fort McIntosh treaties convincing Congress that the Ohio Country was rightfully theirs.

With the signing of this document tension on the frontier spun further out of control. The Ohioans who favored rebellion never supported the original treaties and regarded this new one with equal disdain. The document was signed mostly by aging sachems that had grown tired of war, and the fact that the younger warriors blatantly disregarded their wishes was evidence of how far the Ohio Country had drifted from the values that had regulated it for decades. Some historians believe that Guyasuta himself was at the Fort Harmar conference, but regardless of whether he was present, he agreed with the men that actually signed the document.

The failure of the Treaty of Fort Harmar and the violence that ensued in Kentucky and the Ohio Country was the final straw for the United States; as the frontier was warped by chaotic upheaval those in the east celebrated the election and inauguration of their first president. George Washington was now the single most powerful man in North America, and his first order of business was one that he was all too familiar with. Seven years after winning its independence through the fires of combat, America was preparing for war again.

In 1790 Pittsburgh had established itself as the most populous and civilized town on the American frontier. It was in its time a veritable "Gateway to the West," a title that it would lose as the United States pushed its limits farther away from the bounds of its old colonial borders. Pittsburgh defined the Ohio River valley, and the uniquely shifting qualities of the region had transformed it into a multilingual, multiracial, multiethnic capital of the American frontier.[9]

In and around the three rivers, those very same passages that gave birth to Fort Pitt, now sat a sprawling town. It had its traders and settlers but now it also had schools, churches, and plenty of taverns. Although the coastal society and refinement of the east had begun to flow into the city along the old Forbes Road built a generation earlier, Pittsburgh remained a rough and unfinished place. People and goods came across the mountains in a trickle that was growing stronger every day. The prominent English, German, Scots-Irish, African, and Indian elements of the city combined in an undeniably frontier way. Among the hundreds of people seen traipsing through the muddy streets of the city was Guyasuta.

Guyasuta was far from a celebrity in Pittsburgh, but most white residents recognized him as a major player among the area's shrinking Indian presence. He was far too old to engage in battles of any kind by 1790, and his jaunts through the town were far from dignified. He was crippled with age; decades of war had taken their toll on the tired sachem and left him as a gaunt, withered vision of his former self. Guyasuta maintained a residence just north of the town along the Allegheny River, and when he ventured into what would eventually be downtown Pittsburgh it was usually to replenish his dwindling stores of liquor. He made the trip frequently.

An addiction to alcohol had gripped Guyasuta throughout his life, but because liquor was generally only available in heavy spurts to the Indians of the frontier, he never indulged regularly. Now, though, as Pittsburgh was a permanent settlement, he could drink heavily as often as he wanted. For the previous ten years Guyasuta had developed a reputation in Pittsburgh for his notoriously hard drinking, and when combined with his physical state the once proud warrior appeared more a bumbling fool than great Half-King. Although he was far from his glory days, Guyasuta adhered to the system that gave him so much power to begin with. The Iroquois Confederacy was a divided union, and the council fire had long been extinguished, yet Guyasuta still petitioned local governments as though it burned as brightly as ever. While in the past he had negotiated such measures as profound as war and peace, he had been reduced in 1790 to asking for favors; in reality he was merely begging.

Despite the developments of upheaval farther west in the Ohio Country, and the fact that his own kin was still heavily involved, Guyasuta was remarkably disinterested in these events. A year after the failed Treaty of Fort Harmar, Guyasuta employed a young, literate Seneca to transcribe a message to be delivered to the Pennsylvania state legislature in Philadelphia. While the great orator spoke eloquently, the contents of the letter gave no indication that its sender once led a major rebellion to determine the fate of the frontier. He began it with the ceremonial title *Onas,* or "feather," in the way that had been done since before the Seven Years' War:

> The Sons of my beloved Brother Onas. When I was young and strong our country was full of game, which the Good Spirit sent for us to live upon. The lands which belonged to us were extended far beyond where we hunted. I and the people of my nation had enough to eat and always something to give to our friends when they entered our cabins; and we

rejoiced when they received it from us; hunting was then not tiresome, it was diversion; it was a pleasure.

When your fathers asked land from my nation, we gave it to them, for we had more than enough. Guyasuta was among the first of the people to say, "Give land to our brother Onas for he wants it," and he has always been a friend to Onas and to his children.

Your fathers saw Guyasuta when he was young; when he had not even thought of old age or weakness; but you are too far off to see him, now he is grown old. He is very old and feeble, and he wonders at his own shadow, it is become so little. He has no children to take care of him, and the game is driven away by the white people; so that the young men must hunt all day long to find game for themselves to eat; they have nothing left for Guyasuta; and it is not Guyasuta only who is become old and feeble, there yet remain about thirty men of your old friends, who, unable to provide for themselves or to help one another, are become poor and are hungry and naked.

Guyasuta sends you a belt which he received long ago from your fathers, and a writing which he received but as yesterday from one of you. By these you will remember him and the old friends of your fathers in this nation. Look on this belt and this writing, and if you remember the old friends of your fathers, consider their former friendship and their present distress; and if the Good Spirit shall put it in your hearts to comfort them in their old age, do not disregard his council. We are men and therefore need only tell you that we are old and feeble and hungry and naked; and that we have no other friends but you, the children of our beloved brother Onas.[10]

So often in the study of Indian America one is left with questions that simply cannot be answered. Guyasuta is a man without the benefit of written language. Unlike the prolific writers of his time, Guyasuta leaves us almost nothing throughout the course of his life that indicates his feelings or opinions. In this letter, a letter penned sadly by a Seneca resident of Pittsburgh who was likely too young to recall the triumphs of the man that employed him, we get a glimpse into the great scope of his mind. The words Guyasuta sent to Philadelphia are those of a man who has lost the energy of his youth, and much of the power that came with it. He openly questions the weakness of his body, and has acquiesced to the need for assistance. He is a man reduced, and he has come to terms with the fact that the world around him was continuously changing. Rather than keeping up with the change, the tired Guyasuta was content to sit back and watch.

Following the diplomatic failure of the Treaty at Fort Harmar, President George Washington began to seriously consider using force to suppress any Indian rebellion in the Ohio Country before its increasing momentum threatened the entire nation. Having seen the terrible consequences of Indian raids and wilderness warfare, Washington was anxious to avoid letting them endanger the new republic. When news of violence on the frontier reached the capitol in the wake of the ineffective treaty, Washington wrote to Governor Arthur St. Clair to assess the totality of the damage and detemine whether the Western Confederacy was capable of inciting a full-scale uprising.

The decision for St. Clair was an easy one. Since hostilities had reignited, over fifteen hundred settler families had been killed by the renegade bands of the Ohio Country, and though the Indians were not yet united under one flag, the prospect of war could certainly be the last catalyst that they needed. Another troubling development for St. Clair was the fact that this renewed climate of violence had allowed new war chiefs from the many native groups of the Ohio Country to emerge as viable political leaders. From the practical perspective of control, if the movement only had one symbolic face that one man could be easily neutralized; the fact that many bands now had their own sectional leaders only served to complicate the matter. Among these newly popular figures were the Miami Little Turtle and the Shawnee Blue Jacket; both men had cut their teeth during the American Revolution and now were viewed as the personification of this new struggle among their respective peoples.

For Governor St. Clair the most efficient way to nip this new uprising in the bud was to strike at what he believed to be the geographic heart of the movement at the Miami village of Kekionga. Situated on the site of today's Fort Wayne, Indiana, Kekionga was a major site in this new trend toward violence. But St. Clair's failure to recognize that many other places supported resistance to the United States would have dire consequences. Using Kekionga as his strategic target, St. Clair crafted a plan and presented it to President Washington in New York in August 1790. Although the men disagreed on some aspects of the arrangement, notably whether the cost of a new fort in the region was justified, they agreed that force would need to be applied if the new American nation was to be kept safe and prosperous.

With a blessing from the commander-in-chief himself, St. Clair sounded a clarion call across the frontier and assembled nearly fifteen hundred men at Fort Washington (near present-day Cincinnati) for a punitive mission against the Miami village. The man chosen to lead this venture was General Josiah Harmar, an experienced leader who was present at the signing of the Treaty of Fort McIntosh in 1785 and oversaw the construction of forts throughout the region. Included among his projects was Fort Washington, the very place from which he was preparing to lead his army. Although he was fond of the bottle, it was agreed that he was the best man for the job.[11]

The army that Harmar had at his disposal offers a unique glimpse into the diverse ethnic mixture that was America in the early national period. Made up mainly of immigrants new to the continent, the militia that Harmar prepared for battle was mostly untrained, and entirely untested, with almost no seasoned frontiersmen. Perhaps they knew of the danger of the mission, or they were defending their homes, but whatever the reason they did not join Harmar that fall.

With the approaching winter not far ahead, Harmar and his men designed the expedition to accomplish their goal quickly. If the march on Kekionga was swift, the Americans believed, the larger bands in the area would be unable to spread their talks of confederation during the winter months. That sense of urgency would mean that sacrifices had to be made, and among the most painful were smaller rations of food and almost no training for the freshly armed recruits that Harmar was leading. This costly mistake revealed the overconfidence of the new nation's tiny armed force: they had just defeated an empire, what harm could a meager coalition of Indians be?

Though he was pleased with the pace of the whole measure, Arthur St. Clair never forgot the ever-present potency of that old empire. Still situated on the Great Lakes and garrisoned at Fort Detroit, the British remained present and active in the affairs of the United States and the Indian populations. To ensure that the

Gen. Arthur St. Clair. (*Independence National Historical Park*)

Crown would not react to the expedition, St. Clair sent correspondence to Detroit to reassure its commandant that Harmar's force was acting solely to punish the Indians at Kekionga. The last thing that he needed was an angry British response. If the British were to be aggravated, it could have spelled disaster for his fledgling country; that was a burden St. Clair was not willing to shoulder.

By October 7, Harmar and his motley assortment of militiamen left the confines of Fort Washington, hoping that the expedition would be a short and successful one. The new recruits, through rumor and story, could only speculate on the horrific prospects of an Indian war. Their target, Kekionga, was approximately one hundred and fifty miles to their north, and the Great Miami River would lead them directly to it. In support of Harmar's column was a party of militiamen out of Vincennes, but that force was delayed and their mission ended up being cancelled before it was ever started. The group from Fort Washington was on its own, and their marching orders stood.

After seven days Harmar's force was within striking distance of Kekionga, and as fate would have it some of his Kentucky scouts were able to capture a Shawnee prisoner en route. Following a rather stern interrogation, which some claimed bordered on torture, the rogue warrior informed the Americans that both the Miami and Shawnee were well aware of their intentions. He also added that the warriors of both groups were lying in wait outside Kekionga to ambush Harmar and his men. Having learned the lessons of the past, the following day Harmar dispatched a small party of men under the command of Colonel John Hardin to reclaim the element of surprise and upend the Indian plan; when the men arrived at Kekionga on October 17 they were stunned by the eerie calm of an abandoned village.

It seemed that the residents had used the same scouts that kept them abreast of Harmar's movements to gain valuable intelligence of his advanced column's approach. Kekionga was now a ghost town, and the women and children who lived there had fled to safety within the walls of Fort Detroit. They were welcomed by the British and allowed to store their valuable food and supplies there while the Miami and Shawnee warriors went back to engage Harmar's men. It seemed that the punitive mission that the Americans had so dreaded in the fall of 1790 was easier than they thought, and Hardin's men left the village to return to camp.

On October 19, Hardin led another column back toward Kekionga. With their target left fallow, Harmar and Hardin devised a new strategy to eliminate the adjunct village of the sachem called Le Gris not far away. At midday, scouts for Hardin's column stumbled across a native warrior on horseback and instantly gave pursuit; he was merely a decoy.

Not realizing this fact until it was too late, the Americans followed the excited horseman into the swampy marsh lands of the Eel River, just outside Kekionga, and directly into a trap. Hardin was unaware of his folly and as the Americans were greatly slowed by the mucky floor of the forest they were pounced upon on three sides by the Miami and Shawnees. It was a hectic and sudden explosion of violence by nearly one hundred warriors from the surrounding area, and by the end over sixty Americans were dead. Hardin himself was unharmed, but his surviving officers made it clear that they believed that blame should fall on his shoulders.

The following day Josiah Harmar sent a detachment of three hundred American Regulars and militia on an intelligence mission to pinpoint the exact locations of the warrior forces. They too were attacked and nineteen were killed. At the center of these brutal victories was the rising Miami leader Little Turtle. Though many different sachems vied for power during the formative new Western Confederacy of Indian nations, Little Turtle's actions spoke louder than words. The Americans fled the scene of this second attack in such a hurry that they did not even bury or retrieve their dead. Harmar retreated much farther in order to collect his thoughts at a safe distance, and his disregard for his fallen men turned most of his army against him.[12]

On October 21 Colonel Hardin, still seething from his ambush two days prior, accosted Harmar and demanded four hundred men to collect their dead and punish the Indians. He was granted three hundred, and the next morning they marched to Kekionga. The village was no longer vacant, however, with over a thousand warriors waiting for another showdown with the Americans. When Hardin arrived he was stunned by the number of Miami and Shawnees before him, and he sent a message back to Harmar immediately to send reinforcements. When word reached camp, some indicate that Harmar was slightly intoxicated, others that he was flat-out drunk, but all agreed that he was terribly frightened by the news. Instead of sending the men to assist Hardin, Harmar commanded the rest of his force to form a defensive square around his camp and simply wait. Hardin prepared the attack, fully expecting reinforcements that never came.

Whatever plans Hardin made would never develop, as fiery Little Turtle drew first blood. Outnumbered two-to-one, Hardin's force was sent reeling by the Indian surge, but throughout the pandemonium the American officer remained composed and level-headed. Using sound defensive tactics, Hardin was able to hold out against Little Turtle for three hours under the impression that help was on its way. By the end of the engagement one hundred and eighty Americans were killed or wounded, and the Miami and Shawnees were victorious yet again. The Indians called this event the Battle of Pumpkin Fields, a macabre label due to the fact that the scalped heads of the dead steamed like a field of squash in the autumn. The United States had not fared well thus far, and this fact only emboldened the collective nations.

Harmar was forced to retreat after losing so many of his men, and President Washington was furious. It appeared now that full-scale war was the only option left to deal with the unexpectedly powerful and still-growing Western Confederacy, and assigning it to an incompetent man like Harmar was not a mistake that the president could make twice. Washington wrote, "my mind . . . is prepared for the worst; that is, for expence without honor or profit."[13]

In the year 1791 the arousal of the Western Confederacy of Indian nations continued to evolve and the United States pressed to keep pace with it. Since the disaster of Harmar's campaign, the allied Ohio peoples had been emboldened by their victory and as a result the frontier became nearly void of white settlements. That summer, American diplomat Timothy Pickering struck a perceived monumental deal with Red Jacket at Newtown Point in southwestern New York in which the men brokered a deal of neutrality for the Seneca nation; while Cornplanter was not present at the meeting, his sentiments were echoed by his nephew Red Jacket. Far across the Great Lakes in Canada, Joseph Brant had found himself in a favorable position with the British, and with food and supplies readily available, the fervor to support rebellion in the Ohio Country greatly diminished. For Washington and his Secretary of War, Henry Knox, it had been a successful year as the most prominent leaders in the Iroquois nations, and the majority of their warriors, were decidedly out of the conflict. Their allegiance to the cause was more aligned with establishing their own imperial rule again, and when that failed to improve, whatever confederacy was started at Lower Sandusky had quickly spun far out of their control. In a council at Philadelphia between Washington and Cornplanter, the Seneca succinctly summed up his people's argument, stating they would "till the ground with the plough as the white people do" only "if you mean to leave us and our children any land to till."[14]

The new rebellion, the Western Confederacy, was a decidedly Ohioan experiment. Its key leaders were Little Turtle of the Miami and Blue Jacket of the Shawnee. The land that they fought for was the Ohio Country itself, and gains that they had made were done so without any Iroquois assistance. The Iroquois under Cornplanter, Brant, and Red Jacket were not a real threat by 1791, but Washington was willing to take whatever small victories he could get after almost five years of insurrection on the frontier.

In light of the developments with the Iroquois and with an increasing sense of urgency, President Washington sent another expedition into the Ohio Country in hopes of ending the great Indian uprising. His target again would be Kekionga, as it had become

Little Turtle of the Miami, one of the leaders of the Western Confederacy. (*Ohio Historical Society*)

something of an unofficial capital of the Miami and Shawnees bent on war, and he hoped to avoid the mistake of the previous year. Harmar had been a faithful servant and dutiful leader in the revolution, yet his career in its aftermath had represented a slow tragic decline, ending with a requested court-martial on the charge of negligence of duty following the campaign of 1790. A new venture, one that was certain to repel the Ohioans, would need a strong leader who was familiar with the territory. Washington hoped that Arthur St. Clair himself would be the man to finally find victory.

The governor of the Northwest Territory willingly took on the task of supervising troops, for in eighteenth-century America it was not unheard of to see a major political official leading an army. Washington believed it was his duty to lead the army if necessary, but Governor St. Clair was more than capable of leading this new charge. The president informed St. Clair that he hoped to get this new expedition under way in the summer months of 1791, and Congress voted to raise an entire second regiment in support. For St. Clair it appeared that he had the full support of the executive and legislative branches, but the realities of a modern republic soon took hold. One of the issues with raising a public army was that public monies were necessary, and the United States was still burdened by the heavy debt of the American Revolution. So, while Congress was doubling the size of the army, it slashed soldiers' pay; the result was demoralized, angry young soldiers who were promised one thing and given another. The first regiment was whittled down to fewer than three hundred men, and the new regiment was only able to fill half of its intended ranks. If St. Clair was to be successful against the Ohioans, he would have to overcome the failings of Congress first.

St. Clair would begin his march out of Fort Washington and take a path similar to Harmar's a year earlier, but the situation that he oversaw was problematic from the onset. At his disposal were six hundred American Regulars and eight hundred men drafted on a single six-month term—not enough to confront Little Turtle and Blue Jacket. As governor of the territory St. Clair was able to garner the service of six hundred hardy frontier militiamen. Even this force of almost two thousand men may not have convinced St. Clair that he could be victorious in the days to come. To worsen matters, his men were poorly trained and insufficiently supplied; his horses were local and not suited for combat, and rations of food for the men and feed for their beasts were inadequate. All told, the summer launch that President Washington sought was impossible, and St. Clair did not begin his march until October.

Although Washington actively tried to avoid the pitfalls of 1790, the similarities between St. Clair's and Harmar's campaigns were obvious, starting with how unprepared the rough, green troops were. Shortly after his column began its journey, St. Clair suffered terrible losses due to desertion as nearly six hundred men abandoned their commitments. As they marched, the men saw Indian scouts in the trees around them and were further discouraged by the fears that they were heading into a trap.

After a month of marching northward toward Kekionga, St. Clair found himself in a desperately familiar situation. He had been suffering with a terrible case of gout for much of the journey, and the nagging pain was a constant distraction from his official duties as general. In camp on November 2, the governor had recalculated the strength of his army after weeks of desertion and had only eleven hundred men left; when he left Fort

Washington he had commanded two thousand. Of those that remained, only eight hundred were professional soldiers with just fifty officers to command them. The rest were the untrained, unprepared irregulars.[15]

Some miles away at Kekionga, the enemy that the Americans prepared to face was having more success. Little Turtle had become the face of the resistance among the Miami, and his reputation had grown enormously after the destruction of Harmar's men. Likewise the Shawnee Blue Jacket had gained a following largely carried over from his actions during the American Revolution and subsequent frontier raids. They were able to gather seven hundred warriors anxious to challenge St. Clair for the rights to their own land and to govern themselves. But the news was only getting better: word had come days prior that the Delaware, under the command of great elder chief Buckongahelas, were preparing to join their struggle. He would bring with him almost five hundred men fully prepared to wage war on the United States.

On the morning of November 4 St. Clair's army had established camp near the mouth of the Wabash River. As usual, the unpolished soldiers carried on during the morning preparations and sallied slowly toward their breakfast. Some were still in their sleeping attire and almost none expected much action other than consuming a nearly indigestible meal while the sun continued to rise. In a flash the whooping call of a pan-Indian ambush broke out and overran the camp. At one-thousand men strong the warriors needed little time to completely rout the Americans. Many of the unprepared soldiers were killed on the spot, but the majority fled across the water, leaving their camp and firearms behind.

While the militiamen panicked, the trained Regulars promptly prepared their muskets for firing and rallied into position. On a small elevation overlooking the camp artillery men scrambled to ready their cannon. By 1791 the Ohioans were as versed in European style warfare as the Americans, and while they did not engage in the tactics they certainly prided themselves on disrupting them. Native snipers made quick work of the cannon and their crews, and the remaining Americans on the hill deliberately destroyed the guns so that their enemy could not use them. With little hope for an organized response, the Americans fixed their bayonets and prepared for the worst. The result was a continuous series of charges, blade first, toward their Indian attackers that failed miserably. As the Americans ran at the warriors, the Indians would simply break their lines, scatter, and eventually regroup behind the Regulars and hack them down. The bayonet charge had won many battles before, and would again, but it was only effective if one's enemy held a rigid line. The Indians cared very little for that style of fighting and the Americans paid with their lives.

Eventually St. Clair was forced to call a retreat and his men fled the battle site; their escape was limited, however, by the surging Indians in pursuit. Many of the Americans were slain while running away, and the carnage of the defeat redefined violence and casualty counts on a historic scale. When St. Clair was able to regroup with some of his men at Fort Jefferson a short distance away, the numbers that he tallied were staggering. The death toll indicated that 39 of 50 officers were slain, and 632 out of 920 men had been killed. Another 264 were wounded, and when counting the civilians that followed the army in support a total of 832 Americans had died. The casualty rate was 97 percent.

The battle has never been given an official name in military records, and to this day using figures calculating the ratio of survivors to dead, St. Clair's losses stand as the single worst defeat ever suffered by the United States Army. At best estimates, only twenty-one Indian warriors were killed. For the Americans it was a crushing blow that forced them to consider a reorganization of their entire strategy for controlling the frontier; for the Western Confederacy, however, it affirmed that their cause was just and that victory would soon be theirs. The United States of America seemed on the precipice of defeat, and Indian America was more unified than ever. Rufus Putnam, an influential member of the U.S. Army, wrote, "the Indians began to believe them Selves invinsible, and they truly had great cause of triumph."[16]

By 1792 it had become apparent that after the defeat of St. Clair along at the Wabash, the loose ends of Washington's Indian policy would need to be shored up as quickly as possible. In a great council at Philadelphia, the president sat with the chiefs of the Iroquois yet again, this time to try to gauge their current stance on the Western Confederacy and try to attain their official neutrality once and for all. The diplomat Timothy Pickering had placed great faith in the fact that Cornplanter was not inclined to war, and that he and his Seneca had no interest in rebellion; the other tribesmen, most notably Red Jacket and Joseph Brant, still required convincing.

When the council at Philadelphia got under way, Washington showered the sachems with gifts. Red Jacket discussed his opinions openly with specific concerns about his people's ability to retain control of their traditional lands. Brant, who was something of a renegade living in Canada at the time, used the council to judge what sort of deal the Americans were willing to offer him. As he and his branch of the Iroquois lived in British territory, Brant had developed a unique relationship with the lieutenant governor of Upper Canada, John Graves Simcoe. Washington attempted to persuade Brant and his Iroquois to move back into American territory, going so far as to offer him large tracts of land and a personal pension. For Washington, gaining Brant's favor was particularly vital, as Simcoe led a very pronounced British charge to arm the Indians and press for rebellion as a means of further weakening the fledgling American states. Brant did not accept the president's offer, generally because his people had a strong affinity for the British, but he did acknowledge that only diplomacy would create peace with the Americans; combat, which the Western Confederacy desired, would lead to ruin.[17]

In that meeting Washington accomplished little in the way of an official treaty of neutrality, but he did open up discussions for meaningful diplomacy in the future and a sense that harmony could be achieved through negotiation. For his great efforts, Washington even awarded Red Jacket a special medallion of peace inscribed with an image of the two men shaking hands. While the status of the American-Iroquois relationship was not yet defined, it was now certain that their role in the Indian rebellion would be minimal; that was victory in itself.

Things had not gone so well when negotiation was offered to the Ohioans, though. In April 1792 Washington dispatched Colonel John Hardin, the chief voice of reason during Harmar's campaign, to act as an envoy of peace to the Shawnee. He was welcomed and given shelter for the night in one of their villages under the auspices of diplomatic immunity. As he slept, though, Hardin was murdered in his bed. It was a grisly message that the Ohioans were bent on war and the time for treaties had passed.

For Washington, however, diplomacy among the Iroquois was only a starting point; in the west stood a formidable Indian confederacy primed for all out war on the frontier. In the wake of St. Clair's defeat terror had spread throughout the Ohio Country and murderous raids had disrupted much of the settlement in the region.

Fort Pitt, the thirty-year-old bastion at the three rivers, had fallen into such a state of disrepair that a new fort had to be built nearby, called Fort Fayette in honor of Washington's ally the Marquis De La Fayette. It appeared it would see its primary action against an Indian enemy, and as the only major settlement in the midst of the uprising, it would fall to Pittsburgh to tailor whatever response the president desired.[18]

Washington's major dilemma, echoed by Henry Knox, was that individual state militias were not competent enough to suppress the rebellious Ohio Indians. Since the nation's inception there was an inherent distrust of strong central government among the states, and one of the great precursors of an imperial power was always a powerful, organized national army. For those reasons the strong Anti-Federalist wing of Congress had been reluctant to raise national troops, and instead favored a decentralized arrangement of states organizing their own militias when they decided it was necessary. In the president's mind that strategy was wholly ineffective and had resulted in some of the worst disasters in American military history. It was decided then in Philadelphia that the United States needed a professional standing army, and so it was done.

The failures of leadership had allowed terrible defeats over the previous two years, and Washington gave his search for an officer to lead this new army the highest priority. Harmar had been unprofessional, and St. Clair impatient. Washington sought a man who from his own experience was reliable, faithful, and most of all daring; he needed someone he could trust and who would be willing to break rank and go toe-to-toe with the native warriors who awaited him.

His choice was a monumental one, and he reached back in his own history to find him. General Anthony Wayne had developed a reputation in the American Revolution for being fearless, and perhaps a bit foolhardy. He had led his men into battle valiantly at places like Brandywine, Paoli, and Germantown; he also did hard time in the winter of Valley Forge. While he was a capable man, it was only after he charged the much larger British force of Charles Cornwallis armed with bayonets at Green Spring that he became known as "Mad Anthony" Wayne. Since the end of the war he was spoken of with reverence in taverns across the new nation, and he was a key member of the Georgia state delegation that ratified the U.S. Constitution.[19]

Gen. Anthony Wayne, drawn by James Sharples, Sr., just before the Ohio Expedition. (*Independence National Historical Park*)

When he received word from Washington that he was selected to build, train, and lead the first standing army in American history, it could not have come at a better time. The forty-nine-year-old Wayne had been elected to Congress as a representative of Georgia in 1788, yet when his political opponents challenged his residency requirements his seat was taken away from him. He was tired and worn from the grind of public service, and Washington's charge was the perfect remedy to an overall unfulfilling spell in the political arena. What lay ahead of the veteran general was no ordinary military assignment, however, and it would require all of his vast experience just to begin the long and difficult process.

Washington, Knox, and Wayne agreed that a conventional army would not be substantial enough to inflict meaningful damage on the Western Confederacy and its warriors, and using innovative new methods a plan was developed to create a fighting force unlike any other that had marched before on the North American continent. What they proposed would combine all of the best-known elements of a major land-based army into one brigade-sized body of men. It would mold the collective elements of cavalry, light and heavy infantry, and artillery into one sturdy and mobile fighting force dubbed the Legion of the United States. It was a lofty goal, and Wayne insisted that he be given ample time to train. With no debate from the president, the general set out for Pittsburgh to gather volunteers and recruits who would be the raw materials necessary for him to create such a devastating instrument of destruction.

Beginning in June, Wayne rallied twenty-five hundred men from the remaining elements of the Continental army and new recruits in and around the city of Pittsburgh. His men occupied Fort Fayette along the Allegheny River, and Wayne suddenly came face-to-face with the consequences of training so close to such a populous area. As the old general attempted to keep his young soldiers focused and disciplined, the vices of Pittsburgh drew them away from their goal. As winter approached in November Wayne recognized that with the cold weather came a dramatic increase in downtime, and idle hands were always "the Devil's playground."[20]

Seeking a suitable position to train his men during the winter, Wayne located an empty parcel of ground twenty-miles north of Pittsburgh, near the long-abandoned ruins of Logstown. It was directly up the Ohio River, and its placement was ideal, far enough away that distractions of the city would be out of reach, yet close enough that if endangered, Wayne and his force could retreat to the safety of Fort Fayette. On this site Wayne would establish what would become the United States of America's first basic training encampment, named Legionville.

Throughout the winter of 1792 an empty stretch of ground had been transformed to an advanced training facility. Wayne put his raw recruits through rigorous drills on a daily basis, and was fully aware that while it was done at great delay the result would be a coherent fighting force capable of countering the Western Confederacy of Ohioans. Legionville was a protected position, but it was not a fort in the traditional sense. Around all four sides of the camp was a defensive ditch that totaled more than a mile in length, and at each corner stood a stone redoubt capable of housing thirty-six men. It was guarded on regular shifts by over two-hundred-and-fifty men that stood watch twenty-four hours seven days a week. In total the camp covered thirty-five acres. Among the Legion's soldiers were many soon-to-be prominent figures, including Meriwether Lewis, William Clark, and future president William Henry Harrison.

But for all of its pronounced and powerful features, Legionville was also a place of diplomacy for the local Indian groups. Anthony Wayne was no expert, and he was often guided by terrible prejudices, but over his tenure his skills sharpened greatly when it came to negotiating with the native population. Shortly after his great camp was founded, the general received a visit from Guyasuta, the highest-ranking local representative of a system that no longer existed. Guyasuta still took his duties as Half-King very seriously, yet because of his destitute appearance and bent, shuffling posture Wayne was at first reluctant to hear him. But his news was valuable and even the general recognized that.

Guyastua's audience with Wayne was both personal and political. He first had asked the general if he might spare some extra clothing and supplies, but on a much more serious note he passed on vital intelligence from deeper within the Ohio Country. Only months earlier in September, the Seneca and other allies of the Iroquois marched over five hundred men into the contested region to meet with the Ohioans and attempt to dissuade them from fighting. Their meeting place was an area called the Glaize. Because the Glaize sat at the intersection of two major rivers, the Maumee and Auglaize, it formed a substantial outcropping of land that served as the heart of the community. The rivers, acting as highways, brought many different peoples together, making it a natural rallying point for the Western Confederacy. It was a unique setting that included many small villages surrounding a single British trading post. Since St. Clair's defeat the Glaize had become the primary headquarters of the Western Confederacy.[21]

It was for that reason that in the summer of 1792, before the great council in Philadelphia with the Iroquois, British lieutenant governor John Graves Simcoe had employed his own

Indian agents to stir unrest among the confederacy. The following speech by Alexander McKee was to reassure the natives that if they did choose to rebel, they would be well supplied by His Majesty the King. "You say 'at this Council fire, which is in the centre of your country, is placed the heart of all the Indian Confederacy, to which you have always considered your Father to be joined.' The King your Father from the earliest moments of his reign, has believed this union to be necessary for your welfare."[22]

The British in Canada sought to keep the Western Confederacy as agitated as possible, for in their opinion the rebellious Indians were merely pawns in the larger chess match of retaining control over North America and suppressing their former subjects in the United States. It was no surprise, then, when Cornplanter and Red Jacket arrived at the Glaize in September they were met with sarcastic and caustic responses. In one council, Red Jacket stated, "Brothers, we know that the Americans have held out their hands to offer you peace. Don't be too proud spirited and reject it."

In response, the Shawnee sachem Painted Pole said, "When you left your village you had a bundle of American speeches under your arm . . . all the Nations desire you to speak from your Heart and not from your Mouth. . . . We know what you are about—we see you plainly."[23]

Guyasuta continued to explain to Wayne that during the long council, some members of the Iroquois delegation had been murdered by the hawkish Ohioans, and that that he feared his nephew Cornplanter might be viewed as a turncoat. In truth, the Iroquois and the Ohioans both sought the same peace; however, the Iroquois believed that it could be found through negotiations with the United States, while the Ohioans only put their faith in the blade of their tomahawk. Guyasuta finished his statements, continued his probe for any liquor or clothing that Wayne might have available, and finally returned to his home north of Pittsburgh. It seemed that his remarks made an impact. Wayne wrote to Secretary of War Henry Knox soon after: "I feel uneasy for the safe return of the Cornplanter."[24]

Wayne remained steadfast in his commitment to march out of Legionville during the spring thaw, and he pressed his men throughout the snowy early months of 1793. They had slowly become a formidable unit and the general was quite impressed with his progress. In a way, the Legion had become the talk of the city since its arrival and most in Pittsburgh knew that while they were the most at risk, they also had the nation's strongest military asset just a few miles upriver. In March 1793 Guyasuta again visited Wayne, this time with an Iroquois delegation of the highest importance. He was joined by New Arrow, Big Tree, and most impressively Cornplanter himself.

Cornplanter was without question the head of this party, and his primary reason for visiting Wayne was to attempt to delay his Legion's great invasion until all diplomatic resources had been exhausted. Even as Cornplanter was sneered at and despised by the Ohioans, he still maintained hope that his unique position between the two worlds could spare a terrible amount of bloodshed on both sides. The primary argument of the Western Confederacy, Cornplanter explained, was that the 1768 Treaty of Fort Stanwix should be honored, and that the Ohio River should be a boundary never crossed by the Americans. He dramatically pointed to the flowing waters and stated: "My mind & heart is upon that river, may that Water ever continue to run, & remain the boundary of a lasting peace, between the Americans & Indians on its opposite shores."[25]

His speech was eloquent, but the hardened Wayne was not impressed. Over the past several months he had directed all of his efforts to fulfilling his mission and crafting a well-disciplined army. In his mind treating with the Ohioans was a lost cause, but he tolerated it in the meantime. Now that his Legion was prepared to march, however, his disregard for diplomacy was even greater. He said to Cornplanter in response, "the only means to secure peace—was to be well prepared for war."[26]

But while Wayne and his Legion were ever present outside of Pittsburgh, a storm of another kind was brewing within the city itself. For days rumors had swirled that one of the frontier's greatest heroes would be placed on trial for the murder of a party of Indians from years earlier. Known as the greatest single Indian fighter in all of the Ohio Country, Samuel Brady was the personification of the collective anger, frustration, fear, and hatred felt by hundreds of frontier settlers in 1793.

Brady was a true product of the frontier, and his life was one of great consequence in the larger development of its distinctly unforgiving personality. Brady's father John served valiantly in the Seven Years' War and even marched with Colonel Henry Bouquet during his expedition into the Ohio Country following the siege of Fort Pitt. Born outside of Shippensburg, Pennsylvania, young Samuel learned much from his father, and only added to the legacy of his family name in the American Revolution. Beginning at the age of twenty, Samuel fought in every major conflict of the first two years of the war including Boston, New York, Trenton, Princeton, Brandywine, and Germantown. He wintered at Valley Forge and actively carried out General Washington's orders in the Ohio Country as one of his primary scouts.

After his brother and father were murdered by renegade Indian bands in 1778, Samuel swore his life to avenging the deaths of his kin, and his legend grew from there. He engaged in all kinds of activities throughout the course of the revolution in his campaign for revenge, including raiding Indian villages and rescuing hostages. His greatest single feat, though, and the event that made him a household name, was when he made a remarkable leap across a twenty-foot gorge to escape a pursing warrior party. Brady was the face of rugged, independent resistance among the Americans, and his name was synonymous with its defense. When an American village would be struck and its residents killed, the name of Samuel Brady would be invoked almost instantly; thoughts of what he would have done if he were present consoled the grieving families. He was a living legend, but it appeared in Pittsburgh by 1793 that his time was finally up.

His murder trial took place in a tavern, and while the citizens of Pittsburgh filed in to watch, Brady sat boldly defiant, soaking in the glory of his celebrity status. The judge that day was brought in from Philadelphia and was especially conspicuous in his white powdered wig. The jury was made up of Brady's peers, themselves all products of Pittsburgh's rough countryside. No one expected the charges to stick. At the start of his trial a young woman named Jennie Stupes proudly displayed herself in the tavern, and came to the defense of Brady; thirteen years earlier the defendant had rescued her from Indian captivity.

Perhaps most intriguing of all from this first great trial of the new American frontier was Brady's relationship with General Anthony Wayne. During the American Revolution Wayne had employed Brady as a scout, and he greatly desired his services in the command of his new Legion's reconnaissance parties. Wayne's influence was so strong, in fact, that he convinced Brady to turn himself in under the pretense that he would be easily exonerated in an Ohio Country court. Brady agreed, and while his supporters in the tavern greatly aided his cause, the most convincing testimony came from an unlikely source.

As the last witness took the stand, Brady was surprised to see the withered figure of Guyasuta approach the bar. Many questioned the allegiances of the old sachem, mostly because of his deep history of rebellion in the region. For most observers his testimony was expected to be the lone defense of the Indians whom Brady killed, but when he began to speak they were surprised. Although the murder that brought Brady to trial was known to have been in cold blood, Guyasuta's tired raspy words blatantly vindicated the Indian fighter's actions. The tired sachem claimed that the Indians whom Brady killed were often seen riding stolen horses and bragging of the scalps that they collected.

While it is unlikely that Guyasuta's statement ultimately led to the acquittal of Samuel Brady, the frontiersman was thankful for his efforts. His remarks were so unexpected that his attorney, James Ross, asked Guyasuta why he made such a flattering testimonial. To that, the sachem raised his scarred, brittle hands and clapped, responding, "am I not the friend of Brady?"[27]

It was an unusually revealing moment in the ever-changing history of the Ohio Country, when its boldest defender of Indian rights spoke so highly of its most terrible adversary. Samuel Brady had built a reputation on his careless and blatant abuse of the region's Indians, yet Guyasuta provided an unexpected and glowing endorsement. Historians have generally passed over this event as trivial, while others overemphasize its meaning. It could be viewed as Guyasuta's effort to free Brady with the understanding that he would suppress the Ohio Rebellion, yet the more obvious conclusion is simply that Guyasuta was atoning for his actions of the past. There was a new conflict emerging in the West, and to defend Brady was to separate himself from the Western Confederacy in the most obvious way possible.

For Guyasuta, a change of image in Pittsburgh was sorely needed. Shortly after hostilities in the west had begun in 1790, the citizenry of the region found his presence to be a source of contempt and a convenient target to vent their frustrations. After settling on an especially fertile plot of land along the Allegheny River just north of the city with two wives, Guyasuta found no rest in his retirement. One onlooker wrote an especially scathing opinion in the *Pittsburgh Gazette,* claiming sarcastically: "We are happy to have an opportunity of congratulating our fellow citizens on the arrival in this town of the great, the mighty, and the war-like Giosota the first, king of the Seneca nation; defender of Hannah's-town; protector of the widow and orphan."[28]

To think that the once great champion of Indian autonomy would behave in such a deferential manner is a difficult notion to accept, but happy endings rarely supersede reality. Guyasuta's world of freedom and self-reliance was disappearing, and like the many relationships of his youth, it too would fade away. He was alone, and though his testimony did not make him an equal citizen in the eyes of the Americans that heard it, perhaps it allowed Guyasuta to feel like part of something greater than himself for one last time.

On April 30, 1793, as the Ohio River rushed forward in the spring thaw, General Anthony Wayne stood resolute. In front of him were over two thousand soldiers loading onto dozens of barges preparing to move west. A year earlier these young men were raw, untrained recruits and after a year of hard training they had finally outgrown their temporary camp outside of Pittsburgh. The general had implemented an unrelenting regimen through the winter, and his troops had carved out their progress through the heavy mounds of fallen snow. Now, with the icy landscape melting away, his soldiers descended the Ohio River with confidence. Wayne had done what many viewed as impossible in one calendar year, and the result lay before him, preparing to land at Fort Washington.

When the soldiers touched the waters of the Ohio, Wayne's Legion of the United States became the single largest armed force ever to sail its waters; neither the empire of France or Britain could lay claim to that honor, and for Wayne it was only a further indication that America was destined to rule the continent. Wayne was a patriot of the highest order, and the thought that such a powerful group fell under his control made him feel akin to Caesar. Wayne was not the only leader preparing for a great showdown with his foreign enemy, however; two hundred miles away the Western Confederacy was doing the same.

Since St. Clair's defeat and the increasing presence of the opportunistic British in the Ohio Country, the Western Confederacy of Indian nations had swelled its warrior numbers to fifteen hundred. Little Turtle was the unchallenged leader of the Miami, Blue Jacket of the Shawnees, and Buckongahelas of the Delawares; all of them were viewed as first among equals, and their leadership was only cemented by their ability to lead from the front. They were war chiefs, and many of the warriors believed that whatever the Americans would throw at them next would be their best offering yet. There was a shared sense of destiny among the Ohioans, and the magnitude of the coming battle drew hundreds more from the Ojibwa, Ottawas, and Potawatomi. As the Great Lakes region was fully represented in the Western Confederacy, much more was at stake in this war than just the fate of the Ohio Country.[29]

Since the war had escalated and the Americans had committed troops to the region under Josiah Harmar, the British in Canada had grown quite wary of their new neighbors' advances. In hopes of defending Fort Detroit, a smaller fort was commissioned for construction along the Maumee River called Fort Miami. It was a bold move; despite the fact that the Treaty of Paris gave America rights to all of the western lands, Britain felt confident that with the ongoing Indian rebellion the Americans could do nothing to stop them. Therefore, in 1794 Fort Miami became a popular rallying point for the Western Confederacy and the Crown passed weapons and supplies from its walls in support of the movement. The British were escalating a cold war with the United States through an Indian proxy; that policy was not too different from that used by the Soviets in Vietnam or the Americans in Afghanistan in the 1980s. The steady stream of goods was efficient and effective, and as long as the Indians were willing to fight the Americans, the British did not have to.

Wayne and his Legion landed at the staging point of Fort Washington along the Ohio River, and by the fall of 1793 the general had broken ground on a new fort farther north to give him a more reliable launching point that was much closer to his intended target. Called Fort Greenville (sometimes Green Ville), it was less than one hundred and fifty miles from the powerbase of the Western Confederacy and Wayne hoped it would remain a valuable hub after the hostilities came to a close. For the harshest spells of the winter months Wayne and his Legion encamped in their freshly minted fortification, and as soon as spring returned they continued their march. Twenty-five miles to the north the general oversaw the construction of another new fort dubbed "Recovery" on the site of St. Clair's terrible defeat. In this he was making a double statement. First he was erasing the Indian victories of the past, and more important, with every log laid he solidified in a tangible way that the United States of America would be a permanent reality in the Ohio Country.

What the Americans had created was a vital line of communication ranging from the Ohio River at Fort Washington in the south to Fort Recovery, over one hundred and fifty miles northward. It was just as the French had done on the opposite side of the region in 1753–54, and what General John Forbes mimicked in 1758. By the summer of 1794 Wayne was proving that slow and steady did win the race, and those forts kept his Legion well stocked and ready for anything that the Western Confederacy could devise.

Sensing that the Americans were making progress, Little Turtle, Blue Jacket, and Simon Girty began to devise a plan to stop Wayne before he moved any closer to their position. Few characters on the American frontier incited as much controversy as Simon Girty, who was known as the "White Savage." Originally taken hostage following the 1756 attack on Fort Granville, Girty was readily adopted into the Seneca clan that captured him. In fact, throughout his life Guyasuta would act as one of many mentoring figures to the young convert. For the rest of his life Girty would spark fear and panic in the hearts of the frontier as the white man who became the "other," the physical representation of the savage conquest. To see Girty fighting alongside his Ohioan brethren was entirely expected, but understanding his greater role is more complex. Despite the fact that Girty was often viewed as an eternal enemy of white settlement, he actually represented more of a bridge between his own worlds, white and Indian; he was truly a product of the great frontier of empire.

On June 30, 1794, a pan-Indian force ambushed Fort Recovery in an attempt to sever its vital supply line to Fort Greenville; the results were not what the Indians had hoped for. In every other battle of that great struggle for independence the Indians tore the Americans to pieces, and though they still inflicted damage, the fort allowed Wayne's garrison to survive. The battle at the walls of Fort Recovery marked the end of the Western Confederacy's undefeated streak against their American enemy.

The failed attack on Fort Recovery also revealed some of the great rifts among the native groups. Since the Great Lakes Indians had joined the cause, there was an intense separation between themselves and the Ohioans. When the Fort Recovery attack unraveled and the Americans fended it off, the defeat took a terrible toll on the overall strength of the Indian force. Feeling like the entire venture was now doomed, many of the Great Lakes sachems led their warriors home, leaving Little Turtle and Blue Jacket behind. It was also out of this attack that General Wayne felt compelled to guide his Legion north to confront what remained of the Western Confederacy once and for all.

Wayne's forces moved in a slow and deliberate fashion, and all the while the general was careful not to repeat the mistakes of his predecessors. On July 25, Wayne received news that almost eight hundred hardened Kentucky militiamen were en route to join his men for this great battle that awaited them. It took Wayne's total strength to over three thousand, and with numbers like that even the staunchest opponents were certain to crumble. Along the way the Legion burned every Indian village that they encountered, and effectively cut a swath through the heartland of the new rebellion. By August 8 he built a fort near the Glaize and called it "Defiance." What the Americans did not know, however, was that the disintegration of the Western Confederacy had already begun. Little Turtle believed that Wayne and his Legion were too strong, and the great war chief began to waver. He stated in council: "We have beaten the enemy twice under different commanders. We cannot expect the same good fortune to attend us always. The Americans are now led by a chief who never sleeps. The night and the days are alike to him, and during all the time that he has been marching on our villages . . . we have never been able to surprise him . . . there is something whispers to me it would be prudent to listen to his offers of peace."[30]

The message that Little Turtle sent on that day was done with the knowledge that Wayne's Legion was bearing down on him with every passing hour. Blue Jacket, in response, stated that he would not abandon the cause and that he would assume leadership of the movement. With his dignity on the line, Little Turtle agreed to remain a part of the Western Confederacy, under the conditions that he would only lead his own Miami people. With this came an essential shift in the power and direction of the confederacy, and the Shawnee Blue Jacket began to devise his strategy for defeating the great new challenge that marched toward them.[31]

For the seasoned Blue Jacket there was no question that the battle had to be fought on his terms, for if he met Wayne face to face in the open field it would spell disaster for his warriors. Indian warfare dictated that whatever advantages one could attain in preparation should be taken swiftly, and if an element of surprise was included it only strengthened overall effectiveness. The place that Blue Jacket and Little Turtle chose to fight was a parcel of land near the Maumee River that had seen extensive storm damage years earlier. The landscape was littered with the remains of fallen trees, and the Indians believed that if they could draw Wayne into a skirmish among those tremendous obstacles his numerical advantage could be negated. The British post of Fort Miami was a short distance away, and that made their decision so much the easier. At this site, a place that would be called Fallen Timbers, the Western Confederacy chose to make its great stand against the United States of America; if it failed, it would be its last.

On the morning of August 20, 1794, General Anthony Wayne prepared his men for the battle that awaited them only miles ahead. Through the use of his scouts, the American commander had received word that the confederacy was fully prepared to engage his soldiers, and the Legion of the United States was fully prepared to respond. Two days prior one of his own scouts had been captured and tortured by the natives, and after passing on valuable intelligence regarding Wayne's plans and strength, he was tied to a tree and shot multiple times. It was the first time that Wayne's Legion would engage an enemy on the field of battle, and considering the innovative design of the untested fighting force its performance would be hard to predict, but Wayne was confident.

This battle would be no ambush, Wayne took comfort in that, but it would be fought on the ground selected by the native war chiefs. While the general prepared to engage his foe, the status of the other side was much less promising. Blue Jacket had selected the field of broken forest days earlier, and the warriors had held their position for over three days. They were tired, hungry, and pushed to their limits even before the fighting had begun. Because of the close proximity of Fort Miami, many of the warriors had taken to running back and forth from their battle lines to the British post to retrieve food and deliver it to their comrades; although the system worked, it was anything but efficient and certainly not sustainable.

Knowing that the practical elements of the terrain were already against him, Wayne elected that it would be his men, not the confederacy's, who would begin the battle. The sky was overcast and the air was cold, and "Mad Anthony" Wayne sent his soldiers into motion. His first action was to use the rough but fiery Kentuckians and he sent them howling toward their Indian adversaries. The Indians met their frontier brethren head on. The Battle of Fallen Timbers had begun. Wayne was aware that for all the ambition that the Kentucky militia brought with them, they had been beaten by the Indians before; he therefore

The Battle of Fallen Timbers. (*Library of Congress*)

sent a line of his best Legionnaires following closely behind. The Indians were able to repel the militia and it seemed to Blue Jacket and Little Turtle that the day was to be theirs again. The warriors charged the fleeing Kentuckians and screamed with victory, but were silenced immediately when they crashed headlong into the Legions' first volley of shots.

In their excitement to finish off the retreating Kentuckians, the disjointed native warriors had neglected to reload their rifles, and when they encountered the Legionnaires they had no recourse but to try to do so in the midst of battle. Sensing his opportunity, Wayne ordered that his men rush forth with their bayonets primed, quickly overrunning the Indians. They turned in retreat but the American cavalry chased them down easily. On the other side of the battlefield a party of Anglo-Canadian militiamen, dressed in war paint, fired at the Americans in a desperate attempt to provide vital cover for their fleeing allies; they too were swarmed by Wayne's Legion.[32]

Little Turtle and Blue Jacket tried desperately to rally their warriors, but Wayne's unrelenting pressure caused a general panic, followed by a massive collapse of the Indian line. With hope slipping away the warriors ran swiftly toward the four-bastioned wooden safety of Fort Miami. When they arrived at the British fort, they were horrified to find its front gate closed and locked from the other side. It was a terrible betrayal to the Indians in the midst of a total defeat. The Ohioans slammed their fists on the door screaming to the commandant to let them in, but from inside the garrison he knew that to do so risked inciting a general war against the United States, and that was a war Britain was not prepared to fight. Fort Miami stood coldly as the Ohioans' last hope of escaping the wrath of Wayne's Legion, and with the gates closed many warriors died on its doorstep.[33]

The entire battle lasted less than eighty minutes, yet the damage inflicted by the Legion of the United States was immeasurable. Forty warriors were tallied as dead, and hundreds more were wounded and carried to safety by their surviving comrades. The Western Confederacy had placed its full might into that one battle at Fallen Timbers, and Wayne's onslaught rendered it permanently disabled. With the annihilation of Blue Jacket's army of fifteen hundred warriors came the startling realization that for all of their preparation, and for all of their victories, the only truly effective mechanism of the confederacy's resistance to American expansion into the frontier—their fighting forces—had been destroyed. All that was left was the reckoning.

At the village of Canandaigua, New York, just two months after the carnage at Fallen Timbers, the American diplomat Timothy Pickering stood proudly in the center of an Iroquois delegation of over fifteen hundred people. With him were Cornplanter and Red Jacket, along with their fellow sachems Handsome Lake and Little Beard. For years they had deflected the advances of their Ohioan brethren in their calls for war, and throughout all of the strife they stood firm to their principles; peace and diplomacy were always preferred to combat, and their outcomes were much more effective. The rebellious Ohioans had put their faith in the sword, and as a result they suffered a crushing defeat. But now, after months of deliberations and council, the Iroquois

Confederacy stood proudly beside the new United States of America not as an enemy, but as an ally.

On November 11, less than three months after the great bloodletting in the Ohio Country, Pickering stood as a direct representative of President George Washington to sign a treaty with the Six Nations that would begin a new chapter in the long history of the Haudenosaunee. The Treaty of Canandaigua was celebrated by the Seneca, Oneida, Cayuga, Onondaga, Tuscarora, and Mohawk alike. For their actions and support in suppressing the Western Confederacy, the Iroquois peoples were officially designated as friends of the new United States. The land that they had struggled so valiantly to preserve would be theirs, and western New York would remain the property of the Iroquois nation as long as the American Republic graced the face of the earth. When the treaty was read aloud to the hundreds of Indian families in the village, the Iroquois and Americans were celebrated as equals. It was a union of two nations, one seeking to define itself, and the other to maintain its ancient and historic identity.[34]

The Treaty of Canandaigua marked a monumental shift in the history of the continent, and a stark contrast in competing dreams. To the west, one version of Indian America lay fallow in the ashes of defeat, while only a few hundred miles east another arose renewed, refreshed, and prepared to prosper into the nineteenth century and beyond. As terrible as its antecedents had been and as costly as it was, peace had come at last.

EPILOGUE

North America was changing so fast that General Anthony Wayne could hardly keep pace. Only a year earlier the Ohio Country had been a land of deadly rebellion, and now it was almost peaceful. He had established Fort Greenville in 1794 as his great launching point into the heart of the Western Confederacy, and following his complete victory it was a place of celebration. The Americans present were overjoyed at the prospects of what lay ahead that day, yet the majority of people there felt nothing but the pain of defeat.

Filing in a line to the small post of Fort Greenville were the defeated and broken sachems of the former Western Confederacy. Since the Battle of Fallen Timbers, their alliance had dissolved. They were at one time a massively powerful resistance movement against American expansion; but now they were only a delegation of many tribes prepared to concede as one. As Wayne stood proudly to represent a singular American nation, the chiefs of the Wyandot, Delaware, Shawnees, and Ottawa only spoke for themselves. The Ohioans had been broken by the Legion of the United States, and in its wake came only sorrow.[1]

After the collapse of Little Turtle and Blue Jacket's warriors twelve months prior, the spirit of the Ohioans had been all but extinguished. The fall of 1794 was a definitive moment in Indian America as the Western Confederacy watched the Iroquois achieve their own measure of victory with the Treaty of Canandaigua while they themselves found only defeat.[2]

Around the same time the Ohioans also lost one of their greatest defenders. While the circumstances of his death are unknown, Guyasuta passed away among his tribal family sometime after the American victory at Fallen Timbers. While the Ohioan warriors were being stamped out by Wayne's Legion, the seventy-year-old sachem was likely fading away slowly after a life of struggle. Sources best indicate that he died in the home of his nephew Cornplanter on a plot of land granted to him by the United States for his diplomatic efforts the previous year. His death brought to a close the story of one of Indian America's most influential figures, yet there was little ceremony around his passing. Guyasuta had spent the last five years of his life much diminished from his earlier days, and it was likely that his reputation as an alcoholic blunderer overshadowed his prior achievements.[3]

His life had been defined by his unrelenting commitment to achieving the best for his people, and unlike most of his contemporaries, his upbringing in the unique climate of the Ohio Country allowed him to largely see past the traditional bonds of tribal obligation. In that respect he was a visionary, and while his career was one of both success and failure, he never strayed from his primary objective. In his service to his Ohioan brethren he went to war more than any one man should, and was rarely gratified with a result that he had hoped for. For Guyasuta, his great victory was always a distant vision, and he took to the field of battle knowing that regardless of the outcome that day would only be a small piece in a much larger puzzle of achieving Indian autonomy. It was a cruel irony that one of Guyasuta's last memories was of his dream vanishing with the smoke of Fallen Timbers.

In the year that followed their victory, the United States of America had taken full advantage of their position as conqueror. It was apparent by that point that nothing could stop the expansion and settlement of the Ohio Country, and the only course of action for the war-weary Ohioan sachems was to

The Greenville Treaty Land Cessions, 1794.

accept whatever surrender was available to them. The Iroquois had treated with the Americans at Canandaigua, and although they retained very little in comparison with their traditional homelands the Haudenosaunee still controlled their own destiny; the component parts of the former Western Confederacy had little choice but to capitulate and do the same.[4]

It was under those pretenses that Wayne and the Ohioans met at Fort Greenville on August 3, 1795. Under the auspices of peace, overshadowed by the glaring cloud of callous expansion, the sachems of the Ohio Country filed by one after another to sign away their ancestral hunting grounds. They had chosen a path of war a decade earlier, and now they suffered the consequences. The product of that fateful day was called the Treaty of Fort Greenville, and it represented the end of an entire way of life for thousands of native peoples; the treaty stood as the great ending of an Ohioan struggle that had lasted almost five decades. The mournful result of three generations of war was concluded that day in 1795.

The Treaty of Fort Greenville was at its time the most resolute ever signed by the United States with an Indian delegation, and its many features were far-reaching and thoroughly effective. The agreement served to create an effective boundary between Indian land and territory available to American settlement; though the Ohioans put their full faith into this boundary, there was little doubt that it would be violated by independent white settlers before the ink was dry. The new boundary line was the newest evolution of the frontier, and just as the Treaty of Fort Stanwix had made the limits of western expansion the Ohio River, the Treaty of Fort Greenville would replace it even farther west. This new limitation was extensive, and from its origins at the Cuyahoga River near present-day Cleveland to its conclusion in Kentucky it served to give the United States unrivaled control over the precious lands of the Ohio Country.

This devastatingly large land grab by the Americans was intended to be a punishment brought down on the Western Confederacy. Along with the land concessions, the Americans offered the Ohioans a minor annuity of federal dollars and a regular stipend of valuable commodities. Even in defeat, the need for trade goods to bolster their shattered economy was central to Indian survival. Despite its incredibly destructive particulars, the Treaty of Greenville was presented by the Americans as the only means of remedying the differences between the two competing worlds. Article I read plainly: "Henceforth all hostilities shall cease; peace is hereby established, and shall be perpetual; and a friendly intercourse shall take place between the said United States and Indian tribes."[5]

The stipulations of the treaty, cosigned by Anthony Wayne himself, sealed the fate of the Ohioans forever, and guaranteed the expansion and prosperity of the United States for years to come. With their signatures, the defeated sachems agreed to sign over the Ohio Country completely to the Americans and vacate all of their villages in a massive westward migration into lands that they had no ancestral ties to. The result was a great exodus, and along with the exiles came a new generation's reactions of anger, frustration, and perceived injustice. Among this disaffected group of refugees were new faces to carry on their legacy of resistance, but confrontation was the last thing on the Ohioans' minds at the time. They worried about finding homes, feeding their children, and protecting their possessions while starting over from nothing.

Awaiting them on in the outer reaches of what would become the American Midwest was a world of dismay. As the Ohioans trekked away from the only world they knew, they would encounter new peoples with little openness to absorbing their way of life. Although there would be tensions, it would ironically be their turbulent past that would allow the Ohioans to gain acceptance amongst these tribes; their long history of loss and neglect would soon travel westward on the back of the ambitions of the United States of America. In less than two decades a pair of Shawnee brothers whose father had died at the Battle of Point Pleasant in 1774, Tecumseh and Tenskwatawa, would carry on the native struggle against the encroachment of settlers and rally these western peoples, just as their ancestors had done a generation earlier. Their struggle too would end in failure.

In the conquest of the Ohio Country, and the subsequent dismantling of the Ohioan peoples, the United States had created its blueprint for what it would ultimately describe as Manifest Destiny. The damaging techniques employed in 1795 would be used again and again for almost a century. That August night, as the sachems prepared to explain the Treaty of Greenville to their shattered peoples, there emerged a sorrowful revelation. The sun would rise again over the Ohio Country, but there would not be an Ohioan left to see it. The ground had been broken for the construction of a new America, and the first casualty was the Indian land that Guyasuta had called home.

A sculpture portraying Guyasuta and Washington at their final meeting along the Ohio River in 1770 by artist James West overlooks the city of Pittsburgh. (*Author*)

NOTES

CHAPTER ONE: THE HUNTER

1. Wallace, *Indians in Pennsylvania*, 126.
2. Anderson, *The War that Made America*, 20.
3. Kopper, *The Journals of George Washington and Christopher Gist*, 49.
4. Crytzer, *Major Washington's Pittsburgh and the Mission to Fort Le Boeuf*, 41.
5. James and Stotz, *Drums in the Forest*, 26.
6. Anderson, *The War that Made America*, 22.
7. Anderson, *The War that Made America*, 23.
8. Anderson, *The War that Made America*, 27.
9. Flexner, *George Washington*, 97.
10. Wallace, *Indians in Pennsylvania*, 182.
11. Crytzer, *Major Washington's Pittsburgh and the Mission to Fort Le Boeuf*, 34.
12. Anderson, *The War that Made America*, 34.
13. Kopper, *The Journals of George Washington and Christopher Gist*, 7.
14. Sipe, *The Indian Chiefs of Pennsylvania*, 287.
15. Kopper, *The Journals of George Washington and Christopher Gist, 1753-1754*, 5. Dr. Kevin Kopper has used this short volume to present Washington's journals in a fully annotated form. It is the most thorough examination of the journals ever published.
16. Kopper, *The Journals of George Washington and Christopher Gist*, 12.
17. Kopper, *The Journals of George Washington and Christopher Gist*, 15
18. Hale, *The Indians of Pennsylvania*, 288.
19. Kopper, *The Journals of George Washington and Christopher Gist*, 17.
20. Kopper, *The Journals of George Washington and Christopher Gist*, 40.
21. Wallace, *Indian Paths of Pennsylvania*, 170.
22. Crytzer, *Major Washington's Pittsburgh and the Mission to Fort Le Boeuf*, 74.
23. Flexner, *George Washington*, 66.
24. Kopper, *The Journals of George Washington and Christopher Gist*, 20.
25. Kopper, *The Journals of George Washington and Christopher Gist*, 20.
26. Kopper, *The Journals of George Washington and Christopher Gist*, 20.
27. Sipe, *The Indian Chiefs of Pennsylvania*, 375–376.
28. Kopper, *The Journals of George Washington and Christopher Gist*.
29. Kopper, *The Journals of George Washington and Christopher Gist*, 23.
30. Kopper, *The Journals of George Washington and Christopher Gist*, 26.
31. Kopper, *The Journals of George Washington and Christopher Gist*, 27.
32. Kopper, *The Journals of George Washington and Christopher Gist*, 30.
33. Kopper, *The Journals of George Washington and Christopher Gist*, 31.

CHAPTER TWO: VICTORY ON THE MONONGAHELA

1. Anderson, *The War that Made America*, 43.
2. Dixon, "A High Wind Rising," 41.
3. O'Meara, *Guns at the Forks*, 51.

4. Anderson, *Crucible of War*, 48–49.

5. Dixon, *A High Wind Rising*, 42.

6. Anderson, *The War that Made America*, 49.

7. Dixon, *A High Wind Rising*, 44.

8. Flexner, *George Washington*, 89.

9. Anderson, *Crucible of War*, 63.

10. Dixon, *A High Wind Rising*, 43–44.

11. Dixon, *A High Wind Rising*, 45.

12. Anderson, *The War that Made America*, 50.

13. Dixon, *A High Wind Rising*, 46.

14. Dixon, *A High Wind Rising*, 47. It is in this creative new theory, the idea that Villiers did not simply quit on the greatest potential victory of his young career but was influenced to pull back, that the true measure of this work is revealed. This theory, proposed by historian David Dixon in 2006, underscores the wealth of material missed when native involvement is considered as less than equal to their French and British cohorts.

15. Dixon, *A High Wind Rising*, 47.

16. Wallace, *Indians in Pennsylvania*, 182.

17. Anderson, *The War that Made America*, 61.

18. Anderson, *Crucible of War*, 92.

19. Anderson, *The War that Made America*, 69.

20. Anderson, *The War that Made America*, 69.

21. Kopperman, *Braddock at the Monongahela*, 22.

22. Kopperman, *Braddock at the Monongahela*, 27.

23. Kopperman, *Braddock at the Monongahela*, 52.

24. O'Meara, *Guns at the Forks*, 144.

25. Anderson, *Crucible of War*, 102.

26. Flexner, *George Washington*, 130.

27. Anderson, *The War that Made America*, 70.

28. Kopperman, *Braddock at the Monongahela*, 89.

29. Tilton, *George Washington*, 60.

30. Kopperman, *Braddock at the Monongahela*, 91.

CHAPTER THREE: UNCERTAIN ALLIANCES

1. Anderson, *The War that Made America*, 90.

2. Anderson, *The War that Made America*, 91.

3. Silver, *Our Savage Neighbors*, 87.

4. Anderson, *The Crucible of War*, 150.

5. Sipe, *The Indian Chiefs of Pennsylvania*, 269.

6. Barr, *Victory at Kittanning?* 16.

7. Barr, *Victory at Kittanning?* 22.

8. Anderson, *The War that Made America*, 112.

9. Anderson, *The Crucible of War*, 211.

10. Anderson, *The War that Made America*, 123.

11. O'Meara, *Guns at the Forks*, 185.

12. Quoted in Fisher, *Pennsylvania's Forbes Trail*, 95.

13. Sipe, *The Indian Chiefs of Pennsylvania*, 372.

14. Sipe, *The Indian Chiefs of Pennsylvania*, 373.

15. Stewart, *Sketches of the Character, Manners and Present State of the Highlanders of Scotland*, Vol. 1, 312–313.

16. Sipe, *The Indian Chiefs of Pennsylvania*, 373.

17. Busch, *Reports of the Commission to Locate the Site of Frontier Forts in Western Pennsylvania*, Vol. II.

18. Sipe, *The Indian Chiefs of Pennsylvania*, 374.

19. Sipe, *The Indian Chiefs of Pennsylvania*, 374.

20. Busch, *Reports of the Commission to Locate the Site of Frontier Forts in Western Pennsylvania*, 12.

21. O'Meara, *Guns at the Forks*, 205.

22. Busch, *Reports of the Commission to Locate the Site of Frontier Forts in Western Pennsylvania*, 49.

23. Downes, *Council Fires on the Upper Ohio*, 78.

24. O'Mcara, *Guns at the Forks*, 209.

25. O'Meara, *Guns at the Forks*, 210.

26. Crytzer, *Fort Pitt*, 10.

27. O'Meara, *Guns at the Forks*, 221.

28. Crytzer, *Fort Pitt*, 27.

29. Crytzer, *Fort Pitt*, 29.

30. *Meeting of Minutes from the Provincial Council of Pennsylvania from the Organization to the Termination of the Proprietary Government*, 384.

31. Crytzer, *Fort Pitt*, 29.

CHAPTER FOUR: FIRE ON THE FRONTIER

1. Anderson, *The War that Made America*, 9.

2. Amherst to Johnson, as quoted in Dixon, *Never Come to Peace Again*, 78.

3. Dixon, *Never Come to Peace Again*, 87.

4. *The Papers of Sir William Johnson*, 475.

5. *The Papers of Sir William Johnson*, 488.

6. Anderson, *The Crucible of War*, 488.

7. Anderson, *The Crucible of War*, 422.

8. Anderson, *The Crucible of War*, 506.

9. Calloway, *The Scratch of a Pen*, 12.

10. Anderson, *The War that Made America*, 217.

11. Amherst to Johnson, as quoted in Dixon, *Never Come to Peace Again*, 78.

12. Dixon, *Never Come to Peace Again*, 89.

13. Crytzer, *Fort Pitt*, 88.

14. Wallace, *Indians in Pennsylvania*, 55.

15. Dowd, *Spirited Resistance*, 34.

16. Calloway, *The Scratch of a Pen*, 70.

17. Silver, *Our Savage Neighbors*, 17.

18. Peckham, *Pontiac and the Indian Uprising*, 120.

19. Crytzer, *Fort Pitt*, 77.

20. Downes, *Council Fires on the Upper Ohio*, 120.

21. Crytzer, *Fort Pitt*, 98.

22. Dixon, *Never Come to Peace Again*, 122.

23. Dixon, *Never Come to Peace Again*, 41.
24. *Fort Pitt and Letters from the Frontier*, 93.
25. Amherst to Bouquet, June 6, 1763, *Bouquet Papers*, 6:209.
26. Bouquet to Ecuyer, *Bouquet Papers*, 6:225.
27. O'Meara, *Guns at the Forks*, 236–239.
28. Dixon, *Never Come to Peace Again*, 186.
29. Dixon, *Never Come to Peace Again*, 187.
30. Crytzer, *Fort Pitt*, 118.
31. Bouquet to Amherst, *Bouquet Papers*, 6:344.
32. Dixon, *Never Come to Peace Again*, 196.

CHAPTER FIVE: DREAM OF HIS FATHERS

1. Foley, *The Jeffersonian Cyclopedia*, 784.
2. De Tocqueville, *Democracy in America*, 342.
3. Briggs, *Lincoln's Speeches Reconsidered*, 29.
4. Kopper, *The Journals of George Washington and Christopher Gist*, 212.
5. Calloway, *The Scratch of a Pen*, 73.
6. Dixon, *Never Come to Peace Again*, 210–211.
7. Calloway, *The Scratch of a Pen*, 92.
8. Anderson, *The War that Made America*, 252.
9. Kenny, *Peaceable Kingdom Lost*, 185.
10. Dixon, *Never Come to Peace Again*, 247.
11. Kenny, *Peaceable Kingdom Lost*, 41.
12. Engels, *Equipped for Murder.*
13. Silver, *Our Savage Neighbors*, 94.
14. Sipe, *The Indian Chiefs of Pennsylvania*, 399.
15. Dixon, *Never Come to Peace Again*, 223.
16. Anderson, *Crucible of War*, 552–553.
17. Dixon, *Never Come to Peace Again*, 224.
18. Downes, *Council Fires on the Upper Ohio*, 79.
19. Dixon, *Never Come to Peace Again*, 219.
20. Anderson, *The War that Made America*, 146.
21. Crytzer, *Fort Pitt*, 118.
22. Dixon, *Never Come to Peace Again*, 231
23. Bouquet to Gage, *Bouquet Papers*, 621.
24. Dixon, *Never Come to Peace Again*, 238.
25. Dixon, *Never Come to Peace Again*, 239.
26. Guyasuta to Bouquet, *Bouquet Papers*, 669.
27. Dixon, *Never Come to Peace Again*, 242.
28. Hale, *The Indian Chiefs of Pennsylvania*, 291.
29. Sipe, *The Indian Chiefs of Pennsylvania*, 401.
30. Crytzer, *Fort Pitt*, 153.
31. Anderson, *Crucible of War*, 332.

CHAPTER SIX: UNWAVERING COMMITMENT

1. Kopper, *The Journals of George Washington and Christopher Gist*, 211.
2. Sipe, *The Indian Chiefs of Pennsylvania*, 401.

3. Hoffman, *Simon Girty*, 55–56.
4. Crytzer, *Fort Pitt*, 128.
5. *Dictionary of Canadian Biography*, Volume IV, 408 409.
6. Fitzpatrick, *Writings of Washington*, 2:269.
7. Fitzpatrick, *Writings of Washington*, 2:269.
8. Downes, *Council Fires on the Upper Ohio*, 150–152.
9. Morgan, *Boone*, 137–138.
10. Crytzer, *Fort Pitt*, 145.
11. Downes, *Council Fires on the Upper Ohio*, 160.
12. Crytzer, *Fort Pitt*, 145-146.
13. Edgington to Draper, in *A Documentary History of Lord Dunmore's War*, 17.
14. Judge Henry Holly, in *A Documentary History of Lord Dunmore's War*, 9–11.
15. *American Archives, Fourth Series, Vol. 1*, 479.
16. Crytzer, *Fort Pitt*, 134.
17. Washington, *The Writings of George Washington*, "*To Lord Dunmore*"
18. Downes, *Council Fires on the Upper Ohio*, 154.
19. Anderson, *Crucible of War*, 574–576.
20. Crytzer, *Fort Pitt*, 146.
21. Downes, *Council Fires on the Upper Ohio*, 176–177.
22. Morgan, *Boone*, 150.
23. Sipe, *The Indian Chiefs of Pennsylvania*, 434.
24. Mayer, *Tah-gah-jute: or, Logan and Captain Michael Cresap*, 86.
25. McDonald, "The Battle of Point Pleasant: First Battle of the American Revolution."
26. Kelsay, *Joseph Brant*, 138.
27. Calloway, *The American Revolution in Indian Country*, 137.
28. Crytzer, *Fort Pitt*, 127.
29. Hale, *The Indian Chiefs of Pennsylvania*, 402.
30. Calloway, *The American Revolution in Indian Country*, 29.
31. Hoffman, *Simon Girty*, 105.
32. Calloway, *The American Revolution in Indian Country*, 29.
33. Calloway, *The American Revolution in Indian Country*, 30.
34. Calloway, *The American Revolution in Indian Country*, 30.
35. Hunt, *Journals of the Continental Congress*, 95.

Chapter Seven: The Cause of the Crown

1. Graymont, *The Iroquois in the American Revolution*, vii.
2. Calloway, *The American Revolution in Indian Country*, xiii
3. Calloway, *The American Revolution in Indian Country*, 32. No single historian has shed as much light on the Native viewpoint as Dartmouth's Colin Calloway. His analysis of the Indian, not just northern but western and southern as well, during the Revolutionary period is best seen in this work. It is a masterpiece of scholarship that should be on every historian's bookshelf.
4. Calloway, *The American Revolution in Indian Country*, 38.
5. Kelsay, *Joseph Brant*, 188.
6. Kelsay, *Joseph Brant*, 185.
7. Quoted in Abler, *Cornplanter*, 40.

8. Graymont, *The Iroquois in the American Revolution*, 149.
9. Shannon, *Iroquois Diplomacy on the Early American Frontier*, 116.
10. Watt, *Rebellion in the Mohawk Valley*, 219.
11. Calloway, *The American Revolution in Indian Country*, 33.
12. Kelsay, *Joseph Brant*, 204.
13. Lunt, *John Burgoyne of Saratoga*, 183.
14. Graymont, *The Iroquois in the American Revolution*, 130.
15. Watt, *Rebellion in the Mohawk Valley*, 115.
16. Lunt, *John Burgoyne of Saratoga*, 184.
17. Graymont, *The Iroquois in the American Revolution*, 134.
18. Nickerson, *The Turning Point of the Revolution*, 202.
19. Nickerson, *The Turning Point of the Revolution*, 207.
20. Watt, *Rebellion in the Mohawk Valley*, 316–318.
21. Watt, *Rebellion in the Mohawk Valley*, 177.
22. Watt, *Rebellion in the Mohawk Valley*, 196.
23. Downes, *Council Fires on the Upper Ohio*, 211.
24. Jennings, *The Creation of America*, 243.
25. Crytzer, *Fort Pitt*, 159-161.

CHAPTER EIGHT: THE CAUSE OF HIS PEOPLE

1. Graymont, *The Iroquois in the American Revolution*, 192.
2. Sipe, *The Indian Chiefs of Pennsylvania*, 486.
3. Hoffman, *Simon Girty*, 108.
4. Graymont, *The Iroquois in the American Revolution*, 168.
5. Moyer, *Wild Yankees*, 1.
6. Kelsay, *Joseph Brant*, 218–220.
7. Graymont, *The Iroquois in the American Revolution*, 169.
8. Cruikshank, *Rangers and the Settlement of Niagara*, 49.
9. Moyer, *Wild Yankees*, 2.
10. Kelsay, *Joseph Brant*, 233.
11. Calloway, *The American Revolution in Indian Country*, 129–131.
12. "Instructions to Major General John Sullivan," *The Writings of George Washington*.
13. Williams, *The Year of the Hangman*, xi.
14. Downes, *Council Fires on the Upper Ohio*, 248.
15. Downes, *Council Fires on the Upper Ohio*, 252.
16. Downes, *Council Fires on the Upper Ohio*, 252.
17. Calloway, *The American Revolution in Indian Country*, 139.
18. Calloway, *The American Revolution in Indian Country*, 142.
19. Abler, *Dictionary of Canadian Biography*, Vol. IV.
20. Downes, *Council Fires on the Upper Ohio*, 264.
21. Crytzer, *Fort Pitt*, 163.
22. Kelsay, *Joseph Brant*, 331.
23. Wallace, *Indians in Pennsylvania*, 51.
24. Sipe, *The Indian Chiefs of Pennsylvania*, 404–405.
25. Abler, *Dictionary of Canadian Biography*, Vol. IV.
26. Sipe, *The Indian Chiefs of Pennsylvania*, 404.
27. Crytzer, *Fort Pitt*, 175.

CHAPTER NINE: HE WONDERS AT HIS OWN SHADOW

1. Kelsay, *Joseph Brant*, 359.
2. Downes, *Council Fires on the Upper Ohio*, 292–293.
3. Kelsay, *Joseph Brant*, 373.
4. Hoffman, *Simon Girty*, 273.
5. Downes, *Council Fires on the Upper Ohio*, 300.
6. Downes, *Council Fires on the Upper Ohio*, 302.
7. Downes, *Council Fires on the Upper Ohio*, 298–299.
8. Carnes and Garraty, *American Destiny*, 151.
9. Crytzer, *Fort Pitt*, 170.
10. Gist, *Journals of Christopher Gist*, 212-213.
11. Downes, *Council Fires on the Upper Ohio*, 312.
12. Hoffman, *Simon Girty*, 292–295.
13. Schecter, *George Washington's America*, 233.
14. Shannon, *Iroquois Diplomacy on the Early American Frontier*, 205.
15. Downes, *Council Fires on the Upper Ohio*, 318–320.
16. Downes, *Council Fires on the Upper Ohio*, 320.
17. Shannon, *Iroquois Diplomacy on the Early American Frontier*. 205.
18. Crytzer, *Fort Pitt*, 171.
19. Jortner, *The Gods of Prophetstown*, 64.
20. Hoffman, *Simon Girty*, 321.
21. Jortner, *The Gods of Prophetstown*, 55–57.
22. Willig, *Diplomatic Turning Point in the West*, 52–53.
23. Willig, *Diplomatic Turning Point in the West*, 54.
24. Abler, *Cornplanter*, 91.
25. Abler, *Cornplanter*, 92.
26. Abler, *Cornplanter*, 92.
27. Sipe, *The Indian Chiefs of Pennsylvania*. 408.
28. Baldwin, *Pittsburgh*, 107.
29. Calloway, *The Shawnees and the War for America*, 97.
30. Hoffman, *Simon Girty*, 345.
31. Calloway, *The Shawnees and the War for America*, 102–103.
32. Downes, *Council Fires on the Upper Ohio*, 334–335.
33. Hoffman, *Simon Girty*, 348
34. Shannon, *Iroquois Diplomacy on the Early American Frontier*, 206–208.

EPILOGUE

1 Calloway, *The Shawnees and the War for America*, 109.
2 Jortner, *The Gods of Prophetstown*, 70.
3 Sipe, *The Indian Chiefs of Pennsylvania*, 408.
4 Downes, *Council Fires on the Upper Ohio*, 337.
5 *Text of the Treaty of Greenville, 1795*, Clarke Historical Library, Central Michigan University.

BIBLIOGRAPHY

Abler, Thomas Struthers. *Cornplanter: Chief Warrior of the Allegany Senecas*. Syracuse: Syracuse University Press, 2007.

Anderson, Fred. *Crucible of War: The Seven Years' War and the Fate of Empire in British North America, 1754–1766*. New York: Vintage Books, 2000.

————. *The War that Made America: A Short History of the French and Indian War*. New York: Penguin, 2006.

Baldwin, Leland D. *Pittsburgh: The Story of a City*. Pittsburgh: University of Pittsburgh Press, 1938.

Barr, Daniel P. "Victory at Kittanning? Reevaluating the Impact of Armstrong's Raid on the Seven Years' War in Pennsylvania." *Pennsylvania Magazine of History and Biography* 131.1 (2007): 5–32.

Bouquet, Henry. *The Papers of Henry Bouquet: November 17, 1761–July 17, 1765*. Harrisburg: Pennsylvania Historical and Museum Commission, 1994.

Briggs, John Channing. *Lincoln's Speeches Reconsidered*. Baltimore: Johns Hopkins University Press, 2005.

Busch, Clarence M. *Report on the Commission to Locate the Frontier Forts of Western Pennsylvania, Volume II*. Harrisburg: State Commission of Pennsylvania, 1896.

Calloway, Colin G. *The American Revolution in Indian Country: Crisis and Diversity in Native American Communities*. Cambridge: Cambridge University Press, 1995.

————. *New Worlds for All: Indians, Europeans, and the Remaking of Early America*. Baltimore: Johns Hopkins University Press, 1997.

————. *The Scratch of a Pen: 1763 and the Transformation of North America*. New York: Oxford University Press, 2006.

————. *The Shawnees and the War for America*. New York: Penguin, 2007.

Carnes, Mark C., and John A. Garraty. *American Destiny: Narrative of a Nation*. New York: Pearson Longman, 2008.

Crocker, Thomas E. *Braddock's March: How the Man Sent to Seize a Continent Changed American History*. Yardley, Pa.: Westholme Publishing, 2009.

Cruikshank, Ernest. *The Story of Butler's Rangers and the Settlement of Niagara.* Welland: Tribune Printing House, 1893.

Crytzer, Brady J. *Fort Pitt: A Frontier History.* Charleston: History Press, 2012.

———. *Major Washington's Pittsburgh and the Mission to Fort Le Boeuf.* Charleston: History Press, 2011.

De Tocqueville, Alexis. *Democracy in America.* New York: D. Appleton and Co., 1904.

Dixon, David. "A High Wind Rising: George Washington, Fort Necessity, and the Ohio Country Indians." *Pennsylvania History* 74: 33–51.

———. *Never Come to Peace Again: Pontiac's Uprising and the Fate of the British Empire in North America.* Norman: University of Oklahoma Press, 2005.

Dowd, Gregory A. *A Spirited Resistance: The North American Indian Struggle for Unity, 1745–1815.* Baltimore: Johns Hopkins University Press, 1993.

Downes, Randolph C. *Council Fires on the Upper Ohio.* Pittsburgh: University of Pittsburgh Press, 1940.

Engels, Jeremy. "Equipped for Murder: The Paxton Boys and the Spirit of Killing All Indians in Pennsylvania, 1763–1764." *Rhetoric & Public Affairs* 8.3 (January 2005): 355–381.

Fischer, Laura S. *Pennsylvania's Forbes Trail.* New York: Taylor Trade Publishing, 2008.

Fitzpatrick, John C., ed. *The Writings of George Washington.* Charlottesville: University of Virginia, 1931.

Flexner, James Thomas. *George Washington: The Forge of Experience, 1732–1775.* Boston: Little, Brown, 1965.

Foley, John P. *The Jeffersonian Cyclopedia.* New York: Funk and Wagnalls, 1900.

Ford, Worthington Chauncey, ed. *The Writings of George Washington.* New York: Knickerbocker Press, 1891.

Graymont, Barbara. *The Iroquois in the American Revolution.* Syracuse: Syracuse University Press, 1972.

Halpenny, Frances G., and Jean Hamelin. *Dictionary of Canadian Biography,* Volume IV, 1771 to 1800. Toronto: University of Toronto Press, 1979.

Hoffman, Phillip W. *Simon Girty, Turncoat Hero: The Most Hated Man on the Early American Frontier.* Franklin, Tenn.: Flying Camp Press, 2009.

Hunt, Gaillard, ed. *Journals of the Continental Congress.* Washington, D.C.: Government Printing Office, 1912.

James, Alfred Proctor, and Charles Morse Stotz. *Drums in the Forest: Decision at the Forks, Defense in the Wilderness.* Pittsburgh: University of Pittsburgh Press, 2005.

Jennings, Francis. *The Creation of America: Through Revolution to Empire.* Cambridge: Cambridge University Press, 2000.

Jortner, Adam. *The Gods of Prophetstown: The Battle of Tippecanoe and the Holy War for the American Frontier.* Oxford: Oxford University Press, 2012.

Kelsay, Isabel Thompson. *Joseph Brant, 1743–1807: Man of Two Worlds.* Syracuse: Syracuse University Press, 1984.

Kenny, Kevin. *Peaceable Kingdom Lost: The Paxton Boys and the Destruction of William Penn's Holy Experiment.* New York: Oxford University Press, 2009.

Kopper, Kevin P. *The Journals of George Washington and Christopher Gist: Mission to Fort Le Boeuf.* Slippery Rock, Pa.: Slippery Rock University and Historic Harmony, 2009.

Kopperman, Paul. *Braddock at the Monongahela.* Pittsburgh: University of Pittsburgh Press, 1977.

Lunt, James D. *John Burgoyne of Saratoga.* London: Macdonald and Jane's, 1976.

Mayer, Brantz. *Tah-gah-jute: or, Logan and Captain Michael Cresap.* Baltimore: Maryland Historical Society, 1851.

McDonald, Kenneth. "The Battle of Point Pleasant: First Battle of the American Revolution." *West Virginia History* 36 (1974): 40–49.

Meeting of Minutes from the Provincial Council of Pennsylvania from the Organization to the Termination of the Proprietary Government. Harrisburg, Pa.: Theo Fenn and Co., 1851.

Morgan, Robert. *Boone: A Biography.* Chapel Hill: Algonquin Paperbacks, 2007.

Moyer, Paul. *Wild Yankees: The Struggle for Independence Along Pennsylvania's Revolutionary Frontier.* Ithaca: Cornell University Press, 2007.

Nickerson, Hoffman. *The Turning Point of the Revolution or Burgoyne in America.* Cambridge: Riverside Press, 1928.

O'Meara, Walter. *Guns at the Forks.* Pittsburgh: University of Pittsburgh Press, 1965.

Peckham, Howard Henry. *Pontiac and the Indian Uprising.* Detroit: Wayne State University Press, 1994.

Pencak, William A., and Daniel K. Richter. *Friends and Enemies in Penn's Woods: Indians, Colonists, and the Racial Construction of Pennsylvania.* University Park: Pennsylvania State University Press, 2004.

Shannon, Timothy. *Iroquois Diplomacy on the Early American Frontier*. New York: Penguin, 2008.

Silver, Peter. *Our Savage Neighbors: How Indian War Transformed Early America*. New York: W. W. Norton, 2009.

Sipe, C. Hale. *The Indian Chiefs of Pennsylvania*. Lewisburg, Pa.: Wennawoods, 1998.

Stewart, David. *Sketches of the Character, Manners and Present State of the Highlanders of Scotland*. Vol. 1. Edinburgh: Archibald Constable and Co., 1825.

Sullivan, James. *The Papers of Sir William Johnson*. Albany: University of the State of New York, 1921.

Thwaites, Reuben Gold. *A Documentary History of Dunmore's War*. Madison: Wisconsin Historical Society, 1905.

Wallace, Paul A. W. *Historic Indian Paths of Pennsylvania*. Harrisburg: Pennsylvania Historical and Museum Commission, 1952.

———. *Indians in Pennsylvania*. Harrisburg: Pennsylvania Historical and Museum Commission, 1981.

Watt, Gavin K. *Rebellion in the Mohawk Valley: The St. Leger Expedition of 1777*. Ontario: Dundurn Press, 2002.

Williams, Glenn. *Year of the Hangman: George Washington's Campaign Against the Iroquois*. Yardley, Pa.: Westholme Publishing, 2005.

Willig, Timothy D. "Diplomatic Turning Point in the West: The Six Nations and the Ohio Confederacy, 1792-1794." *Preserving Tradition and Understanding the Past: Papers from the Conference on Iroquois Research, 2001-2005*, chapter 5 (2010): 49–60.

ACKNOWLEDGMENTS

As an undergraduate I had the privilege to study under David Dixon at Slippery Rock University, and it was his passionate and unrivaled expertise and guidance that has allowed me to become the historian that I am today. I was not unique in that regard. As a teacher and mentor David Dixon mentored hundreds of students over his long career at SRU, and his tenure serves as a sterling example of passion, commitment, and resilience for educators everywhere. Although only a select few of his pupils have gone on to pursue history as a profession, his legacy lives on through his brilliant scholarship and a litany of fond memories that will forever be associated with him.

In 2005, David Dixon published *Never Come to Peace Again: Pontiac's Uprising and the Fate of the British Empire in North America*, a book that revolutionized our understanding of the role of the American Indian in the earliest days of the American experience. As a follow up, *Pennsylvania History* printed his groundbreaking article "A High Wind Rising: George Washington, Fort Necessity, and the Ohio Country Indians," in which transformative reinterpretation (when wielded correctly) revealed itself to be a historian's most powerful tool. Prof. Dixon's writings have defined my professional style and interests and I do my best to continue his efforts with my own students. To honor his work and legacy I dedicate this book to him.

I would like to thank my publisher, Bruce H. Franklin, Noreen O'Connor-Abel for her copyediting, Tracy Dungan for his maps, and Trudi Gershenov for her cover design.

This book would not have been possible without the love and support of my wife Jennifer. She has remained patient with me through all of the writing, research, and rewriting that went into its pages, and for that I am thankful. I would also like to express my gratitude for the hospitality and patience of my family and friends, too many to list here. You know who you are, and I hope that you know how much your support has meant to me.

INDEX